WORLD OF LANGUAGE

Marian Davies Toth   Nancy Nickell Ragno   Betty G. Gray

Contributing Author – Primary   Elfrieda Hiebert
Contributing Author – Vocabulary   Richard E. Hodges
Contributing Author – Poetry   Myra Cohn Livingston

Consulting Author – Thinking Skills   David N. Perkins

SILVER BURDETT GINN

NEEDHAM, MA   PARSIPPANY, NJ

Atlanta, GA   Irving, TX   Deerfield, IL   Santa Clara, CA

Acknowledgments

Cover: James Needham

Contributing Writers: Sandra Breuer, Judy Brim, Wendy Davis, Anne Maley, Marcia Miller, Anne Ryle, Gerry Tomlinson

Contributing artists: Anthony Accardo, Angela Adams, Ernest Albanese, Robert Alley, Victor Ambrus, George Baquero, Bob Barner, Howard Berelson, Alex Bloch, Kristine Bollinger, Denise Brunkus, Robert Casilla, Gwen Connolly, Doug Cushman, Renee Daily, Susan David, Betsy Day, Nancy Didion, John Dispenza, Susan Dodge, Michele Epstein, Simon Galkin, Tom Garcia, Marika Hahn, Diane Dawson Hearns, Dennis Hockerman, Marilyn Janovitz, Sue Johnston, Bernadette Lau, Dora Leder, Ron LeHew, Bruce Lemerise, Vickie Lerner, Morrissa Lipstein, Karen Loccisano, Richard Loehle, Claude Martinot, Barbara Maslen, Darcy May, Verlin Miller, Kathy Mitchell, Les Morrill, Gabriele Nenzione, John Nez, Bob Roper, Rosenkrans/Hoffman, Marge Sanfilippo, Claudia Sargent, Bob Shein, Joel Snyder, Barbara Steadman, George Ulrich, Joe Veno, Alexandra Wallner, Richard Walz, Larry Winborg, Fred Winkowski, Lane Yerkes.

Picture Credits: All photographs by Silver Burdett & Ginn (SB&G) unless otherwise noted. **Unit 1:** 6: Dan DeWilde for SB&G. 15: © Michael S. Yamashita/Westlight. 17: *Royal Tide I,* 1960, 96 x 40 x 8 in. 44: All by Dan DeWilde for SB&G. 49: *More Stories Julian Tells* by Ann Cameron. Illustrated by Ann Strugnell. Reprinted by permission of Alfred A. Knopf, Inc. **Unit 2:** 60: Jim Pickerell for SB&G 76: *l.* © Jerry Jacka, courtesy Coltar Bay Indian Arts Museum, Grand Teton National Park, Wyoming; *t.r.* Terry E. Eiler; *b.r.* Michal Heron. 80–82: Jim Pickerell for SB&G. 86: *t.* Lee Boltin; *b.* Art Resource. 87: Courtesy Kip and Ron Grangier. 88: Jim Pickerell for SB&G. 94: Jim Pickerell for SB&G. 98: All by Dan DeWilde for SB&G. 103: *When Clay Sings* by Byrd Baylor. Jacket illustration copyright © 1972 by Tom Bahti. Reprinted with permission of Charles Scribner's Sons, an imprint of Macmillan Publishing Company. **Unit 3:** 143: © Jeff Gnass/The Stock Market, 1990. 148: All by Dan DeWilde for SB&G. 153: *Sky Songs* by Myra Cohn Livingston. Illustrated by Leonard Everett Fisher. Reprinted by permission of Holiday House, Inc. **Unit 4:** 178: © B&B, 1956 art from the archives of Brown & Bigelow, Inc. 198: All by Dan DeWilde for SB&G. 203: *Ribsy* by Beverly Cleary, copyright © 1964. Illustrated by Louis Darling. Reprinted by permission of Morrow Junior Books (a division of William Morrow and Company, Inc.) **Unit 5:** 234: From *Beauty and the Beast* by Marianna Mayer, illustrated by Mercer Mayer. Illustration copyright © 1978 by Mercer Mayer. Reproduced with permission of Four Winds Press, an imprint of Macmillan Publishing Company. 256: All by Dan DeWilde for SB&G. 261: *Weaving of a Dream* by Marilee Heyer. Copyright © 1986 by Marilee Heyer. All rights reserved. Reprinted by permission of Viking Penguin, Inc. **Unit 6:** 301: *b.l.* Courtesy of the Texas Memorial Museum; *t.r.* Martin/Scala/Art Resource; *b.r.* Courtesy of the Southwest Museum, Los Angeles, Calif. #CT.138. 312: All by Dan DeWilde for SB&G. 316: Courtesy of the New-York Historical Society. 317: *My Prairie Year* by Brett Harvey. Copyright © by Brett Harvey. Reprinted by permission of Holiday House, Inc. **Unit 7:** 338: *t.* Heather Angel; *m.* Salvatore Giordano III; *b.* William E. Ferguson. 339: *t.* © Wolfgang Kaehler 1988; *m.* Bill Griffin/IMAGERY; *b.* Robin Smith/Shostal Associates. 366: All by Dan DeWilde for SB&G. 371: *Helen Keller* by Stewart Graff. Used by permission of Dell Books. (A division of Bantam, Doubleday, Dell Publishing Group, Inc.) **Unit 8:** 386: NASA. 387: NASA. 389: From *The Grand Tour,* copyright © 1981 by Ron Miller and William K. Hartmann. Reprinted by permission of Workman Publishing. All rights reserved. 406: NASA. 412: All by Dan DeWilde for SB&G. 417: *The Planets in our Solar System* by Franklyn M. Branley (Thomas Y. Crowell). Jacket art copyright © 1987 by Don Madden. Reprinted by permission of Harper & Row Publishers, Inc. 477: Claire Rydell for SB&G. **Dictionary:** 445: The Bettmann Archive. 448: Steve Terrill. 449: *l.* From *The Fairy Tales of The Brothers Grimm,* illustrated by Arthur Rackham, Doubleday & Co., 1909. Reprinted by kind permission of Mrs. Barbara Edwards; *l. inset* The Bettmann Archive; *r.* Hans Reinhard/Bruce Coleman. 450: John Elk III/Bruce Coleman. 453: Historical Pictures Service. 454: The Bettmann Archive. Every effort has been made to locate the original sources. If any errors have occurred, the publisher can be notified and corrections will be made.

Silver Burdett Ginn
A Division of Simon & Schuster
160 Gould Street
Needham Heights, MA 02194

3 4 5 6 7 8 9 -VH- 00 99 98 97 96

INTRODUCTORY UNIT

UNIT 1   USING LANGUAGE TO NARRATE

PART 1 LANGUAGE AWARENESS ◆ SENTENCES

PART 2 A REASON FOR WRITING ◆ NARRATING

UNIT 2　　USING LANGUAGE TO INFORM

UNIT 3   USING LANGUAGE TO CREATE

PART 1   LANGUAGE AWARENESS ◆ NOUNS

PART 2   A REASON FOR WRITING ◆ CREATING

UNIT 4   USING LANGUAGE TO PERSUADE

UNIT THEME: Pets

Literature Model: Socks

vii

UNIT 5   USING LANGUAGE TO IMAGINE

PART 1   LANGUAGE AWARENESS ◆ VERBS

PART 2   A REASON FOR WRITING ◆ IMAGINING

UNIT 6   USING LANGUAGE TO RESEARCH

PART 1   LANGUAGE AWARENESS ◆ VERBS

PART 2   A REASON FOR WRITING ◆ RESEARCHING

UNIT 7 USING LANGUAGE TO DESCRIBE

PART 1 LANGUAGE AWARENESS ◆ ADJECTIVES

PART 2 A REASON FOR WRITING ◆ DESCRIBING

UNIT 8   USING LANGUAGE TO CLASSIFY

PART 1   LANGUAGE AWARENESS ◆ SENTENCES

PART 2   A REASON FOR WRITING ◆ CLASSIFYING

WRITER'S REFERENCE BOOK

AWARD LITERATURE WINNING

"A Curve in the River"
from *More Stories Julian Tells*
by Ann Cameron

North America

Atlantic Ocean

Pacific Ocean

South America

"The Sleeping Prince"
from *Clever Gretchen and Other Forgotten Folktales*
by Alison Lurie

Socks
by Beverly Cleary

Through Grandpa's Eyes
by Patricia MacLachlan

LITERATURE

Most poets like to ~
around them. Sometir~
things like bugs and~
these poets talk to~
them. What surpr~
the poets say?

AWARD
WINNING
AUTHOR

LITERATURE

FROM

Socks

by BEVERLY CLEARY

KITTENS
25¢ or
BEST OFFER

DAILY
NEWS

DAILY
NEWS

13

182

LITERATURE: Story

Introductory Unit

Literature in Your World

Literature is a key. It unlocks your imagination. It opens your mind to a world of ideas. With literature, you can enter any time or any place. You can meet people you would never meet… share ideas with great thinkers…have marvelous adventures! Literature is indeed a key — a key to your wonderful world and to the world of language.

Writing in Your World

Writing and reading work together. They are partners, a team. Writers are readers, and readers are writers. Sometimes you write for your readers. Sometimes you write just for yourself. Writing helps you share your ideas. Writing helps you explore your thoughts and feelings. Writing helps you grow.

Writing is thinking. Writing helps you find out about your world. Writing can help you to change it! Writing is powerful. It is a powerful tool in your world and in the wonderful world of language.

What Is a Writer?

A writer is anyone who writes. *You* are a writer. Sometimes you write for others. Other times you write just for yourself. Here are three kinds of writing. You will try them this year.

Writing to Inform ♦ Writing can help you get something done. For example, you might write directions to explain how to get to your house.

Writing to Create ♦ You might use your imagination to write a poem or story.

Writing to Express Yourself ♦ You can write to express what you think or feel — to explore your ideas. This kind of writing is a kind of talking to yourself.

Many writers use a journal when they write just for themselves. This is a good idea for you, too.

Journal Writing

A journal is a writer's best friend. Carry one with you. Then you will be ready to

- jot down an idea
- practice different kinds of writing
- express yourself in words
- write what you think about a book, a movie, a song
- record your impressions of things you see and do

A journal can be a special notebook or a book you make by stapling paper in a folder. Once you have your journal, use it right away. In this book you will find many ideas for journal writing.

Introducing the Writing Process

Sometimes you want to write something to share with others. You want to make it really good. Using the writing process will help you do your best.

When you use the writing process, you go through the process of writing step by step. You do not expect to just sit down and write a perfect paper. Instead, you take time to think, to plan, to get ideas. Later you go over what you have written. You make changes and corrections.

With each step of the writing process, you are given *strategies*. These are helpful plans — ways of working. They show you how to get ideas, how to get started and keep going, how to improve your writing, and how to share it.

Think, Read, Speak, Listen, Write

At the end of each unit, you will use the writing process to write something to share with others. You will be well-prepared by the lessons in that unit.

- A **Thinking Skill** lesson gives a strategy to use in reading and writing.
- A **Literature** lesson gives you a writing model.
- A **Speaking and Listening** lesson helps you develop skills for using language orally.
- The **Writing** lessons explain the kinds of writing you will do as you use the writing process.
- Two **Connection** lessons help you apply the grammar and literature to writing.

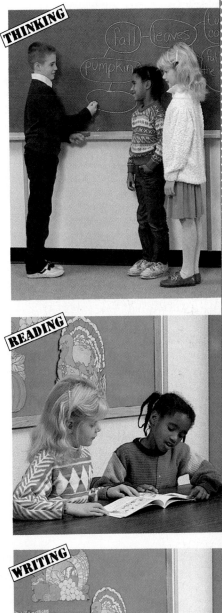

Using the Writing Process

WRITER'S HINT

As you write, keep these two things in mind:

1. Purpose Why are you writing? To tell a story? To describe something? To give information?

2. Audience Who will read what you write? Someone your own age? Someone younger? An adult?

Write a Description

On the next four pages you will preview the writing process and have a chance to try each stage. The stages are: *prewriting, writing, revising, proofreading,* and *publishing*.

Writers often start by prewriting and end by publishing. They may, however, go back and forth among the other stages. With each stage there is an activity for you to do.

Read the Writer's Hint now. For your description your *purpose* is to describe something you are wearing. Your *audience* is your classmates.

1 Prewriting ◆ Getting ready to write

Have you ever said, "I don't know what to write about"? Don't worry. Most writers feel that way before they start writing. There are lots of ways to get ideas. You can brainstorm or draw an idea cluster. You can keep a journal or interview someone.

PREWRITING IDEA

Using Your Senses

Choose something you have on that is interesting to describe. Don't tell anyone what it is.

Observe. If you choose a button on your sweater, for instance, look at it closely. What details do you see? How does it feel when you touch it? Does it make a sound if you tap it? Does it have a smell? Write down everything you notice. Your notes can be just words.

2 Writing ◆ Putting your ideas on paper

You have your writing topic. You have your notes. A blank page is staring at you. How can you get started?

The important thing is just to start writing. Don't worry if your ideas are out of order. Don't worry about spelling right now. Later you can make changes to improve and correct your writing.

WRITING IDEA

Starting with a Question

Put your prewriting notes in front of you. How can you begin? You might begin with a question such as *Can you guess what is unusual about this button?* Next use your notes to describe what you have chosen. Tell how it looks, sounds, feels, smells, and maybe tastes. Then add an ending sentence, such as *Even a small button is interesting when you really study it.*

3 Revising ♦ Making changes to improve your writing

Reading to yourself is important to do when you revise your writing. Think about your purpose. Did you really describe something you are wearing? Or did you forget to describe and start telling a story? Think about your audience. Will your classmates understand what you wrote?

Next read your writing to a partner. Then ask your partner to make suggestions and ask questions. Think about what your partner suggests. Finally, make the changes *you* feel are important.

REVISING IDEA

Read to Yourself and Read to a Partner

First read your description to yourself. Think about your purpose and audience. Did you really write a description? Will your classmates be able to "see" what you describe? Make changes to improve your description. You can cross out words and write in new words. You can draw arrows to show where to move words or sentences. Your writing may look very messy at this point. That is all right.

Next read your description to a partner. Ask, "*What part did you like best? Is there any part that you would like to know more about?*" Listen to the answers. Then make the changes *you* think will improve your description.

4 Proofreading ◆ Looking for and fixing errors

After you have made sure your writing says what you want it to say, proofread it. Look for errors. Check capital letters and punctuation, indenting, and spelling. Then make a clean copy in your best handwriting.

PROOFREADING IDEA

One Thing at a Time

It's hard to look for every kind of error at once. Check for one thing at a time. First check indenting, then capitalization, then punctuation. Check your spelling last.

5 Publishing ◆ Sharing your writing with others

There are many ways to share your writing. You may read it aloud to others. You may record it with a tape recorder or post it on a bulletin board. One of the best parts of writing is sharing what you wrote with others.

PUBLISHING IDEA

A Guessing Game

Take turns reading your descriptions aloud. In place of the name of your object, though, say a nonsense word you make up, such as *glump*. See how well you have described your objects. Can your classmates tell what it is?

UNIT ONE

USING LANGUAGE TO
NARRATE

PART ONE

Unit Theme *Messages*

Language Awareness Sentences

PART TWO

Literature "A Curve in the River" by Ann Cameron

A Reason for Writing Narrating

Writing
IN YOUR JOURNAL

WRITER'S WARM-UP ◆ You have probably sent many messages. You may have written a note or a letter. Why do people send messages? How many ways can you think of to send messages? Write in your journal about sending messages. Tell about your favorite way to send them.

Part of the following message is invisible. What words could you use to finish the message?

I go camping in ____ . At night it's ____ .
I like to ____ . Please, call ____ .

1 Writing Sentences

Read the paired groups of words below. In each pair one group of words is a sentence. The other group of words is not a sentence.

The spy watched the queen.	**Sentence**
Mixed lemon juice and water.	**Not a Sentence**
Then the woman.	**Not a Sentence**
She wrote a message on the paper.	**Sentence**
The spy looked at the paper.	**Sentence**
The blank paper on the desk.	**Not a Sentence**

Each sentence above tells a complete thought. The other groups of words do not tell complete thoughts. They are not sentences.

> **Summary** ◆ A **sentence** is a group of words that tells a complete thought. Use complete sentences in your writing.

Guided Practice

Tell which groups of words below are sentences.

1. The spy could not read the queen's message.
2. The message was invisible.
3. Tricked the spy and his helpers.

Practice

A. Write *sentence* or *not a sentence* for each group of words below.

4. You can write invisible messages.
5. Lemon juice or juice and water.
6. White paper and a nail.
7. A nail can be used as a pen.
8. The lemon juice for ink.
9. You could write a message to your friend.
10. The message will be invisible at first.
11. The heat from the iron.
12. The lemon juice will turn brown.
13. Then your message will be visible.
14. You and your friend.
15. You can write secret messages.
16. You can mail them to your friends.
17. Will read the message.

B. Match a group of words from each column below to make a complete thought. Write each sentence.

18. The writer   are easy to read.
19. Some books   was hanging on the wall.
20. The calendar   used the typewriter.
21. Pencils   helped her see.
22. Her glasses   are made of wood.

Apply • **Think and Write**

From Your Writing ◆ Read what you wrote for the Writer's Warm-up. Count the number of sentences you wrote.

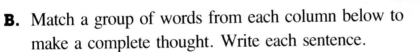

✎ **Remember** to be sure each sentence you write tells a complete thought.

GETTING STARTED

What is black and white and "red" all over?
Change the order of the words below to answer the riddle.
white and "read" A newspaper black is and all over.

2 Word Order in Sentences

Read each group of words below. The two underlined groups of words make sense. The words in these sentences are in the right order.

> Wrote class a newspaper our. <u>Our class wrote a newspaper.</u>
> News the paper the tells. <u>The paper tells the news.</u>

Changing the order of words sometimes changes the meaning of a sentence. Read the sentences below. Which sentence tells about the picture?

> Emma has a picture of Tim.
> Tim has a picture of Emma.

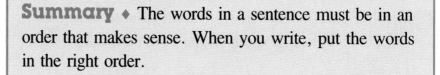

Summary ◆ The words in a sentence must be in an order that makes sense. When you write, put the words in the right order.

Guided Practice

Arrange each group of words in an order that makes sense.

1. has newspaper four Our pages school.
2. stories for We write the paper.
3. page pictures has Every.
4. about events tells The paper.
5. The read children paper the.

Practice

A. The groups of words below do not make sense.
Change the order of the words to make sense.
Write each sentence.

    6. paper the work on We school.
    7. The pictures paper has many.
    8. stories write the We.
    9. The ready is paper.
  10. sell paper graders Third our.

B. Change the order of the underlined words. Write each
new sentence. Notice how the meaning changes.

  11. The paper has <u>many</u> stories but <u>few</u> pictures.
  12. The <u>reporter</u> interviewed the <u>detective</u>.
  13. Two <u>pictures</u> are worth a thousand <u>words</u>.
  14. We <u>sort</u> and <u>deliver</u> the papers.
  15. The <u>first</u> page is longer than the <u>last</u> page.

C. Read the sentences below. Then write new sentences
by changing the word order.

  16. The teacher gave the reporter a paper.
  17. The letter was longer than the story.
  18. Jim told Sandy about the movie review.
  19. The editor wrote a letter to the readers.
  20. Jill will type and edit each story.

Apply ◆ Think and Write

Sentence Sense ◆ Write sentences about working on a
newspaper. Trade papers with a partner. Does the order of
the words in each sentence make sense?

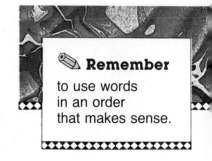

✎ **Remember**
to use words
in an order
that makes sense.

♦ GETTING STARTED ♦

Ask alphabetical questions, such as *Is Audrey an astronaut?*
The answers must be alphabetical, too:
No, Audrey is an actress.

3 Statements and Questions

Some sentences are statements. A statement is a sentence that tells something. Read the statement below. Notice that it begins with a capital letter and ends with a period.

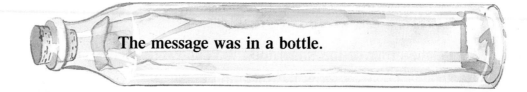

The message was in a bottle.

Some sentences are questions. A question is a sentence that asks something. Read the question below. Notice that it begins with a capital letter and ends with a question mark.

■ **Where was the message?**

> **Summary** ♦ The first word of a sentence begins with a **capital letter**. A **statement** is a sentence that tells something. It ends with a period (**.**). A **question** is a sentence that asks something. It ends with a question mark (**?**).

Guided Practice

Tell if each sentence is a statement or a question.

1. Messages can be sent in many different ways.
2. Have you ever put a message in a balloon?
3. Some pigeons are trained to carry messages.

Practice

A. Read each sentence below. If the sentence tells something, write *statement*. If the sentence asks something, write *question*.

4. Messages can be written or spoken.
5. We can use codes to send secret messages.
6. Do you know a secret code?
7. Have you ever heard of the Morse code?
8. It uses dots and dashes.
9. Messages can be sent by telegraph.
10. Can a flashlight be used to send Morse code?
11. Are smoke signals one kind of code?
12. Do you know what the smoke signals mean?
13. Listen to the beat of the drums.
14. Each drumbeat is part of a secret message.

B. Write each sentence. Begin each sentence with a capital letter. Use periods and question marks correctly.

15. has Irma mailed her invitations
16. i should call her
17. will David write to her
18. can you leave a message
19. she will get our messages tomorrow

Apply ◆ Think and Write

A Partner Interview ◆ Find a partner to interview. Write two questions. Trade questions and write statements to answer them. Read your questions and answers to each other.

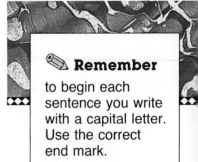

✏️ **Remember**

to begin each sentence you write with a capital letter. Use the correct end mark.

GETTING STARTED

Play "Simon Says." Tell people to clap their hands, stamp their feet, touch their knees, wiggle their noses.

4 Commands and Exclamations

Some sentences are commands. A command gives an order. Read the command below. Notice that it begins with a capital letter and ends with a period.

■ **Tell me what you want.**

Some sentences are exclamations. An exclamation shows strong feeling. Read the exclamation below. Notice that it begins with a capital letter and ends with an exclamation mark.

■ **I want this blue bike!**

> **Summary** ◆ A **command** is a sentence that gives an order. It ends with a period (.). An **exclamation** is a sentence that shows strong feeling. It ends with an exclamation mark (!). You can use commands and exclamations to make your writing more interesting.

Guided Practice

Tell if each sentence is a command or an exclamation.

1. This game is fun!
2. Come to Cabot's Cycle Shop this week.
3. I like this bike!

Practice

A. Read each sentence below. If it gives an order, write *command*. If it shows strong feeling, write *exclamation*.

   4. Speedy Bikes are better than all the others!
   5. Save your money to buy a Speedy Bike.
   6. Get a three-speed or a ten-speed Speedy.
   7. Every child likes Speedy Bikes best!
   8. Buy a Speedy Bike today.

B. Write each command or exclamation correctly.

   9. buy this new cereal
   10. this cereal tastes great
   11. remember to shop at Manny's Market
   12. everyone wants that new toy
   13. don't be left out

C. Rewrite each sentence as a command.

   EXAMPLE: You probably could hurry up.
   ANSWER: Hurry up.

   14. You can brush your teeth with Bright-White.
   15. We usually buy Best Loaf Bread.
   16. You can get Puffy Pops at the grocery store.
   17. He likes to shop at E-Z Stores.
   18. She decided to buy a Speedy Bike.

Apply ◆ Think and Write

An Advertisement ◆ Work with a partner. Write an advertisement for Bright-White Toothpaste or Speedy Bikes. Use both commands and exclamations.

✎ **Remember** to use different kinds of sentences to express your ideas.

Think of ways to complete a sentence that begins *Old MacDonald . . .* (Hint: *Old MacDonald picked the corn. Old MacDonald plowed the field.*)

5 Sentence Parts

Every sentence has two parts. Read each sentence below. The blue part names someone or something. It is called the subject of the sentence. The green part tells what the subject is or does. It is called the predicate of the sentence.

1. **People** **communicate without words.**
2. **They** **can give messages with their eyes.**
3. **Young children** **use their hands when they talk.**

People is the subject in sentence **1**. The predicate is *communicate without words*. What are the subjects in sentences **2** and **3**? What are the predicates in sentences **2** and **3**?

Summary ◆ A sentence has two parts. The **subject** names someone or something. The **predicate** tells what the subject is or does. When you write, be sure each sentence has a subject and a predicate that make sense together.

Guided Practice

Find the subject and the predicate in each sentence below.

1. A friendly person | stands near you.
2. An angry friend | turns away from you.
3. Your body | can show your feelings.

Practice

A. Write *subject* if the subject is underlined. Write *predicate* if the predicate is underlined.

    4. <u>Our faces</u> communicate feelings.
    5. <u>A frown</u> can mean several things.
    6. You <u>may see anger in a frown.</u>
    7. <u>Eyebrows</u> can show surprise.
    8. Tight lips <u>mean anger or impatience.</u>

B. Write each sentence. Draw a line between the subject and the predicate.

    9. Some people show surprise with their mouths.
    10. A smiling face sends a happy message.
    11. Your eyes can show sadness.
    12. Eyes sparkle with delight.
    13. Your face sends messages.

C. Match each subject to a predicate. Write the sentences.

Subjects	**Predicates**
14. The angry boy	clapped her hands.
15. The delighted woman	clenched his fists.
16. A frightened child	raised her eyebrows.
17. The loving father	ran from the big dog.
18. The surprised girl	smiled at the baby.

Apply ◆ **Think and Write**

Sentence Puzzles ◆ Write sentences about body language. Cut each sentence apart between the subject and the predicate. Trade sentences with a partner. Put the sentences back together again.

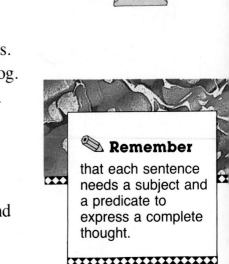

✎ **Remember**
that each sentence needs a subject and a predicate to express a complete thought.

GETTING STARTED

Make up riddles about your favorite story characters.
EXAMPLE: *What mouse has human parents?*
ANSWER: *Stuart Little has human parents.*

6 Subjects in Sentences

The picture shows ways of communicating. Read the sentences below. The blue part of each sentence is the subject. It names someone or something that is giving a message.

1. The instruments give information to the pilot.
2. Diane gives information to the control tower.

The instruments is the subject of sentence **1**. *Diane* is the subject of sentence **2**.

Name a subject to complete the sentence below. Remember, your subject should name someone or something.

3. _____ wrote a message on the computer.

> **Summary** ♦ The **subject** of a sentence names someone or something. When you write, vary the subjects of your sentences.

Guided Practice

The subject is underlined in each sentence below. Think of a different subject. Say each new sentence.

1. Traffic lights help drivers.
2. Police officers receive messages on their radios.
3. Funny movies entertain people.

Practice

A. The subject is underlined in each sentence. It names someone or something. Think of a different subject. Write each new sentence. Then underline the subject.

> **EXAMPLE:** The <u>TV show</u> explained earthquakes.
> **ANSWER:** The <u>filmstrip</u> explained earthquakes.

4. This <u>poster</u> advertises the circus.
5. Some great <u>songs</u> were on the program.
6. The <u>TV announcer</u> reported the news.
7. My <u>name</u> is on the bracelet.
8. The <u>red car</u> honked as a warning.

B. Add a subject to each word group below. Write each complete sentence.

9. ___ controls the traffic.
10. ___ gives the weather report.
11. ___ contains news from my cousin.
12. ___ makes a safety suggestion.
13. ___ shows the price of sneakers.
14. ___ gave the time and place of the party.
15. ___ had my home address.
16. ___ shows the name of the company.
17. ___ can read the train schedule.
18. ___ has a colorful picture.

Apply ◆ Think and Write

Dictionary of Knowledge ◆ Read about Paul Revere in the Dictionary of Knowledge. Write sentences telling when he lived, where he rode on his horse, and what message he carried.

✎ **Remember**
that the subject of each sentence needs to be clear.

Tell a story about Curious George. Tell who he is and what he does. Take turns adding sentences.

7 Predicates in Sentences

The predicate of a sentence tells what the subject is or does. Read the sentences below. The predicate of each sentence is in green.

1. Chim is a good artist.
2. Chim paints a picture.

In sentence **1** *is a good artist* is the predicate. It tells what Chim is. In sentence **2** *paints a picture* is the predicate. It tells what Chim does.

The predicate in the sentence below is missing. What predicate can you add to complete the sentence?

■ **3.** An artist ____ .

> **Summary** ◆ The **predicate** of a sentence tells what the subject is or does. When you write, add variety by using a different predicate in each sentence.

Guided Practice

The predicate is underlined in each sentence below. Think of a different predicate. Say the new sentence.

1. Some painters <u>use oil paints.</u>
2. Other artists <u>make sculptures of wood or metal.</u>
3. Many people <u>are at the art museum.</u>

Practice

A. The predicate is underlined in each sentence. It tells what the subject is or does. Think of a different predicate. Write each new sentence. Then underline the predicate.

EXAMPLE: The children <u>enjoyed the story.</u>

ANSWER: The children <u>wrote a poem.</u>

4. Our class <u>visited the city park.</u>
5. Some wood sculptures <u>were near the entrance.</u>
6. A famous sculptress <u>created the art.</u>
7. The artist <u>was Louise Nevelson.</u>
8. Her art <u>expressed her feelings.</u>

B. Add a predicate to each word group below. Write each complete sentence.

9. The art museum ____ .
10. Many artists ____ .
11. A well-known pianist ____ .
12. The graceful dancer ____ .
13. Modern painters ____ .
14. My favorite picture ____ .
15. The visiting actors ____ .
16. Some poems ____ .
17. The photographs ____ .
18. Our school orchestra ____ .

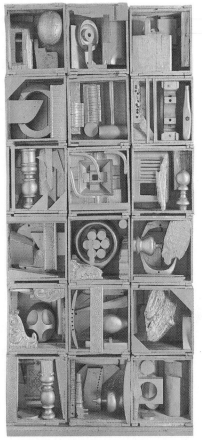

ROYAL TIDE I
Wood sculpture painted gold by Louise Nevelson
Private Collection. Photography Courtesy of the Pace Gallery.

Apply ◆ Think and Write

"I-Do-This" Sentences ◆ Write sentences about one of your talents, such as singing or playing an instrument. Underline each predicate. Read your sentences to a partner.

✎ **Remember**
to make the predicates of your sentences as interesting as you can.

GETTING STARTED

There are many ways to say that something is good. What other words could you use for *good* in this sentence?

John was a good guitar player.

VOCABULARY ♦
Using the Thesaurus

A **thesaurus** is a book of synonyms, or words that have almost the same meaning. The entry words in a thesaurus are listed in alphabetical order, just like a dictionary. For each entry word, many synonyms are listed. The last part of the entry lists words that mean the opposite of the entry word. Words that have opposite meanings are called *antonyms*. You will learn more about synonyms in Unit 7 and more about antonyms in Unit 8.

When you write, you can use a thesaurus to choose clear and interesting words. Study the thesaurus entry.

Entry word ——— **wet**—covered with water or another

Example Sentence ——— liquid; not yet dry. Gina used a wet cloth to wipe the sticky table.

damp—having some water. These clothes are still too damp to wear.
humid—having water vapor in the air. If the kitchen is humid, turn on the fan.

Synonyms ——— *moist*—slightly wet. Newly planted seeds should be kept in moist soil.
soaked—wet throughout. We had soaked feet because we forgot to wear boots.
soggy—heavy from being wet. This soggy oatmeal tastes awful!

Antonyms ——— ANTONYMS: arid, dry, parched

Building Your Vocabulary

Name the entry word above and find its example sentence. How many synonyms are listed? How many antonyms?

Practice

A. Use the thesaurus entry in this lesson. Choose a different synonym to replace *wet* in each sentence.

    1. It wasn't raining, but the air was very <u>wet</u>.

    2. After the downpour the boys were thoroughly <u>wet</u>.

    3. The book was so <u>wet</u> that I could hardly lift it.

    4. The clothes were almost dry but still <u>wet</u>.

B. Turn to the Thesaurus that begins on page 456. Choose a word to replace each underlined word below.

    5. The autumn air is very <u>cool</u>.

    6. The river seemed very <u>dirty</u>.

    7. Some gymnasts can <u>jump</u> high in the air.

    8. Our friends from Vermont are always very <u>nice</u>.

C. Use the Thesaurus to answer the questions.

    9. Which synonym of *bad* means "not right"?

    10. Which synonym of *rest* means to "sleep lightly"?

    11. Which synonym of *run* begins with *s*?

Language Corner ◆ Palindromes

Did you know that some words are spelled the same both forward and backward? These words are called **palindromes**.

Did, pop, and *radar* are palindromes. Can you think of others?

How to Combine Sentences

Two sentences that repeat words can be combined, or joined, into one sentence. You can use the word *and* to combine them. *Andy* is the subject of each sentence below. The sentences tell about two things Andy did.

1. Andy wrote a letter. Andy mailed it today.
2. Andy wrote a letter and mailed it today.

Sentence **2** uses the word *and* to combine two short sentences into one strong sentence.

You can also use the word *and* to combine sentences that have the same predicate. Read the sentences below. Which words are not repeated when these two short sentences are joined?

3. Roy spoke French. My cousin spoke French.
4. Roy and my cousin spoke French.

The Grammar Game ◆ Can you join each pair of sentences to make one strong sentence? What word will you add to each pair?

◆ Lia hummed cheerfully. Lia snapped her fingers.
◆ The conductor bowed to the audience.
The musicians bowed to the audience.

Working Together

Combining sentences can make your writing stronger. Work together as a group on activities **A** and **B**.

In Your Group

♦ Let everyone share ideas.
♦ Don't interrupt each other.
♦ Listen to each other carefully.
♦ Help the group finish on time.

A. Use the word *and* to combine any two sentences of the group's choice. How many different sentences can you write?

We told jokes.   We watched movies.
We popped corn.   We told funny stories.
We made piñatas.   We visited a science lab.

B. Use two names joined by *and* to complete each sentence. Choose names of group members.

1. ___ listened carefully.   **4.** ___ shared ideas.
2. ___ didn't interrupt.   **5.** ___ helped a lot.
3. ___ read quietly.   **6.** ___ walked softly.

WRITERS' CORNER ♦ Stringy Sentences

Sometimes the word *and* is used too often. Stringy sentences are too long and hard to read.

STRINGY: **Sal made the beds and washed the dishes and emptied the trash and swept the floor.**

IMPROVED: **Sal made the beds and washed the dishes. Sal emptied the trash and swept the floor.**

Read what you wrote for the Writer's Warm-up. Look for short sentences that could be joined by *and*. Look for stringy sentences, too.

LINCOLN PROCLAIMING THANKSGIVING
painting by Dean Conwell
Louis A. Warren Lincoln Memorial Library and Museum,
Fort Wayne, Indiana.

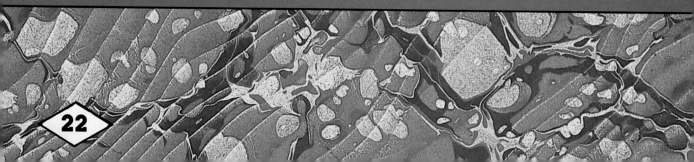

USING LANGUAGE
TO
NARRATE

═══ **PART TWO** ═══

Literature   "A Curve in the River" by Ann Cameron

Composition Narrating

CREATIVE
Writing

FINE ARTS ◆ Dean Conwell painted this picture of President Abraham Lincoln. Lincoln is signing a message about a new holiday. Americans will now celebrate Thanksgiving as a national holiday. If you could proclaim a new holiday, what would it be? Would it be in the summer? The winter? Write a message to proclaim your new holiday.

CREATIVE THINKING ♦
A Strategy for Narrating

A PREDICTION CHART

Telling a story is sometimes called narrating. After this lesson you will read part of a story, "A Curve in the River." Then you will write a story about an event in your own life.

In "A Curve in the River," Julian is the storyteller. He is narrating something he did, so he uses the word *I*. This is how he begins.

> This is something I learned in school: . . . The whole earth is mostly water—three-quarters ocean. . . . And using water—streams and rivers and oceans—anybody could put a message in a bottle and send it all the way around the world.

A prediction is something you think is going to happen. Julian put a message in a bottle. Then he thought about, or predicted, what would happen to it. He predicted that the bottle would go all around the world.

Learning the Strategy

You often make predictions. For example, suppose you are in the library. You look at a book. You predict that you will enjoy it.

Sometimes you can predict several things that might happen. Suppose you are at the zoo. A zookeeper asks if

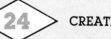

you want a camel ride. How many things can you predict
might happen? How can predicting help you decide?

Do any of your predictions ever come true? It can be fun
to find out. A prediction chart can help. It might look like
this.

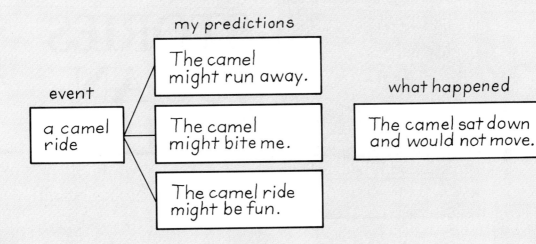

Using the Strategy

A. Think about things you think might happen in school
today. Make a prediction chart about them. Later, finish
the chart by telling what really happened.

B. In "A Curve in the River," Julian puts a message in a
bottle. Then he puts the bottle in the river. He wants
someone far away to find it and read it. What do you
think might happen? Make a prediction chart. Fill in
your predictions. Then, after you have read the story,
fill in what really happened.

Applying the Strategy

- How do you figure out what might happen?
- When might you want to make a prediction?

LITERATURE

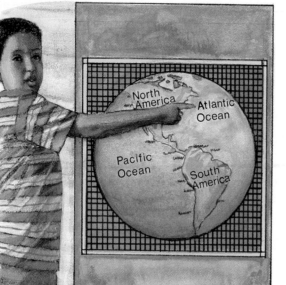

FROM

MORE STORIES JULIAN TELLS

by ANN CAMERON

Once there was a boy named Julian. Like you, Julian has some secrets to keep. Like you, he has some stories to tell about his adventures. Here is one of Julian's stories.

A Curve in the River

This is something I learned in school: The whole body is mostly water.

We think we're solid, but we're not. You can tell sometimes from your blood and tears and stuff that what you're like inside isn't what you're like outside, but usually you'd never know.

Also, the whole earth is mostly water—three-quarters ocean. The continents are just little stopping places. And using water—streams and rivers and oceans—anybody could put a message in a bottle and send it all the way around the world.

That was my secret project.

So Julian carried out his secret project. He wrote a message with his address and phone number. He put the message in a bottle. Then he threw the corked bottle in the river and watched it go out of sight.

Every day after that, Julian kept thinking about his secret project. He thought about his bottle floating to faraway places. He imagined writing letters to the person who found it. He saw himself in other countries, visiting his new friend.

A week later, Julian's friend Gloria called him with some news. She had found his bottle at her house, just down the street. Julian's bottle had not gone around the world after all. It had stayed right there in the neighborhood!

Julian was too upset to talk to Gloria after that. Julian's father noticed and asked Julian what was wrong. Here is how Julian tells the rest of his story.

Then I decided to tell my father about the bottle and how Gloria found it. It didn't matter anymore to keep it a secret. The secret was over.

"That's too bad," my father said. "But it's not Gloria's fault."

"She found the bottle," I said. "She must be laughing at me for trying such a stupid idea."

"It's not a stupid idea," my father said. "You just had bad luck. You know what your problem is? It's the curve in the river. Your bottle got stuck on that curve, and it didn't have a chance."

I felt a little better. I went to see Gloria.

"I wanted to give you your bottle back," Gloria said. Then she added, "I thought it was a great idea, sending a message in a bottle."

"Well, it's a good idea, but it's a no-good idea because of the curve in the river. The bottle couldn't get around it," I explained.

"I guess it couldn't," Gloria said.

"Julian," my father said, "I have to make a long trip in the truck Saturday. I have to pick up some car parts. I'm going to go past the big bridge down the river. Would you like to ride along?"

I said I would.

"You know," my father said, "there's something we could do. We could walk out on the bridge. And if you wanted, you could send a new message. Your bottle would have a good chance from there. It's past the curve in the river."

I thought about it. I decided to do it. And I told my father.

"You know," he said, "if you don't mind my advice—put something special about yourself in the bottle, for the person who finds it."

"Why?" I asked.

"It'll give the wind and the water something special to carry. If you send something you care about, it might bring you luck."

I was working on my new message. And then I thought about Huey and Gloria. I thought how they might want to send bottles too. It didn't seem so important anymore that I be the only one to do it.

And that's what we did. We all got new bottles, and we put something special in each one. We each made a picture of ourselves for our bottle.

And in his, Huey put his favorite joke:
Where does a hamburger go on New Year's Eve?
To a meat ball.

In hers, Gloria put instructions on doing a cartwheel.

In mine, I wrote instructions for taking care of rabbits.

We added our addresses and phone numbers and pushed in the corks tightly. We were ready for Saturday.

The bridge was long and silver and sparkled in the sun. It was so big that it looked like giants must have made it, that human beings never could have. But human beings did.

My father parked below the bridge. "From here we have to walk," he said.

We got out of the truck, which always smells a little bit of dust, but mostly of the raisins Dad keeps on the dashboard.

We walked in the outside walkers' lane to the middle of the river. Cars whizzed past. We each had our bottle in a backpack.

The bridge swayed a little. We could feel it vibrate. My father held Gloria's and Huey's hands. I held Gloria's other hand.

"It's scary, but it's safe," my father said.

We held on to the bridge railing and looked over the side. The green water slid under us very fast. For a minute it seemed like the bridge was moving and the water was standing still.

We unpacked our bottles.

"Don't just throw them over the side," my father said. "Make some wishes. Sending messages around the world is a big thing to do. Anytime you do a big thing, it's good to make wishes."

We did.

I don't know what Huey or Gloria wished. I wished our bottles would sail along together. I wished they wouldn't get trapped in seaweed or ice, or hit rocks. I wished we'd make new friends on the other side of the world. I wished we'd go to meet them someday.

"Ready?" my father said.

Together we threw our bottles over the side. They made a tiny splash. They looked very small, but we could see them starting toward the ocean.

They were like Columbus's ships. I hoped they'd stay together a long, long time.

Library Link ◆ *To learn about some other exciting adventures, read* More Stories Julian Tells *by Ann Cameron.*

Reader's Response

Do you think Julian had a good idea? Tell why or why not.

MORE STORIES JULIAN TELLS

Responding to Literature

1. Imagine that you will send a message in a bottle. What message will you write? Draw a picture of your bottle. Write your message inside.

2. Julian sent a message in a bottle. If you could send a message, how would you send it?

3. What happened to the three bottles? What would you like to know? Write questions. Then choose your favorite question. Read it to your classmates.

Writing to Learn

Think and Predict ◆ Julian hoped he would make new friends on the other side of the world. Pretend you have sent a message in a bottle. What will happen to it? Copy the chart below. Fill in the details.

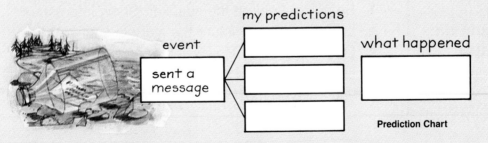

my predictions

event

sent a message

what happened

Prediction Chart

Write ◆ Write about sending your message. Tell what you thought would happen.

♦ **GETTING STARTED** ♦

Start a "Story Round" by finishing this sentence:
When I was in the first grade, _____ .
Take turns adding sentences to the story.

SPEAKING and LISTENING ♦
Telling a Story

Stories are important. Long before there were books, people told stories. Before writing was invented, storytellers told tales. People listened and remembered. They retold the stories to their children. Do you know stories told by your parents?

Telling a story can be as much fun as listening to a story. It is fun to share stories that you enjoy. Try it. Follow the guidelines below to tell and listen to a good story.

Telling a Story	1. Have a good beginning. 2. Tell the story events in order. (Not: "Oh, I forgot to tell you something that happened first.") 3. Look at your listeners. Speak so everyone can hear. 4. Show feeling with your voice, face, and actions. 5. Practice aloud, in front of a mirror if you wish.
Being an Active Listener	1. Be polite. Look at the speaker. Show interest. 2. Listen to enjoy. Picture the story in your mind. 3. Listen to predict. How will the story end? 4. Listen to help the speaker. Tell the speaker what you enjoyed most. Ask questions, too.

Summary ♦ When you tell a story, have a good beginning. Tell the events in order. Be an active listener by thinking, "How will the story end?"

Guided Practice

Read aloud these sentences from "A Curve in the River." Read each sentence with a feeling of excitement. Speak clearly so that your listeners can hear you easily.

1. I kept thinking about my secret project.
2. My bottle was supposed to travel around the world.
3. It's good to make wishes.

Practice

A. Say these sentences from the story with feeling. Choose from the feelings below. See if your listeners can tell which feeling you are showing.

fear	amazement	surprise	anger
wonder	sadness	joy	excitement

4. The whole body is mostly water.
5. That was my secret project.
6. I was working on my new message.
7. Where does a hamburger go on New Year's Eve?
8. The green water slid under us very fast.

B. Use the guidelines in this lesson. Take turns telling about stories you have read. When it is your turn to listen, try to predict how the story you hear will end.

Apply • Think and Write

A Tongue Twister ◆ Practice speaking clearly. Write a tongue twister. Begin as many words as you can with the same letter: Bob broke both bottles. See how fast you can say your tongue twister clearly.

> ✏️ **REMEMBER**
> to listen to predict how a story will end.

Think about the story "Little Red Riding Hood." Play "Who? Where? When?" Ask and answer questions about the story.

WRITING ◆
Story Characters and Setting

Every story has one or more characters. The characters are the people or animals in a story. The story is about them. The characters may be true to life or they may be make-believe.

Every story also has a setting. The setting is when and where the story takes place. A story's setting might be your hometown at this very moment. It might be a space station on another planet!

Characters and setting work together in a story, no matter what kind of story it is.

> **Summary** ◆ **Characters** are the people or animals in a story. **Setting** is when and where the story takes place. Writers try to make the characters and the setting seem real to the reader.

Guided Practice

Tell if each of the following is a story character or a story setting.

1. Huey
2. a bridge over a river
3. in Dad's truck
4. Gloria
5. Julian's house

Practice

A. Write *character* or *setting* to show which part of a story each item describes.

6. Snoopy and Lucy
7. midnight in the swamp
8. your kitchen
9. King Midas
10. a friendly dragon
11. Mario's house
12. Ferdinand the Bull
13. an underwater cave
14. Never-Never Land
15. the Little Red Hen

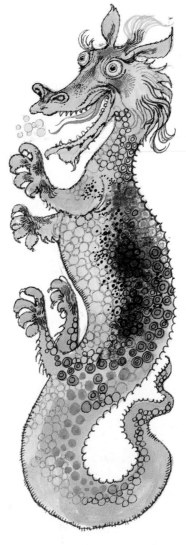

B. These sentences are from "A Curve in the River." For each one, write *character* or *setting* to show which part of the story the sentence fits.

16. I'm going to go past the big bridge down the river.
17. And then I thought about Huey and Gloria.
18. The bridge was long and silver and sparkled in the sun.
19. My father held Gloria's and Huey's hands.
20. I don't know what Huey or Gloria wished.

C. Put on your wishing cap. If you could be any character from any book, who would you be? Why? What time would you choose to live in? What place? Write about your choices.

Apply • **Think and Write**

Dictionary of Knowledge ♦ Read about Mark Twain in the Dictionary of Knowledge. Suppose you wrote a true-life story about him. Write one thing you would say about him. Then write about the setting you would use. Tell its time and its place.

✏ **REMEMBER**

to carefully plan the setting and characters of your story.

♦ GETTING STARTED ♦

Here is a story beginning: <u>Maria rushed to catch the bus for school.</u> What could go wrong? What else could go wrong? How will the story end?

WRITING ♦
A Story Plot

You know that a story has characters and a setting. A story must also have a plot. A plot is the series of events in the story. It answers these questions: *What happened? What happened after that? And after that? How does the story end?*

A plot has three parts: a beginning, a middle, and an ending. At the beginning the main character is given a problem to solve. In the middle of the story, the character tries to solve the problem. But things go wrong. Excitement builds. The ending of the story tells how the character solves the problem.

A Plot

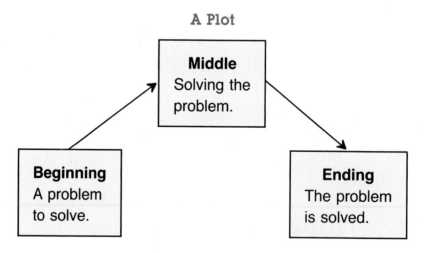

Middle
Solving the problem.

Beginning
A problem to solve.

Ending
The problem is solved.

> **Summary** ♦ A **plot** is the series of events in a story. It tells what happens. A writer needs to plan a story's plot—its beginning, middle, and ending.

Guided Practice

Do you remember the story about Goldilocks and the three bears? Each event pictured is part of the story. Put the story in order by its beginning, middle, and ending.

1. The bears return home and find Goldilocks.
2. The three bears take a walk in the woods.
3. Goldilocks enters the bears' house and eats Baby Bear's food.

Practice

A. The events below tell another story. In which part of the story does each event belong? Write beginning, middle, or ending for each event.

4. Only the birds answered her cries for help.
5. She walked for miles, looking for the trail.
6. Gloria went camping with her friends.
7. Gloria accidentally wandered off from camp. She was lost!
8. She heard a noise. It was Mrs. Eldridge, their leader, finding her at last.

B. Write the five events for **Practice A** in the correct order to tell a story.

Apply • Think and Write

Story Parts ♦ Write a sentence you could use to begin a story about yourself. Then write a sentence that tells about a problem you could solve in your story.

> ✎ **REMEMBER**
> to plan a beginning, middle, and ending for your story.

Focus on Story Order

Read this paragraph about "A Curve in the River." You read part of this story earlier in the unit.

He waited. Who would find the bottle? He waited, he wondered. He wrote a note. He corked the bottle and threw it in the river. Julian had a secret project. He put it in a bottle that had a cork. He put his name and address on it. His question was answered.

What happens in the story? It is not easy to tell, is it? The problem is that the events are not told in order. The order does not make sense. Can you fix the paragraph? Here is one way to do it. Notice how the underlined words help put the story in order. They are clue words.

Julian had a secret project. *First* he wrote a note. He put his name and address on it. *Next* he put it in a bottle that had a cork. *Then* he corked the bottle and threw it in the river. *After that* he waited. *While* he waited, he wondered. Who would find the bottle? *Soon* his question was answered.

The Writer's Voice ◆ Now it is clear what Julian was doing. The events are arranged in order. The underlined words tell you something, too. What do they tell you about each event?

Working Together

Telling a story in order helps to make the story clear. Work with your group on activities **A** and **B**.

A. Arrange the sentences below in story order. Watch for clue words.

 1. On Saturday, we sent our bottles down the river.
 2. Then we added our addresses and phone numbers.
 3. First, we all got new bottles.
 4. Finally, we pushed in the corks tightly.
 5. We each wrote something to put in our bottle.

B. Suppose your group found a message in a bottle. Where would you find the bottle? What would the message say? What would you do? As a group, write a story about your make-believe adventure. Use words such as *first* and *then* to show the order in which things happen.

In Your Group

- ◆ Make sure everyone knows the directions.
- ◆ Give your ideas to the group.
- ◆ Ask others to talk.
- ◆ Thank people for their ideas.

THESAURUS CORNER ◆ Word Choice

Copy the sentences below. Use the Thesaurus to replace each word in dark type with a good synonym. Underline each clue word that shows story order.

We had a good week. First, we went to an auto **show.** Next, we saw a circus with **funny** clowns. Then we saw a **bright** fireworks display. Finally, we took a brief **trip** to my uncle's farm.

WRITING PROCESS

NARRATING

Writing a Personal Narrative

A narrative is a story. Personal narratives are stories that people tell about themselves. In these stories the writers call themselves *I* or *me*.

In the story "A Curve in the River," Julian told about how he put a message in a bottle. He told what he did. He also told how he felt. These details made his story seem very real.

Know Your Purpose and Audience

MY PURPOSE

In this lesson you will write a personal narrative. Your purpose will be to write a story about something that happened to you.

MY AUDIENCE

Your audience will be your classmates. Later you and your classmates can tell your stories. You can also put them together in a book.

1 Prewriting

Prewriting is getting ready to write. First choose a topic. Then gather ideas about your topic.

Choose Your Topic ♦ Can you remember the first time you went to school? Those ''firsts'' in your life are important. Make a list of ''firsts'' that you remember. Then circle the one you like best.

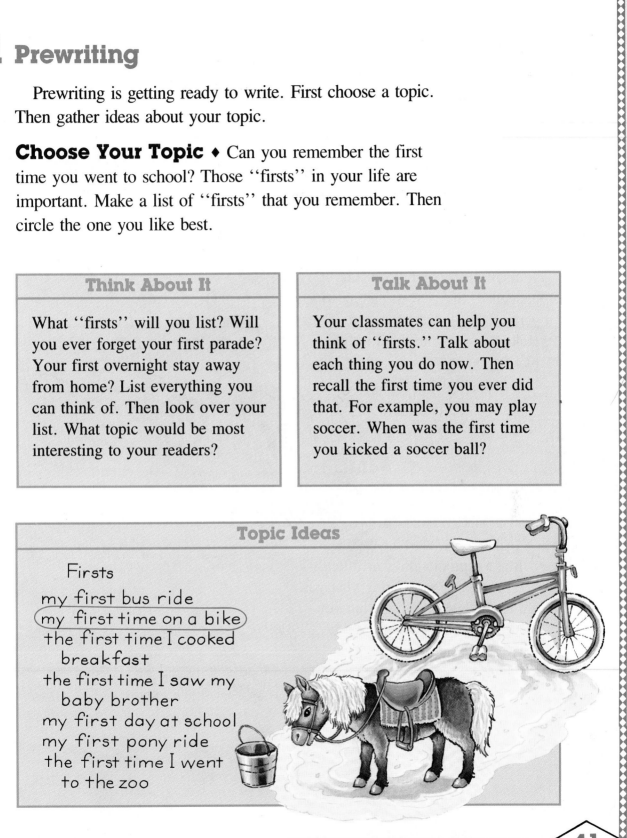

Think About It

What ''firsts'' will you list? Will you ever forget your first parade? Your first overnight stay away from home? List everything you can think of. Then look over your list. What topic would be most interesting to your readers?

Talk About It

Your classmates can help you think of ''firsts.'' Talk about each thing you do now. Then recall the first time you ever did that. For example, you may play soccer. When was the first time you kicked a soccer ball?

Topic Ideas

Firsts
my first bus ride
my first time on a bike
the first time I cooked breakfast
the first time I saw my baby brother
my first day at school
my first pony ride
the first time I went to the zoo

Choose Your Strategy ♦ How can you gather ideas about your topic? Here are two ways to get ideas. Read both. Then decide which you want to try.

PREWRITING IDEAS

CHOICE ONE

A Memory Search

Do a memory search. Draw yourself at the time your story happened. Show your picture to a partner. Tell what happened. Then make notes. Write them on your picture.

Model

running dog
Dad helped
hit a bush
SLOW DOWN!

CHOICE TWO

A Prediction Chart

Make a prediction chart like this one for your story. Write what you did as the event. Write what you predicted would happen. Write what really did happen.

Model

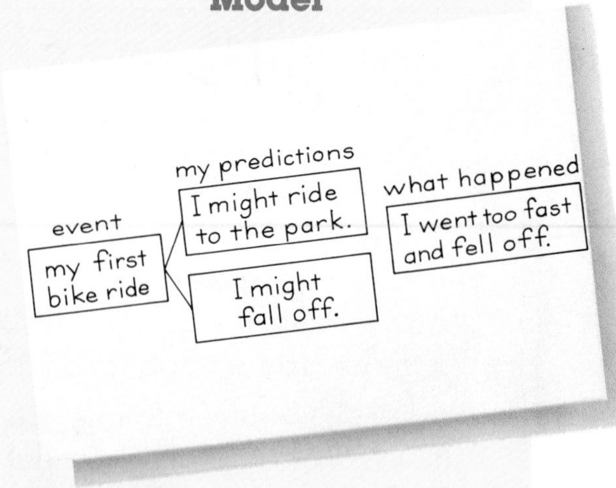

event
my first
bike ride

my predictions
I might ride
to the park.

I might
fall off.

what happened
I went too fast
and fell off.

2 Writing

Writing is putting your ideas on paper. First look at the picture or chart you made. This will help you remember your story. Then begin writing your story. You might start like this.

- ♦ I'll never forget the day I ____.
- ♦ The first time I ____.

After you start, write what happened next. End with what happened last. Don't worry about mistakes. You can go back later to make changes.

Sample First Draft ♦

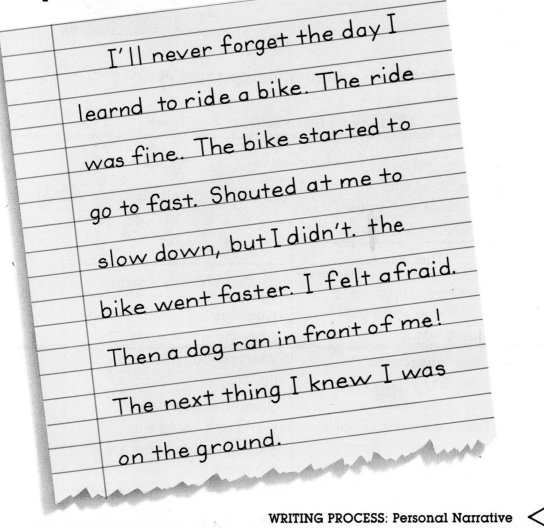

I'll never forget the day I learnd to ride a bike. The ride was fine. The bike started to go to fast. Shouted at me to slow down, but I didn't. the bike went faster. I felt afraid. Then a dog ran in front of me! The next thing I knew I was on the ground.

3 Revising

Here is an idea to help improve your narrative.

REVISING IDEA

FIRST Read to Yourself

Think about your purpose. Did you tell about something that happened to you? Will your audience understand your story? Make a wavy line ∿∿∿ under any parts you want to fix.

Focus: Is your story in correct story order?

THEN Share with a Partner

Ask a partner to be your first audience. Read your story aloud. Then ask your partner for ideas. The guidelines below may help.

The Writer

Guidelines: Read aloud slowly. Think about your partner's suggestions.

Sample questions:
- What was your favorite part of my story?
- **Focus question:** Should I make the order clearer?

The Writer's Partner

Guidelines: Listen carefully while the writer reads. Give your opinion honestly, but politely.

Sample responses:
- The part I liked was ____.
- I wasn't sure about the order of ____.

WRITING PROCESS: Personal Narrative

Revising Model ◆ Look at the sample story that is being revised. Notice the revising marks. The writer used them to show himself the changes he wants to make.

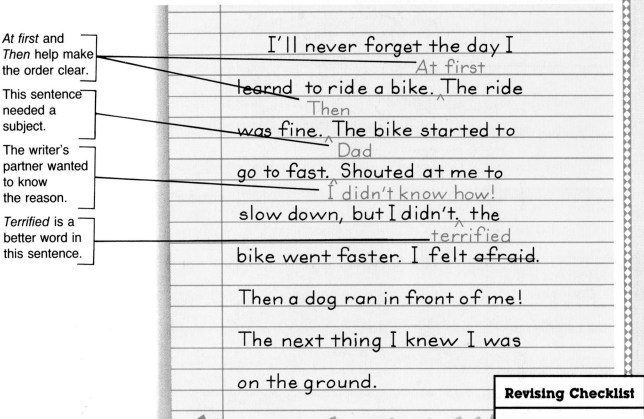

At first and *Then* help make the order clear.

This sentence needed a subject.

The writer's partner wanted to know the reason.

Terrified is a better word in this sentence.

> I'll never forget the day I
> ~~At first~~
> ~~learnd~~ to ride a bike. The ride
> Then
> was fine. ∧ The bike started to
> Dad
> go to fast. ∧ Shouted at me to
> I didn't know how!
> slow down, but I didn't. ∧ the
> terrified
> bike went faster. I felt ~~afraid~~.
>
> Then a dog ran in front of me!
>
> The next thing I knew I was
>
> on the ground.

Read the revised story above. Read it the way the writer decided it *should* be. Then revise your own story.

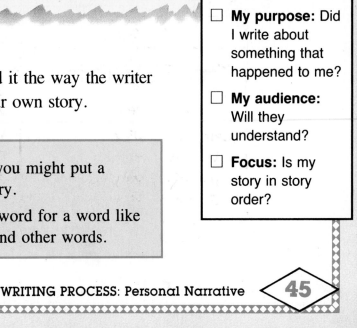

Revising Checklist

☐ **My purpose:** Did I write about something that happened to me?

☐ **My audience:** Will they understand?

☐ **Focus:** Is my story in story order?

Grammar Check ◆ Sometimes you might put a question or exclamation in your story.

Word Choice ◆ Is there a better word for a word like *afraid*? A thesaurus can help you find other words.

4 Proofreading

Proofreading is looking for and fixing errors. A reader needs a neat, correct copy to read.

Proofreading Model ♦ Below is the sample story. The new red marks are proofreading marks.

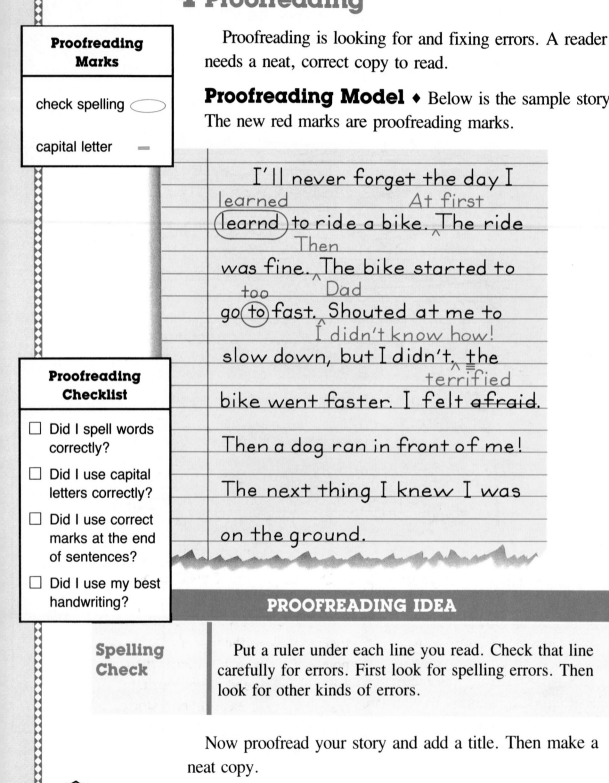

I'll never forget the day I
~~learnd~~ *learned* to ride a bike. ^*At first* The ride
was fine. ^*Then* The bike started to
go ~~to~~ *too* fast. ^*Dad* Shouted at me to
slow down, but I didn't. ^the *I didn't know how!*
bike went faster. I felt ~~afraid~~ *terrified*.

Then a dog ran in front of me!

The next thing I knew I was

on the ground.

PROOFREADING IDEA

Spelling Check

Put a ruler under each line you read. Check that line carefully for errors. First look for spelling errors. Then look for other kinds of errors.

Now proofread your story and add a title. Then make a neat copy.

5 Publishing

Publishing means sharing your writing with others. Below are two ways you can share your writing.

Learning to Ride

I'll never forget the day I learned to ride a bike. At first the ride was fine. Then the bike started to go too fast. Dad told me to slow down, but I didn't. I didn't know how! The bike went faster. I felt terrified. Then a dog ran in front of me! The next thing I knew I was on the ground.

PUBLISHING IDEAS

Share Aloud

You might enjoy telling your story aloud. Look at your audience. Speak slowly and clearly. Then ask each of your classmates to write one word that describes your story. Is it funny? Maybe it is scary.

Share in Writing

Draw a picture of your favorite part of your story. Then put everyone's stories and pictures together. Keep them in a nice notebook or box. Put them where everyone can read them. During free time, read each other's stories. Tell each writer what you liked best about his or her story.

Writing Across the Curriculum Social Studies

In this unit you wrote about yourself. You wrote about something you predicted. Then you wrote what really happened. In social studies books, you often read about famous people. You can predict what probably happened to them. Then you can find out what really happened.

Writing to Learn

Think and Predict ♦ Admiral Richard Byrd was the first person to go to the South Pole. What do you think the trip was like? Think about temperatures, the clothing he needed, and the animals he might have seen. Make a prediction chart. Write things you think might have happened to Byrd.

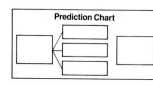

Prediction Chart

Write ♦ Pretend you were chosen to go with Admiral Byrd. Use your prediction chart to help write about the trip.

Writing in Your Journal

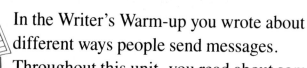

In the Writer's Warm-up you wrote about different ways people send messages. Throughout this unit, you read about some messages people sent in unusual ways. In your journal, write about a kind of message you would like to receive.

BOOKS TO ENJOY

Read More About It

More Stories Julian Tells *by Ann Cameron*
Julian has lots of adventures. You read about
one of them in this unit. Read the book. You
will read how Julian wishes for Smokey the
Bear to appear. Will Smokey appear?

Koko's Kitten *by Francine Patterson*
Can a real gorilla send messages? Koko can.
She has been taught sign language. Koko signs
to tell how much she loves her pet kitten.

Book Report Idea   Story Shape

Tell about a book you have
read with words and with
shape.

Create a Story Shape
Choose a special shape that
fits some part of the story.
Cut the shape out of paper.
Write the title and author in
the shape. Add some details
about the story. Be sure to tell
why you liked your book.

UNIT REVIEW

Unit 1

Sentences   *pages 4–17*

A. Write *yes* if the word group is a sentence. Write *no* if the word group is not a sentence.

1. Are at camp.
2. Our tent is green.
3. Two people.
4. It stays dry inside.

5. We had a campfire.
6. Slept on the ground.
7. We saw the stars.
8. The fireflies.

B. Write each group of words in sentence order.

9. I show a watched TV.
10. with me it watched Tina.
11. show funny The was.
12. a car cat A drove.

13. Tina laughed I and.
14. the liked We show.
15. long It was hour an.
16. over The is show.

C. Write each sentence correctly. Use a capital letter and put the correct mark at the end.

17. is the mail here
18. this letter is for you
19. read it to me
20. your uncle wrote it

21. is he in Alaska
22. he sent a picture
23. it shows a bear
24. the bear is fishing

D. Write *subject* if the subject is underlined. Write *predicate* if the predicate is underlined.

25. <u>The baby</u> waved.
26. I <u>made a funny face</u>.
27. <u>The little girl</u> smiled.

28. <u>We</u> played catch.
29. The ball <u>bounced away</u>.
30. She <u>ran after it</u>.

Thesaurus *pages 18–19*

E. Read these Thesaurus entries. Answer the questions.

---

moist—slightly wet; damp. The puppy's nose feels <u>moist</u>.
ANTONYM: dry

31. What is the entry word?
32. What is the antonym for the entry word?

---

arrive—reach a certain place. I will <u>arrive</u> home before lunch.
ANTONYM: leave

33. What is the entry word?
34. What is the antonym for the entry word?

Story Order Words *pages 36–37*

F. Write the sentences in story order. Watch for words that help put the events in order.

35. Last I looked in the mailbox.
36. I looked everywhere for the hidden message.
37. First I peeked under an old bucket.
38. Then I peered under the mat on the porch.
39. Next I went up on the porch.

Plot, Character, and Setting *pages 34–37*

G. Write *plot, character,* or *setting* to show which part of a story each item describes.

40. the rabbit and the fox
41. a golden beach at sunset
42. visited his grandfather to cheer him
43. the rocky beach
44. saves the town from a flood
45. Mr. Melrose

Famous Sayings

Find the three famous sayings in the puzzle. Write each sentence.

Secret Messages

Here is a way people send secret messages. A sentence is broken into five-letter groups. No end marks or capital letters are used.

Lee wants to meet you tomorrow.
leewa ntsto meety outom orrow

Write the secret message hidden in the four sentences below. (Hint: The first sentence is a statement. The second is an exclamation. The third is a question. The fourth is a command.) Add end marks and capital letters.

marsh aisco mingt omyho useto night
sheha sthes urpri sebox
canyo ugeth ereby eight
donot telld ebbie

Unit 1 Extra Practice

1 Writing Sentences

p. 4

A. Read each word group. For each pair, write the word group that is a sentence.

1. **a.** P.T. Barnum started the first American circus.
   b. Was the greatest showman of all time.

2. **a.** He took Tom Thumb to cities everywhere.
   b. Forty inches tall and weighed seventy pounds.

3. **a.** Most large circuses have three rings.
   b. Became larger over the years.

4. **a.** The clowns stay together in Clown Alley.
   b. Brightly colored clothes and feathers.

5. **a.** Hard to make people laugh.
   b. Today clowns are part of the circus.

6. **a.** Many funny clown policemen.
   b. Some clowns do tricks on horseback.

7. **a.** There are three kinds of clowns.
   b. Baggy pants, white face, and tramp.

8. **a.** Juggling, riding, and other things to learn.
   b. There is a school for clowns in Venice, Florida.

9. **a.** No two clowns can dress up exactly alike.
   b. Some funny faces and some sad faces.

10. **a.** White face and a floppy hat to wear.
    b. Emmett Kelly was a famous clown with sad eyes.

11. **a.** Clowns perform between the main acts.
    b. A very important job.

12. **a.** Dan Rice was the first great American clown.
    b. Invited to visit President Abraham Lincoln.

2 Word Order in Sentences *p. 6*

A. Use each group of words to make a sentence. Write each sentence.

1. We animals have.
2. pony small The is.
3. big The are dogs.
4. A mice cat chases.
5. quack ducks Our.
6. has The bell a cow.
7. spots has calf The.
8. clover chew Cows.
9. Hens eggs lay.
10. crows The rooster.
11. are pigs fat Six.
12. sheep gives A wool.
13. farm our love I.
14. wants calf The dinner.
15. to barn They walk the.
16. red The is barn.

B. Change the order of the underlined words in each sentence. Notice how the meaning changes. Write each new sentence.

EXAMPLE: **The cat jumped in front of the kitten.**
ANSWER: **The kitten jumped in front of the cat.**

17. The turkey chased the goose.
18. My aunt looked at my puppy.
19. The pony was bigger than the calf.
20. The barn is behind the house.
21. The dog ran after the cat.

C. Two words in each sentence below should trade places. Write them. Then write the sentence correctly.

22. The book picked up a man.
23. I teeth my brush every day.
24. Please dog the walk.
25. She rode her town into bike.

3 Statements and Questions   *p. 8*

A. Read each sentence. Write *statement* if it tells something. Write *question* if it asks something.

1. Jan read about Christopher Columbus.
2. Who was Christopher Columbus?
3. Where was Columbus born?
4. Columbus was born in Italy.
5. How many ships did he have?
6. Columbus had three small ships.
7. Columbus thought the world was round.
8. How many times did Columbus sail from Spain?
9. He made four trips to look for new lands.
10. How long did his first trip take?
11. Columbus sailed for more than two months.
12. Columbus was a great sailor.

B. Write each sentence. Begin each sentence with a capital letter. Use periods and question marks correctly.

13. where did Christopher Columbus land
14. he landed on islands near Florida
15. who paid for his voyages
16. the queen of Spain gave him money
17. columbus was looking for India
18. he wanted to bring back spices
19. why were spices so important in 1492
20. people used spices to keep food safe
21. they also used spices to make perfume
22. did Columbus find cinnamon and pepper
23. the real treasure of Columbus was the New World

4 Commands and Exclamations

A. Read the sentence below. Write *command* if it gives an order. Write *exclamation* if it shows strong feeling.

1. Throw the ball to me.
2. I love baseball games!
3. The runner is out!
4. Watch the player on first base.
5. Give the bat to Jill.
6. This is a close game!
7. Show Mario your new catcher's mitt.
8. Eileen saw a great baseball team!
9. Tell me which team she saw.
10. What exciting players the Atlanta Braves are!
11. Tell me if Eileen saw the catcher.
12. He is such a terrific player!

B. Each sentence below is a command or an exclamation. Write each sentence correctly.

13. how thrilling the World Series game was
14. it was won by a grand-slam home run
15. name the teams in California
16. one player hit three home runs
17. show Chen your baseball cards
18. you have so many baseball cards
19. what a great place New York is
20. visit the Baseball Hall of Fame
21. tell me how to get there
22. we can't wait to see the museum
23. borrow a map from my older sister

5 Sentence Parts

p. 12

A. Read each sentence. Write *subject* if the subject is underlined. Write *predicate* if the predicate is underlined.

1. The <u>children</u> ride to the library.
2. They <u>are returning some books.</u>
3. The <u>red book</u> is due today.
4. Maria <u>read a book about bicycles.</u>
5. She <u>saw a funny picture.</u>
6. An <u>old bicycle</u> had a huge front wheel.
7. The <u>seat</u> was very high.
8. The rider <u>looked frightened.</u>
9. Bicycles <u>are used all over the world.</u>
10. Some <u>riders</u> travel for days on bicycles.
11. <u>France</u> has a long race every year.
12. The race <u>is over two thousand miles long.</u>
13. Many people <u>ride through five countries.</u>
14. <u>They</u> pedal over high mountains.
15. <u>We</u> saw pictures of the race.
16. Whole families <u>were watching the race.</u>
17. A <u>boy</u> was waving a flag at the riders.
18. The flag <u>was red, white, and blue.</u>

B. Write each sentence. Draw a line between the subject and the predicate.

19. Some early bicycles had no pedals.
20. Riders pushed with their feet.
21. One old bicycle had wooden wheels.
22. The ride was bumpy and uncomfortable.
23. The bicycle was called a boneshaker.

6 Subjects in Sentences

p. 14

A. The subject is underlined in each sentence below.
Think of a different subject. Write each new sentence.

1. A bird can fly.
2. Jets can fly fast.
3. My kite flies high.
4. Planes fly over towns.
5. A helicopter landed.
6. The crow flew away.

B. The subject is underlined in each sentence. Think
of a different subject. Write each new sentence.
Then underline the subject.

EXAMPLE: **The robin flew away without a sound.**
ANSWER: **Three geese flew away without a sound.**

7. The eagle has very strong wings.
8. Crows can fly for hours.
9. My kite got caught in the tree.
10. The plane was in the air for ten hours.
11. The glider landed in the middle of a field.

C. Add a subject to each word group below. Write each
complete sentence.

12. ____ went to the airport.
13. ____ carried a heavy suitcase.
14. ____ fastened their seat belts.
15. ____ pressed his nose to the window.
16. ____ fell asleep after the plane took off.
17. ____ was served for lunch during the trip.
18. ____ flew to Chicago last week.
19. ____ waved at the plane from the ground.
20. ____ picked us up at the airport.

7 Predicates in Sentences

A. The predicate is underlined in each sentence. Think of a different predicate. Write each new sentence. Then underline the predicate.

EXAMPLE: **Sunshine helps a garden grow.**
ANSWER: **Sunshine is good for plants.**

1. The garden is in the backyard.
2. Joan pulls out many weeds.
3. She wears thick gloves and a hat.
4. The flowers have a wonderful smell.
5. A worm crawls through the dirt.
6. A garden needs rich soil.
7. Carrots grow under the ground.
8. Three watermelons grew last year.
9. A rake is an important tool.
10. Some plants grow on thick vines.

B. Add a predicate to each word group below. Write each complete sentence.

11. A beautiful butterfly ——— .
12. The rain ——— .
13. Red juicy tomatoes ——— .
14. Tall corn plants ——— .
15. Tiny ladybugs ——— .
16. A hungry rabbit ——— .
17. A pumpkin pie ——— .
18. My older brother ——— .
19. Green leafy lettuce ——— .
20. Tasty peppers ——— .
21. My family ——— .

USING LANGUAGE
TO
INFORM

PART ONE

Unit Theme   *Creative Activities*

Language Awareness   Nouns

PART TWO

Literature   "Dear Ranger Rick"

A Reason for Writing   Informing

Writing
IN YOUR JOURNAL

WRITER'S WARM-UP ◆ How are you creative? Do you sing or draw? Do you build things? Do you invent plays with your friends? How do you feel when you create something? Is it easy or hard? Write in your journal about being creative. Tell what you like best about it.

1 Writing with Nouns

Laura read an article about carving. It said:

▌Carvers use many different tools.
▌People see beautiful carvings in museums.

The underlined words in the sentences are nouns. They name persons, places, or things.

Look at the chart. It shows what each noun names.

Names of Persons	Names of Places	Names of Things
carvers, people	museums	tools, carvings

Can you add a noun to each section on the chart?

Look at the underlined noun in the sentence below. Tell if it names a person, a place, or a thing.

■ We met Aaron at the park.

> **Summary** ◆ A **noun** names a person, place, or thing.

Guided Practice

Find the nouns in these sentences.

1. The sculptor worked at home.
2. A friend bought some wood.
3. The model was displayed at the fair.

Practice

A. One of the words in each pair is a noun. The nouns name persons, places, and things. Write the nouns.

4. rehearsed, costume
5. pretty, actress
6. stage, large
7. light, above
8. sticky, paint

9. speech, across
10. repeated, teacher
11. loud, Jamie
12. curtain, heavy
13. song, now

B. Write each sentence below. Underline the nouns.

14. The class acted out a story.
15. Tia and Rico were in the program.
16. The actors wore colorful costumes.
17. The boys and girls performed for their parents.
18. A large audience filled the gym.

C. Write the sentences. Use a noun to complete each sentence.

19. Everyone clapped at the end of the ____ .
20. The ____ loved the play.
21. Parents with cameras took ____ .
22. The ____ brought refreshments.
23. The actors ate refreshments in the ____ .

Apply ♦ Think and Write

From Your Writing ♦ Read what you wrote for the Writer's Warm-up. Choose a noun you used that names a thing. Draw a picture of the thing. Label its parts with other nouns.

> ✎ **Remember**
> that nouns give information about persons, places, and things.

♦ GETTING STARTED ♦

Make up riddles about things in the classroom that can be used for music, art, or plays.

EXAMPLE: *I see three tools for painting. What do I see?*
ANSWER: *easel, brushes, paints*

2 Singular Nouns and Plural Nouns

Some nouns name one person, place, or thing. Other nouns name more than one person, place, or thing. Look at the underlined nouns below.

1. We sang a new <u>song</u>.
2. The <u>songs</u> were easy to learn.

The noun *song* in sentence **1** names one thing. It is a singular noun. The noun *songs* in sentence **2** names more than one thing. It is a plural noun. When you write, add *-s* to most singular nouns to form the plural.

> **Summary** ♦ A **singular noun** names one person, place, or thing. A **plural noun** names more than one person, place, or thing. Add *-s* to form the plural of most nouns.

Guided Practice

Tell if each underlined word is a singular or a plural noun.

1. <u>Jennifer</u> is learning to play a <u>violin</u>.
2. Her <u>brothers</u> play the <u>flute</u> and the <u>oboe</u>.
3. They had a <u>concert</u> for their <u>parents</u>.
4. They used the <u>deck</u> as a <u>stage</u>.
5. The <u>neighbors</u> enjoyed the <u>performance</u>, too.

Practice

A. Read each sentence. Write *singular* if the underlined noun names one person, place, or thing. Write *plural* if it names more than one person, place, or thing.

6. Our <u>teacher</u> gave each of us some clay.
7. We molded the clay into <u>pots</u>.
8. Our pots dried in a <u>week</u>.
9. We painted colorful <u>designs</u> on them.
10. I use my clay pot as a <u>vase</u>.

B. Write each sentence. Use the correct form of the noun in ( ).

11. A kiln is an ____ . (oven, ovens)
12. You can dry ____ in a kiln. (pot, pots)
13. Two ____ work in this studio. (potter, potters)
14. They share one ____ . (kiln, kilns)
15. Pottery needs many ____ to bake. (hour, hours)

C. Write the plural form of each noun below. Write sentences using five of these plural nouns.

16. artist	**19.** hand	**22.** animal
17. cup	**20.** bowl	**23.** decoration
18. jar	**21.** vase	**24.** candlestick

Apply ◆ Think and Write

Noun Exchange ◆ Write sentences describing an art project. Exchange papers with a partner. List the nouns you find in each other's sentences. Tell whether each noun is singular or plural.

✎ **Remember**
that many plural nouns are formed by adding *-s*.

GETTING STARTED

Play the "What's Better?" game. Use these words: *berry, party, dress, story, cherry, sandwich, penny, bunny, peach, pony, wish,* and *puppy.*

EXAMPLE: *What's better than one story? Lots of stories.*

3 Spelling Plural Nouns

Look at the words *dress, box, bench,* and *sash.* They are singular nouns. They end in *ss, x, ch,* and *sh.* The plural of these nouns is formed by adding *-es.*

dress	box	bench	sash
dress<u>es</u>	box<u>es</u>	bench<u>es</u>	sash<u>es</u>

Look at the words *berry* and *party.* They are singular nouns that end in a consonant and *y.* To form the plural, change the *y* to *i* and add *-es.*

berry	party
berr<u>ies</u>	part<u>ies</u>

Some nouns change their spelling to form the plural.

woman	man	foot
women	men	feet

Summary ♦ Add *-es* to form the plural of nouns that end in *ss, x, ch,* or *sh.* If a noun ends in a consonant and *y,* change the *y* to *i* and add *-es* to form the plural.

Guided Practice

Spell the plural form of each singular noun below.

1. class   **2.** tax   **3.** inch   **4.** man   **5.** story

Practice

A. Write the plural form of each singular noun.

6.	boss	**11.**	branch
7.	fox	**12.**	woman
8.	glass	**13.**	canary
9.	pony	**14.**	lunch
10.	foot	**15.**	sash

B. Write each sentence below. Use the plural form of the noun in ( ).

16. I enjoy working on my ____ at home. (hobby)

17. Mary Kwan takes ____ in embroidery. (class)

18. My neighbor sews ____ of cloth into quilts. (patch)

19. She saves ____ of fabric scraps. (box)

20. I know six embroidery ____ . (stitch)

C. Use the plural form of each of these nouns in a sentence. Write the sentences.

21. penny **22.** ax **23.** man **24.** dish **25.** sandwich

Apply ◆ Think and Write

A Noun Chart ◆ Make a chart like this.

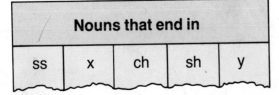

Nouns that end in				
ss	x	ch	sh	y

List singular nouns in each column of the chart. Exchange charts with a friend. Write the plural form of each noun on your friend's chart.

✎ **Remember**
to pay attention to the spelling of plural nouns.

Name something you like about your favorite actor, character, singer, artist, or musician.

EXAMPLE: *I like Jiminy Cricket's voice.*

4 Singular Possessive Nouns

Do you remember the story of the puppet Pinocchio? Read the sentences about him and his maker, Geppetto.

1. The <u>head of the puppet</u> is carved from wood.
2. The <u>tools of Geppetto</u> are very sharp.

The underlined words in **1** tell you that the puppet has a head. In **2** you find out that Geppetto owns tools. The sentences below tell the same things in fewer words.

3. The <u>puppet's head</u> is carved from wood.
4. <u>Geppetto's tools</u> are very sharp.

You know that the singular noun *puppet* names one thing. The word *puppet's* in sentence **3** is a possessive noun. It shows that something belongs to the puppet. What does the puppet have? An apostrophe and *s* was added to *puppet* to form the possessive noun *puppet's*. Can you find the possessive noun in sentence **4**?

> **Summary** ◆ A **possessive noun** shows ownership. To form the possessive of a singular noun, add an apostrophe and *s* ('s).

Guided Practice

Spell the possessive form of each singular noun.

1. aunt   **2.** baby   **3.** Mr. May   **4.** goalie   **5.** cat

Practice

A. Write the possessive form of each singular noun. Remember to add an apostrophe and *s* (**'s**).

6. Pinocchio
7. writer
8. child
9. author
10. father

11. fairy
12. marionette
13. Dr. Acosta
14. girl
15. classmate

B. Write each sentence below. Use the possessive form of the singular noun in ( ).

EXAMPLE: Dad sanded ____ bookshelf. (Marty)
ANSWER: Dad sanded Marty's bookshelf.

16. The ____ hobby is wood carving. (mayor)
17. I borrowed the ____ tools. (carver)
18. ____ picture frame was hand carved. (Mrs. Lum)
19. The ____ desk has gold handles. (queen)
20. Dad carved a box for ____ birthday. (Mother)

C. Use the possessive form of each noun below in a sentence.

21. puppet
22. puppy

23. prince
24. tree

25. peacock

Apply • Think and Write

Information from Pictures ◆ Write about each of the puppets shown on this page. Use possessive nouns in your sentences.

✎ **Remember**
that possessive nouns show that a person or thing owns something.

How many different kinds of musicians' instruments can you squeeze on a bus?

EXAMPLES: *four pianists' pianos, five harpists' harps*

5 Plural Possessive Nouns

Plural nouns have a special form to show ownership. Read these sentences.

1. The musicians will bring the instruments.
2. The musicians' instruments are packed.

In sentence **1**, *musicians* is a plural noun. It ends in *s*. In sentence **2**, *musicians'* is a possessive noun. It ends with an apostrophe.

The plural possessive *musicians'* shows that something belongs to the musicians. What belongs to the musicians?

Study the nouns in the chart. Notice how the plural possessive nouns are formed.

Plural Nouns	Plural Possessive Nouns
boys bands sisters	boys' bands' sisters'

Summary ♦ To form the possessive of a plural noun that ends in *s*, add an apostrophe (').

Guided Practice

Spell the possessive form of each plural noun.

1. singers **3.** artists **5.** painters
2. dancers **4.** players **6.** carvers

Practice

A. Write the possessive form of each plural noun.

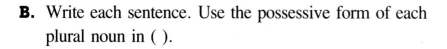

   7. actors

   8. girls

   9. poets

  10. directors

  11. violinists

B. Write each sentence. Use the possessive form of each plural noun in ( ).

  12. The ____ parts were difficult. (soloists)

  13. The ____ voices were very clear. (singers)

  14. The audience applauded the ____ show. (students)

  15. We appreciated the ____ hard work. (teachers)

  16. Everyone enjoyed the ____ cookies. (parents)

C. Use the possessive form of each plural noun below in a sentence.

  17. brothers

  18. drummers

  19. friends

  20. marchers

Apply ◆ **Think and Write**

Dictionary of Knowledge ◆ Find the entry for animation. Read about how animation is used in cartoons. Write sentences about animals that could be used in a cartoon. Use plural possessive forms, such as *chipmunks' teeth*, *kittens' paws*, and *rabbits' ears*.

> **Remember**
> that plural possessive nouns show that people or things own something.

Out is a very useful word. Put *out* in front of these words. What new words do you get? *cry, do, field, fit, grow, law, live, line, number, run, side, smart.*

VOCABULARY ♦
Compounds

Some words are formed from two smaller words. The new word is called a **compound**. Read these sentences.

1. Kip likes to be <u>outdoors</u>.
2. He likes to watch <u>wildlife</u>.

In sentence **1** *outdoors* is a compound. It is formed from *out* and *doors*. What two words form the compound *wildlife* in sentence **2**?

The two smaller words in each compound help to tell what the compound means.

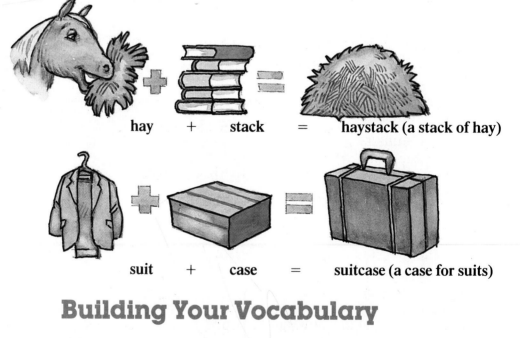

hay + stack = haystack (a stack of hay)

suit + case = suitcase (a case for suits)

Building Your Vocabulary

What two words form each compound below?

1. skateboard
2. barefoot
3. wheelchair
4. applesauce
5. grandfather
6. haircut

Practice

A. Write a compound for each pair of pictures below.

1.
2.
3.

B. **4–7.** Use the words below to form four compounds.

tip	sun	rain	high
way	toe	shine	fall

C. Find two compounds in each sentence below. Then write the two words that form each compound.

   8. We play volleyball in the afternoon.
   9. The snowdrift covered the sidewalk.
   10. We had oatmeal for breakfast.
   11. Aaron plays baseball and basketball.
   12. A bluebird sat on our clothesline.

Language Corner ♦ Word Histories

Have you ever seen a hummingbird? It moves its wings so fast that they seem to make a humming sound. What other birds' names do you know that tell how the birds sound or look?

How to Revise Sentences with Nouns

You have been using nouns to name persons, places, and things. When you write sentences, choose nouns that tell exactly what you mean. Read the sentences below. Which sentence is more exact?

1. Kelly drew a building.
2. Kelly drew a skyscraper.

Both sentences use nouns to tell about Kelly's picture. But the noun in sentence **2** tells <u>exactly</u> what Kelly drew. Try to use exact nouns in your writing. They will help to give information to your reader.

What exact nouns name the buildings in this picture?

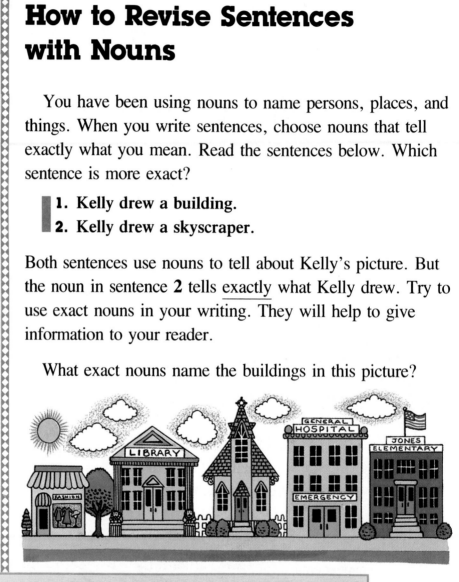

The Grammar Game ◆ Write three exact nouns for each word below. Time yourself.

| toy | clothes | fruit |
| sport | animal | vegetable |

Working Together

Do activities **A** and **B** as a group. You will see how exact nouns give clear information.

In Your Group

- Help explain directions.
- Make sure everyone understands.
- Agree or disagree in a nice way.
- Record everyone's ideas on a list.

A. Look at the chart. Replace each word in each column with at least one exact noun.

person:	relative	worker	athlete
place:	store	room	house
thing:	insect	plant	bird

B. Use exact nouns to replace the words in ( ). Then write the paragraph again using different exact nouns. How many new paragraphs can your group write?

Last week Lyn and Gino went to the (place). They saw their favorite (person) buying a (thing). They were so excited!

WRITERS' CORNER ♦ Fuzzy Sentences

Without exact nouns, sentences are fuzzy, or unclear. Using exact nouns will improve your writing. They will help your reader understand what you mean.

FUZZY: Kareem road a thing to the place.
IMPROVED: Kareem rode a bicycle to the museum.

Read what you wrote for the Writer's Warm-up. Can you replace any words with more exact nouns?

USING LANGUAGE
TO
INFORM

=== **PART TWO** ===

Literature   "Dear Ranger Rick"

A Reason for Writing Informing

CREATIVE

Writing

FINE ARTS ◆ Native Americans in the Southwest made the items pictured at the left. One is done with beadwork. One is a silver belt buckle, and one is a woven mat. Which item appeals to you the most? Write a story about it. You could tell a story about who created the item. You could tell a story about the person who used it.

CRITICAL THINKING ◆
A Strategy for Informing

AN OBSERVATION CHART

One reason for writing is to give information. After this lesson you will read a letter. It is from Kip Grangier. Kip gives information about how he carves birds from wood. Later you will write a letter explaining how to do something.

Kip gives many details about how he makes the birds. Here is part of what he wrote.

> I use many coats of paint mixed with water. This makes the carving look softer, like the way real feathers look.

How does Kip know what real feathers look like? He has to look at real birds. He has to observe, or notice, details about them. Observing real birds helps him make birds from wood. Observing details also helps him explain how he works.

Learning the Strategy

Observing details can help you. Suppose you go to a carnival. What details could you remember about what you see there? Suppose you go to a parade. Can you remember details to tell your friends?

An observation chart can help you remember details. Here is one you might make about the parade.

	The Parade
What I Saw	a band in red uniforms fire engines boy scouts and girl scouts
What I Heard	drums, trumpets, cymbals, flutes fire engine sirens people cheering and clapping

Using the Strategy

A. Pick an object in the classroom. Make an observation chart about it. Leave the top line blank. Write headings on one side. They might be *Where It Is* and *What It Looks Like*. Write details for each heading. Then trade charts with a classmate. Can your classmate guess your object?

B. Can you imagine how Kip makes birds? Before you read Kip's letter, make an observation chart. Write *Bird Carving* at the top. Write *Materials* at the side. Fill in the materials you think Kip uses. Write *Steps* at the side. Fill in what you think Kip does. Then read the letter to find out if you are right.

Applying the Strategy

- Did your partner guess your object for **A,** above? How did you help your partner guess what it was?
- When might making an observation chart help you?

DEAR RANGER RICK

from *Ranger Rick* magazine

Perryhawkin Road
Princess Anne, Maryland 21853
September 19, 1987

Dear Ranger Rick,

Something very exciting happened to me last year. I won first prize in the novice, or beginners', group at the World Championship Wildfowl Carving Competition in Ocean City, Maryland. I am the youngest person ever to win at this competition. My entry was a carving of an emperor penguin and its chick.

I became interested in carving by watching my dad carve. My first carving was of a bufflehead duck. Dad had started it, but our poodle got it and put teeth marks in it, so Dad threw it away. I took the bird out of the trash and finished it. Dad told me what to do. I was three years old then.

Dad is my carving teacher. When I make mistakes, he shows me how to fix what's wrong instead of giving up. I look through my *Ranger Rick* magazines and wildlife books to find pictures of birds to carve. Then I make drawings of the way I want my carving to look. I'm not allowed to use dangerous tools like a power saw, so Dad cuts out pieces of wood for me to carve. After that I'm on my own.

I use different carving tools to chip off pieces of wood and smooth the carving. Then I use a carving knife and chisels to cut in details. Next I sand the wood until it's as smooth as glass. Then I use a wood burner to burn in tiny feather lines.

The painting is last. It's my favorite part, but it's also the hardest. Dad helps me mix the colors of paint that I need. I use many coats of paint mixed with water. This makes the carving look softer, like the way real feathers look. When the painting is finished, so is the bird.

I really like learning about wildlife. My wood carving is one way of doing that.

Your friend,
Kip Grangier

Library Link ♦ *If you enjoyed Kip's letter, you might like to read more of the interesting articles and letters found in* Ranger Rick *magazine.*

Reader's Response

If you were Kip, how would you feel about your carving?

DEAR RANGER RICK

Responding to Literature

1. Kip likes to make wood carvings. Tell about one thing you like to make or do.

2. Find a picture of a bird or an animal that you might like to carve. Make a color sketch of it.

3. Kip says that painting the figures is his favorite part. If you carved figures, what would be your favorite part? Tell why.

Writing to Learn

Think and Remember ♦ Exciting things happened to Kip. Some exciting things might have happened to you recently. List three exciting things that you remember. Then make an observation chart about one exciting thing that happened to you.

1. I went to the zoo.
2. I saw a hummingbird.
3. I baked a loaf of bread.

Zoo	
What I Saw	goats people waterfall bears
What I Heard	birds calling children laughing monkeys chattering

Observation Chart

Write ♦ Use the details you recorded and write about your experience.

Take turns giving and following directions. Start by giving three directions at a time, such as *stand*, *yawn*, and *wink*. Then add more. See how many directions your listeners can remember and follow.

SPEAKING and LISTENING ◆
Directions

"Punch a hole in the clay. Roll it into a ball first."

Joe is giving Dave directions. He is telling him how to make a clay bowl. But Joe's directions are not clear. How can he improve his directions? Read the guidelines below to find out.

How to Give Clear Directions	1. Keep directions easy, but give all the steps. 2. Give the steps in order. Use words like *first*, *second*, *next*, and *last* to show the correct order. 3. Ask if there are any questions.
How to Listen to Directions	1. Listen to remember the directions in order. 2. Picture yourself doing each step. 3. Repeat the directions to yourself. 4. Ask questions if you need to.

Summary ◆ Give clear directions that tell the steps in order. Listen carefully so that you will understand and remember directions.

Guided Practice

Help Joe put his directions in order. Say the directions in order. Tell what words helped you know the order.

1. Next, make the hole larger until the clay is shaped like a bowl.
2. First, roll a lump of clay into a ball.
3. Then work the clay out and up to form the sides.
4. Last, make a handle from a thin roll of clay.
5. Second, punch a hole in the clay ball.

Practice

A. Listen as your teacher or a partner reads Joe's directions in order. Pretend you have the clay in your hands. Act out each step. Then answer these questions.

6. Are the directions complete?
7. Should the directions give more details?
8. Is there anything you did not understand?
9. What title would you give the directions?

B. With a partner, take turns giving and following directions. Choose an activity that is easy to do. For example, tell how to draw a happy face, how to make a paper hat, or how to tie a shoelace. Ask your partner to follow your directions <u>exactly</u>, doing <u>only</u> what you say.

Apply • Think and Write

Written Directions ♦ What do you know how to do? Write the directions in order for a friend. Start by writing *How to _____* .

✎ **Remember**
to give and follow directions in order.

GETTING
STARTED

Take turns trading information. One person can name a subject. The next person can say one sentence about it.

EXAMPLE: *Elephants*

Elephants are huge animals.

WRITING ◆
A Paragraph

You know that a sentence tells a complete thought. Sometimes the thought is simple. One sentence can tell everything you want to say. But what if you want to say more? What if you want to give directions or explain something? Then you need to write a group of sentences. You need to write a paragraph.

A paragraph is a group of sentences about one main idea, or topic. All the sentences in the paragraph tell about that main idea. Can you see why writing a paragraph helps you focus on your main idea? It helps your reader focus on the main idea, too.

A paragraph is easy to spot. The first word of a paragraph is *indented*, or moved in. When you are ready to begin a new main idea, you start a new paragraph. You indent the first word.

The Chinese people are known for their beautiful jade carvings. Jade is a stone that is dark green to almost white. Since early times, the Chinese have made jade carvings. They carve jewelry, vases, bowls, and statues out of jade.

Summary ◆ A **paragraph** is a group of sentences about one main idea. The first word of a paragraph is indented.

Guided Practice

Tell the main idea of this paragraph. Give it a title.

Kip Grangier had an exciting year when he was eight years old. First, he won a wood-carving championship. Next, he was on several television shows. Then he was invited to the White House to show a painted Easter egg he had made.

Practice

A. Read each paragraph. Then write its main idea.

1.   Ivory is a hard, white material from the tusks of elephants and other animals. Ivory lasts a long time. It may be carved and shaped with tools. Ivory has a smooth surface that has a glowing finish when polished. Carved ivory is valuable.

2.   Most elephant ivory comes from eastern Africa. This is a high-quality ivory known for its whiteness. Ivory from eastern Africa is not brittle and is good for carving.

B. If you were a wood-carver, what animal, bird, or fish would you carve? Why would you choose it? Write a paragraph about your choice. Underline your main idea. You might wish to begin this way.

If I were a wood-carver, I would carve a _____ .

Apply ◆ Think and Write

Dictionary of Knowledge ◆ Read about Africa's famous Ivory Coast. Then write a paragraph about what you would most like to see if you visited it.

✎ **Remember**
that all the sentences in a paragraph tell about the same idea.

GETTING STARTED

Tell about an object in your classroom, but don't name it. First, tell what it is used for or what it does. Then tell two or three other things about the object. See who can name the object first.

WRITING ◆

Main Idea and Details

WARD FOUNDATION
WORLD
CHAMPIONSHIP
WILDFOWL CARVING
COMPETITION
1986
OCEAN CITY, MARYLAND

FIRST IN CATEGORY

DECORATIVE
MINIATURE
WILDFOWL

NOVICE CLASS

You know that a paragraph has one main idea. Usually one sentence in the paragraph tells what the main idea is. That sentence is called the topic sentence. It is often the first sentence of the paragraph. All the other sentences add details about the main idea. Read this sample paragraph.

> Something very exciting happened to me last year. I won first prize in the novice, or beginners', group at the World Championship Wildfowl Carving Competition in Ocean City, Maryland. I am the youngest person ever to win at this competition. My entry was a carving of an emperor penguin and its chick.

Summary ◆ The **topic sentence** tells the main idea of a paragraph. The other sentences add details about the main idea.

Guided Practice

Answer these questions about the paragraph above.

1. What is the topic sentence of the paragraph?

2. Which sentences add details?

3. Should the paragraph talk about penguins? Why or why not?

4. What would be a good title for the paragraph?

Practice

A. Sentences **5–9** are topic sentences. For each one, write a sentence that gives a detail about it.

> **5.** Some of my favorite things are red.
> **6.** Artists are lucky people.
> **7.** You need to be careful when you carve wood.
> **8.** Carvings decorate many things.
> **9.** Clay is easy to work with.

B. Write a topic sentence for each idea below.

EXAMPLE: your favorite art activity

ANSWER: Paper sculpture is my favorite art activity.

10. the kind of music you like best
11. a photograph you would like to take
12. the funniest song you know
13. a book you really enjoyed
14. a trip you would like to take

C. Write a paragraph. Begin with one of the topic sentences you wrote for **Practice B**. Then add at least two sentences that give details about the main idea. Remember to indent the first word of your paragraph.

Apply ♦ Think and Write

A Paragraph ♦ Write a paragraph about one of the ideas below. Don't forget to tell what your paragraph is about in your topic sentence.

a happy day   making a sand castle
a grouchy day   making a mask

✎ Remember
to use a topic sentence that tells the main idea.

Avocado Avenue, Bean Boulevard, and Rutabaga Road are some streets in Salad Springs. Make up similar street names for another pretend place. How about Colorville?

WRITING ♦

A Friendly Letter

201 Conner Road
Darby, Montana 59829
April 23, 1991

Dear Emily,
    Thanks for the loom. I'm weaving an Indian rug now. Can you come to our school crafts fair on May 9? You'll like the projects, especially mine! Please say yes!

        Your friend,
        Greg

The heading of Greg's letter tells his address and the date. Notice the comma between the city and state. Also notice the comma between the date and the year.

The greeting says "hello" and the closing says "good-by." A comma follows each of these parts. The first word of each begins with a capital letter.

The body is the main part of the letter. It is a paragraph, so the first word is indented.

What does the signature tell?

Summary ♦ A **friendly letter** has five parts: the heading, greeting, body, closing, and signature.

Guided Practice

Tell where commas are needed. Then tell which letter part each group of words belongs in.

1. Portland Maine   **3.** Your pal

2. Dear Matthew   **4.** January 9 1991

Practice

A. Write the name of the letter part in which each word or word group belongs.

  5. Sincerely,   **9.** September 15, 1990

  6. How are you?   **10.** 106 Rancho Drive

  7. Powell, Wyoming 82435   **11.** Peter

  8. Dear Grandmother,   **12.** I love the paint set.

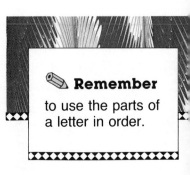

B. Write each part of the letter below correctly. Arrange the parts properly. The letter on page 90 is a model.

> February 3 1990   6342 Stark Avenue
> Dear Aunt Lynne   Cortland Ohio 44410
> I'm getting better with my new camera. I took some pictures of my cat. Now I don't cut off her head!
> Love Martina

C. Pretend Greg wrote to you. Answer his letter. Use all five parts of a friendly letter. Remember the commas.

Apply ⬩ Think and Write

A Friendly Letter ⬩ Write a friendly letter to someone you know. You may wish to mail your letter. Turn to page 476 to find out how to address an envelope.

> ✎ **Remember**
> to use the parts of a letter in order.

Focus on Telling *How-to*

You read Kip's letter to Ranger Rick earlier in this unit. Kip gave information in the letter. He told how to carve a bird from wood.

As you read his letter, what did you see? Did you see him carry out each step? Did you see the bird take shape? Chances are you did, because Kip gave clear directions. How did he do this?

1. *Kip gave the steps in order.* He told what he did *first, next,* and so on. (Think about why this is important.) Kip used these words to help show order: *first, next, after, then, until, last.*

2. *Kip gave details.* He did not just write, "I paint the bird last." He gave exact details. He told exactly how he does the painting.

The following details make the picture clear:

♦ Kip's Dad helps him mix the colors of paint.
♦ Kip uses many coats of paint mixed with water.
♦ Kip's method of painting makes the carving look softer.
♦ It makes the feathers look real.

The Writer's Voice ♦ How-to directions tell how to do or make something. What can you make or do that is special? Tell your classmates how to do it.

Working Together

Good how-to directions are in step-by-step order. They give enough details to make each step clear. As a group, work on activities **A** and **B**.

A. Discuss how to get ready for school in the morning. What are some of the things you have to do? Name four or five things. Write them down in any order. Then, as a group, arrange them in proper order. Compare your group's list with the lists of other groups.

B. Suppose a friend does not know how to make a sandwich. Discuss how to make a sandwich. Put the steps in order. Add details to make it clear. For example:

♦ What kind of bread will you use?

♦ Will you use butter or some other kind of spread?

♦ What else goes on the sandwich? How much of it?

In Your Group

♦ Have everyone share ideas.
♦ Write down ideas on a list.
♦ Remind people to listen carefully.
♦ Keep the group on the subject.

THESAURUS CORNER ♦ Word Choice

Write the mixed-up sentences below in proper order. Replace each noun in dark type with a better synonym. Use the Thesaurus and the Thesaurus Index.

Above all, he must keep in mind a **picture** of each play. The **conductor** of a football team must stay calm at the **tip** of the game. He must also ignore the **noise** of the crowd.

Writing a How-to Letter

Kip Grangier likes to carve birds. He carves birds so well that he won a prize. In his letter to *Ranger Rick* magazine, Kip tells how he does it.

Know Your Purpose and Audience

MY PURPOSE

In this lesson you will write a friendly letter. Your purpose will be to explain how to do something. It should be an activity that you do well.

MY AUDIENCE

Your audience can be a friend or a relative. Later you can read your letter aloud to classmates. You can also mail or deliver your letter.

1 Prewriting

First you need to choose a topic. Then use a plan to gather details for your letter.

Choose Your Topic ♦ What do you like to do in your free time? Do you draw, read, or play games? Make a list of your activities. Then circle the topic you like best.

Think About It

You might try thinking about the seasons when you make your list. What do you do for fun in the summer? Do you do something different in the winter? Look at your list again. Decide what would be the most fun to tell about. Circle that as your choice.

Talk About It

Working with a partner can help you make your list. First write the names of all the seasons. Under each, list the things you do in that season. Your partner can help you remember all the things you do.

Topic Ideas

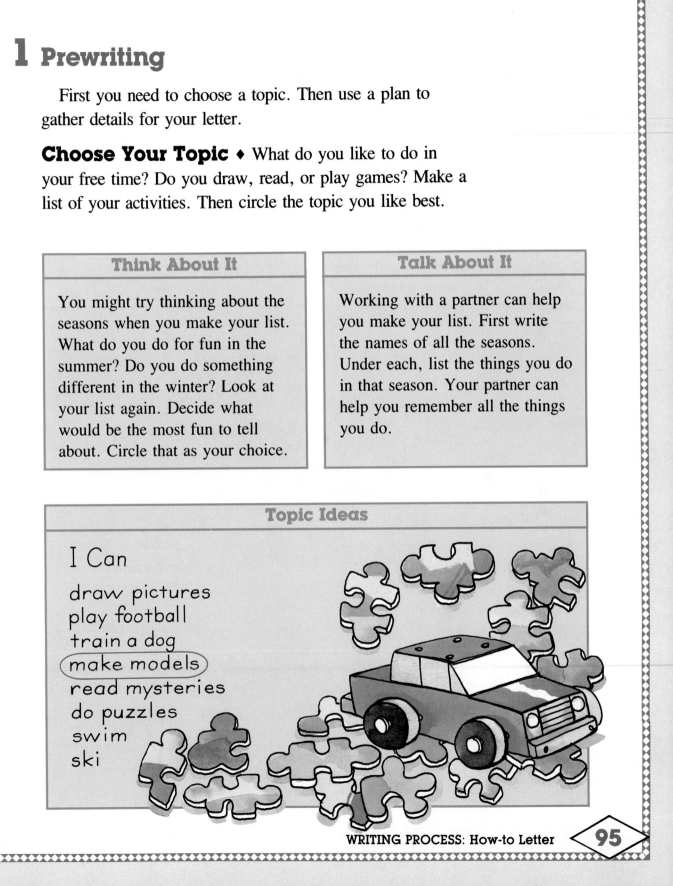

I Can

draw pictures
play football
train a dog
(make models)
read mysteries
do puzzles
swim
ski

Choose Your Strategy ♦ Below are two plans for gathering details. Read both of them. Then decide which idea you will use.

PREWRITING IDEAS

CHOICE ONE

A Cluster Map

Make a cluster map like the one shown here. In the middle write your topic. Write as many details as you can around it.

Model

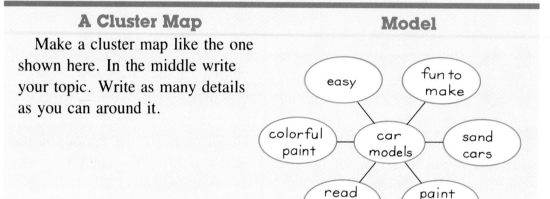

CHOICE TWO

An Observation Chart

Close your eyes. Picture yourself doing what you do well. Picture the materials. Picture the steps. Then make an observation chart like this one.

Model

Making a Model	
Materials	model sandpaper bright paint
Steps	1. read directions 2. sand model 3. paint model

2 Writing

Look at your cluster map or observation chart. Then start to write your letter. Tell the main idea in your first sentence. You might start like this.

- ♦ I really like to ____.
- ♦ In my free time I ____.

Add supporting details. Give the steps in order. Use order words like *first*, *next*, and *last*.

Sample First Draft ♦

In my free time I make modle cars. They are not too hard to build. The directions tell you how to make the body. then you sand and paint every thing. This part is really the most fun.

3 Revising

Here is an idea to help you improve your letter.

REVISING IDEA

FIRST Read to Yourself

As you read, remember your purpose. Is your letter about how to do something? Think of your reader. Will that person understand it? Circle any parts of the letter you would like to improve.

Focus: Did you include enough details? Did you give the details or steps in the right order?

THEN Share with a Partner

Ask a partner to read your letter silently. Then ask for comments. These guidelines may help.

The Writer
Guidelines: Ask your partner for ideas.
Sample questions: • What is the most interesting part? • **Focus question:** Should I add any more details?

The Writer's Partner
Guidelines: Suggest changes in a helpful way.
Sample responses: • It would be interesting to tell about ____. • Maybe you could add some details about ____.

Revising Model ♦ The body of this letter is being revised. Can you understand the writer's changes?

The writer remembered to add an important detail.

Construct is a stronger word than *make*.

Everything is a compound.

The writer's partner thought this was interesting.

> In my free time I make
>
> modle cars. They are not too
> ~~First you must read the directions.~~
> hard to build. ⋀The directions
>   construct
> tell you how to ~~make~~ the body.
>
> then you sand and paint
>   everything
> every thing. This part is really
> ~~You get to choose the color and~~
> the most fun. ⋀   decorations.

Read the body of the letter with the writer's changes. Read it the way the writer wants it to be. Then revise your own letter.

Grammar Check ♦ Sometimes you can write two words together as a compound.

Word Choice ♦ Sometimes there is a stronger word for a word like *make*. A thesaurus can help you choose words.

Revising Checklist

☐ **My purpose:** Did I write a letter about how to do something?

☐ **My audience:** Will the person who reads my letter understand it?

☐ **Focus:** Did I give enough details? Did I give the steps in the right order?

4 Proofreading

Proofreading Marks

check spelling ⬭

capital letter ═

Proofreading can help make your letter neat and correct. It helps your reader understand what you wrote.

Proofreading Model ♦ Here is the sample letter body. The new red marks are proofreading marks.

In my free time I make

model

(modle) cars. They are not too

First you must read the directions.

hard to build. The directions

construct

tell you how to make the body.

then you sand and paint

everything

every thing. This part is really

You get to choose the color and

the most fun.   decorations.

Proofreading Checklist

☐ Did I spell words correctly?

☐ Did I use capital letters correctly?

☐ Did I use correct marks at the end of sentences?

☐ Did I use my best handwriting?

PROOFREADING IDEA

Punctuation Check

Look at the first letter of each word. Is it the right letter? Should it be a capital letter? Correct the first letters of words in your writing.

Proofread the body of your letter. Check the heading, greeting, closing, and signature. Be sure to put commas and capital letters in the right places. Then make a neat copy.

5 Publishing

Would you like to share your how-to letter? Below are two ways you can do it.

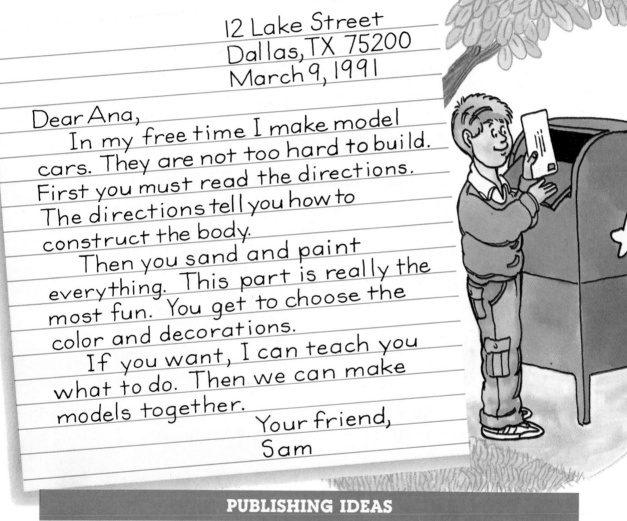

12 Lake Street
Dallas, TX 75200
March 9, 1991

Dear Ana,
   In my free time I make model cars. They are not too hard to build. First you must read the directions. The directions tell you how to construct the body.
   Then you sand and paint everything. This part is really the most fun. You get to choose the color and decorations.
   If you want, I can teach you what to do. Then we can make models together.
                     Your friend,
                     Sam

PUBLISHING IDEAS

Share Aloud	Share in Writing
Read your letter aloud to a few classmates. Ask them what they learned from your letter. Let each listener answer.	Mail or deliver your letter. Be sure to address the envelope correctly. Perhaps you will get a letter back!

CURRICULUM
·CONNECTION·

Writing Across the Curriculum Art

In this unit you wrote a letter explaining how to do something. You had to explain the activity step by step. An observation chart can help you think about the steps in any activity.

Writing to Learn

Think and Observe ◆ Do you know how to draw a house? Could you tell a first grader how? Draw a picture of a house. Then make an observation chart. Look at your picture. Write what you see. Write what you did when you drew it.

Observation Chart

Write ◆ Use the information in your chart. Write directions for a first grader. Tell how to draw a house.

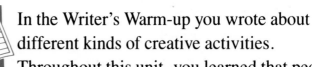

Writing in Your Journal

In the Writer's Warm-up you wrote about different kinds of creative activities.
Throughout this unit you learned that people can be creative in many ways. Have you discovered some new hobby or activity that you might like to try? Write about it in your journal.

BOOKS TO ENJOY

Read More About It

When Clay Sings *by Byrd Baylor*
Early Indians of the southwest United States made designs on clay pots. The author explains what the designs meant and how the pots were used.

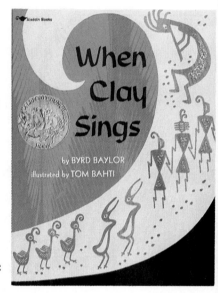

Louis Braille *by Stephen Keeler*
Read about a very special kind of creative activity. A French man used his creativity to solve a big problem. He invented a way for blind people to be able to read. Learn how he made his ideas happen.

Book Report Idea   Author Letter

Write a letter. Tell an author how you felt about the book he or she wrote.

Write a Letter to the Author ♦ Everyone loves to get mail, especially when they are not expecting it. Write a letter to the author of the book you read. Inform the author of what you liked about the book.

> May 11, 1991
>
> Dear Mr. Smith,
>   I really liked your story about the magic violin. When I read it, I

UNIT REVIEW

Unit 2

Nouns *pages 62–71*

A. One of the words in each pair is a noun. Write the nouns.

1. soon, game   4. bike, sleep   7. near, knee
2. card, maybe   5. desk, open   8. clay, hot
3. new, horse   6. next, hall   9. sing, chin

B. Write *singular* or *plural* for each underlined noun.

10. A new <u>picture</u> is on the wall.
11. It is next to the front <u>door</u>.
12. The picture shows some <u>workers</u>.
13. They are looking at a big <u>sign</u>.
14. It tells <u>visitors</u> about our town.
15. After <u>lunch</u> I'll show you the picture.
16. Then we can find the <u>library</u>.

C. Write the plural form of each noun.

17. watch   21. foot   25. box
18. kiss   22. story   26. ranch
19. tax   23. woman   27. glass
20. penny   24. flash   28. dish

D. Write the possessive form of each noun.

29. horse   32. trains   35. store
30. ponies   33. chairs   36. drivers
31. army   34. mother   37. wind

Compounds   *pages 72–73*

E. Write the two words that form each compound.

38. flashlight   **40.** supermarket

39. barnyard   **41.** campfire

Topic Sentences   *pages 88–89*

F. Write the topic sentence for the paragraph.

42.   It is a very hot day. The sun is shining brightly. The flowers are wilting. The sidewalk is burning my feet.

Main Idea and Details   *pages 88–89*

G. Write *main idea* if the sentence tells a main idea. Write *detail* if the sentence tells a detail.

43. I'm getting ready for the kite-flying contest.

44. I made a kite in the shape of a butterfly.

45. Dad made a long tail for the kite.

Friendly Letters   *pages 90–91*

H. Label each part of the letter. Write *closing, signature, body, heading,* or *greeting*.

46. 3 Lamson Place
Cambridge, Massachusetts 02139
February 12, 1990

47. Dear Wei,

48. You moved away four weeks ago. I miss you a lot. Do you like your new house? Write and tell me all about it.

49. Your friend,

50. Patrick

· CUMULATIVE ·
REVIEW

Sentences   *pages 4–17*

A. Write *yes* if the word group is a sentence.
Write *no* if the word group is not a sentence.

1. We walked quickly.
2. To the beach.
3. The sea gulls.
4. They flew over the waves.
5. They caught fish.
6. The baby gulls.

B. Write each group of words in sentence order.

7. float Gulls easily.
8. big are They birds.
9. follow ships Some gulls.
10. deck on the gull is A.

C. Write each sentence correctly. Use a capital letter and put the correct mark at the end.

11. we saw a dark gull
12. is it young
13. how big it is
14. gulls are strong
15. can gulls dive
16. they stand on rocks
17. where do they sleep
18. here is a gull's egg

D. Write *subject* if the subject is underlined. Write *predicate* if the predicate is underlined.

19. Most gulls stay near the ocean.
20. They fly inland during storms.
21. Many other birds live near salt water.
22. I saw some eider ducks once.
23. Sandpipers are interesting birds.
24. They run along the beach very fast.

Nouns *pages 62–71*

E. Write the noun in each pair of words.

25. planet, explore   **29.** after, moon
26. gazing, star   **30.** wheel, loud
27. see, telescope   **31.** in, rocket
28. sun, far   **32.** earth, across

F. Write *singular* if the underlined noun is singular.
Write *plural* if the underlined noun is plural.

33. I see three <u>rockets</u>.
34. The <u>astronauts</u> are inside.
35. One huge <u>engine</u> started.
36. I'm standing on top of a <u>box</u>.
37. One <u>rocket</u> leaves the launching pad.
38. My <u>watch</u> is broken.
39. Mom took <u>pictures</u> of the lift-off.

G. Write the plural form of each noun.

40. launch   **45.** ax
41. brush   **46.** copy
42. man   **47.** watch
43. mix   **48.** army
44. wish   **49.** class

H. Write the possessive form of each noun.

50. women   **55.** family
51. book   **56.** tape
52. radio   **57.** Mrs. Maxwell
53. controllers   **58.** foot
54. directors   **59.** table

Tracking Plural Nouns

Use the clues below to figure out eight plural nouns.

1. You wear them on your feet. _ h _ _ _ _
2. You drink from them. _ _ _ s _ _ _ _
3. You can blow them out. _ a _ _ _ _ _ _
4. You sit on these in parks. _ _ _ c _ _ _ _
5. These are found in bird nests. _ g _ _
6. Gifts often come in these. _ _ x _ _
7. Five of these are worth a nickel. _ _ n _ _ _ _
8. Horses live on these farms. r _ _ _ _ _ _

An Imaginary Animal

The animal in the picture is a zother. It is made up of several animals. For example, it has a zebra's stripes. Write five other animals' parts that you can see in the zother.

Unit 2 Extra Practice

1 Writing with Nouns
p. 62

A. One of the words in each pair is a noun. Write the nouns.

1. towel, hot
2. under, clams
3. later, seashore
4. Erin, walked
5. sun, above
6. scary, lobster
7. shark, salty
8. starfish, bumpy
9. roared, shells
10. sand, when

B. Write each sentence below. Underline the nouns.

11. The family went to the beach.
12. Some joggers ran on the sand.
13. Ann built a castle.
14. Seaweed floated in the water.
15. Fish swam near the shore.
16. Diego and Paul swam in the ocean.
17. Their eyes hurt.
18. The water tasted like salt.
19. Birds walked along the rocks.
20. A gull carried a fish in its mouth.
21. The divers found beautiful shells.
22. A crab crawled on the shore.
23. A family had lunch at the beach.
24. The children unfolded a blanket.
25. Sand was in their shoes.
26. A surfer rode on the waves.
27. The surfboard was made of wood.
28. A swimmer dived into a wave.
29. The children rode on rubber rafts.

2 Singular Nouns and Plural Nouns

p. 64

A. Read each sentence. Write *singular* if the underlined word is a singular noun. Write *plural* if the underlined word is a plural noun.

1. They looked at a <u>star</u>.
2. The bright <u>stars</u> twinkled.
3. The <u>telescope</u> makes many more stars visible.
4. The <u>sun</u> is a very bright star.
5. The <u>planets</u> travel around the sun.
6. We saw three <u>satellites</u> last month.
7. <u>Comets</u> look like flaming balls with tails.
8. <u>Saturn</u> is the planet that has rings around it.
9. <u>Meteors</u> are pieces of stone in space.
10. In Arizona a large <u>meteor</u> fell to the ground.
11. It made a huge <u>hole</u> in the ground.
12. Some <u>visitors</u> took pictures.
13. My <u>brothers</u> looked through a telescope.
14. They saw the <u>planet</u> named Jupiter.
15. Jupiter has four large <u>moons</u>.
16. Jupiter is much larger than <u>Earth</u>.
17. No <u>person</u> from Earth has been to Jupiter.

B. Write each sentence. Use the correct form of the noun in ( ).

18. Mars is the red ____ . (planet, planets)
19. Mercury has long, bright ____ . (day, days)
20. A ____ on Mercury is very cold. (night, nights)
21. The Milky Way is made of many ____ . (star, stars)
22. Earth has only one ____ . (moon, moons)

3 Spelling Plural Nouns

p. 66

A. Write the plural of each singular noun.

1.	dress	**9.**	baby
2.	party	**10.**	ranch
3.	bush	**11.**	butterfly
4.	woman	**12.**	church
5.	ash	**13.**	tax
6.	penny	**14.**	glass
7.	lunch	**15.**	man
8.	crash	**16.**	fox

B. Write each sentence below. Use the plural form of the noun in ( ).

17. Many ____ have Thanksgiving parades. (city)

18. The marchers' ____ get very tired. (foot)

19. We sat on ____ and watched a parade. (bench)

20. Some ____ have special dinners. (family)

21. We set the table with nice ____ . (dish)

22. Leslie poured water into tall ____ . (glass)

23. Kelly ate some ____ . (cranberry)

24. We'll eat turkey ____ next week. (sandwich)

C. Write the plural form of the words in ( ). Write the sentence.

25. They grow (strawberry) and (cranberry) on that farm.

26. You can see (blueberry) growing on those (bush).

27. The (man) and (woman) pack them in (box).

28. Many (family) from several (city) buy them.

29. We have served (raspberry) for many (lunch).

4 Singular Possessive Nouns   *p. 68*

A.   Write the possessive form of each singular noun.

1.	Eric	**9.**	grandfather
2.	lady	**10.**	Ms. Elliott
3.	boy	**11.**	parrot
4.	owl	**12.**	hen
5.	king	**13.**	Dr. Ray
6.	cousin	**14.**	boy
7.	gull	**15.**	rooster
8.	Susan	**16.**	duck

B.   Write each sentence below. Use the possessive form of the noun in ( ).

EXAMPLE: **We looked at ____ book. (Marco)**
ANSWER: **We looked at Marco's book.**

17.   ____ favorite bird is the kiwi. (Ellen)
18.   The ____ feathers look like hair. (kiwi)
19.   The kiwi is the ____ enemy. (worm)
20.   The peacock is the ____ cousin. (chicken)
21.   A ____ tail is beautiful. (peacock)
22.   A ____ beak is large and strong. (heron)
23.   Once ____ uncle saw an eagle in a tree. (Ralph)
24.   The ____ nest was very large and high. (eagle)
25.   My ____ book is about ostriches. (friend)
26.   An ____ neck is long and thin. (ostrich)
27.   ____ garden has a birdbath. (Miss Gold)
28.   She calls it her ____ spa. (cardinal)
29.   The red ____ feathers are bright. (bird)
30.   ____ aunt has a pet shop. (Tammy)
31.   My ____ canary came from there. (teacher)

5 Plural Possessive Nouns

p. 70

A. Write the possessive form of each plural noun.

1.	parents	**9.**	teachers
2.	boys	**10.**	writers
3.	sisters	**11.**	speakers
4.	dogs	**12.**	friends
5.	runners	**13.**	families
6.	players	**14.**	dancers
7.	actors	**15.**	cats
8.	girls	**16.**	artists

B. Write each sentence below. Use the possessive form of the plural noun in ( ).

17. The ____ trumpets are made of brass. (boys)

18. The ____ clarinets look alike. (twins)

19. The ____ stands are metal. (musicians)

20. The ____ feet move to the music. (players)

21. Those ____ voices are too soft. (singers)

22. Even the ____ sound was louder. (flutes)

23. The ____ songs were familiar to us. (students)

24. We watched both ____ marching bands. (schools)

25. I loved the ____ oompah sounds. (tubas)

26. Elena liked the ____ uniforms. (bands)

27. The ____ uniforms looked colorful. (marchers)

28. The ____ buttons were shining brightly. (jackets)

29. Two ____ hats blew off in the wind. (girls)

30. Several of the ____ pom-poms blew onto the field. (cheerleaders)

31. The ____ assistants chased after them. (coaches)

32. The ____ whistles blew shrilly. (referees)

USING LANGUAGE TO
CREATE

=== **PART ONE** ===

Unit Theme *Nature*

Language Awareness Nouns

=== **PART TWO** ===

Literature *Poetry*

A Reason for Writing Creating

Writing
IN YOUR JOURNAL

WRITER'S WARM-UP ◆ What about nature interests you the most? Are there animals that you like? Do you like flowers and other things that grow? Do you like weather or the moon and stars? Write in your journal about nature. Tell what it is about nature that interests you the most.

GETTING STARTED

Name three cities or states you would like to visit. Name some people you would like to meet during your trip.

1 Common Nouns and Proper Nouns

You know that a noun names a person, place, or thing. Some nouns name a particular person, place, or thing.

> **1.** The <u>poet</u> wrote about an <u>animal</u>.
> **2.** <u>A.A. Milne</u> wrote about <u>Winnie-the-Pooh</u>.

In sentence **1**, *poet* and *animal* are common nouns. They do not name a particular poet or animal. In sentence **2**, *A.A. Milne* and *Winnie-the-Pooh* are proper nouns. They name a particular poet and a particular animal. Sentence **2** shows how proper nouns can add detail to your writing.

Proper nouns may have more than one word. Each important word begins with a capital letter.

■ **Nikki Giovanni**   **Robert Frost**   **Gulf of Mexico**

> **Summary** ♦ A **common noun** names any person, place, or thing. A **proper noun** names a particular person, place, or thing.

Guided Practice

Tell if each noun is a common noun or a proper noun.

1. Charleston   **3.** gorilla   **5.** building

2. school   **4.** Banana Park   **6.** Ash Hill School

Practice

A. Copy the underlined nouns from the sentences below. Write *common* beside each common noun. Write *proper* beside each proper noun.

   7. Byron Parker lives in the city of Atlanta.
   8. He is a student at King Elementary School.
   9. Byron has one brother and two sisters.
 10. His family also has a dog named Rex.
 11. Each morning Byron walks Rex in Adams Park.
 12. Last January there was a huge snowstorm in Georgia.
 13. Workers were sent home early from their jobs.
 14. Peachtree Avenue was completely covered with snow.
 15. On Tuesday Byron wrote a poem about the storm.

B. Each sentence below has two nouns. Write the nouns. Then write *common* or *proper* beside each noun.

 16. The girl lives in a small town.
 17. Louise Simpson lives in Maywood.
 18. South Carolina is a beautiful state.
 19. The poet walks in Pine Forest.
 20. Uncle Bob likes poems.

C. Write a proper noun for each common noun listed below.

 21. boy **22.** school **23.** river **24.** city **25.** country

Apply • Think and Write

From Your Writing ♦ List all the nouns you used in the Writer's Warm-up. Tell if each noun is a common noun or a proper noun.

> ✏️ **Remember**
> to use proper nouns to add detail to your writing.

2 Names and Titles

The names of people and pets are proper nouns. Each word in each name below begins with a capital letter.

■ **Walt Whitman**   **Rover**   **Sandra**

Titles are sometimes used with the names of people. Notice the underlined titles below.

Ms. Lucy Ruiz   **Mr. Alvin Moore**   **Mrs. P. Owens**
Miss Jan Wint   **Dr. Maya T. Chu**

Some titles are abbreviations. An **abbreviation** is a shortened form of a word. For instance, *Dr.* is the abbreviation for *Doctor*. Many abbreviations begin with a capital letter and end with a period.

An **initial** is the first letter of a name. An initial may stand for a person's name. It is written with a capital letter and is followed by a period. Notice the initials in *Mrs. P. Owens* and *Dr. Maya T. Chu.*

Summary ◆ Each word in the name of a person or pet begins with a capital letter.

Guided Practice

Tell how to write each name correctly.

1. polly c evans   **3.** ms julia sims   **5.** mr r j verona

2. mrs g brooks   **4.** dr brian hall   **6.** rin tin tin

Practice

A. Write each poet's name correctly.

> **7.** laura e richards
> **8.** mr eugene field
> **9.** miss elizabeth barrett
> **10.** robert browning
> **11.** dr william c williams
> **12.** ms eve merriam
> **13.** clement c moore
> **14.** robert louis stevenson

B. Write each sentence correctly.

> **15.** dr helen m greer writes about wildlife.
> **16.** moira sheehan writes poems.
> **17.** ms sheehan's poems are about woodland animals.
> **18.** My favorite poem is about mr charlie chipmunk.
> **19.** I took some violets to mrs barbara lang.
> **20.** Her daughter, miss jenny b lang, was there.
> **21.** She read me a poem by aileen fisher.
> **22.** ms fisher's poem is called "Fall."
> **23.** Another poem about fall is by carl sandburg.
> **24.** elizabeth m roberts wrote a poem called "The Hens."

C. 25–27. Name each animal in the picture. Give each animal a title, first name, middle initial, and last name.

Apply • Think and Write

Names of People ♦ Write the names of two adults and three children you know. Use titles with the adults' names. Use middle initials with three of the names.

✎ **Remember**
to use capital letters to begin names and titles.

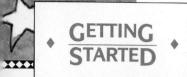

Name a street, town, city, or state for each letter of the
alphabet. It can be a real or imaginary place.
EXAMPLES: *Allen Street, Brownsville, California.*

3 Place Names

Names of particular places are proper nouns. Look at the
proper nouns in the sentences below. Notice that each word
in each name begins with a capital letter.

> My grandparents live on West Preston Road in Dallas.
> Dallas is a city in Texas.
> Flowers bloom along the River Walk in San Antonio.

Look at the map below. Find the place names. How does
each word in each name begin?

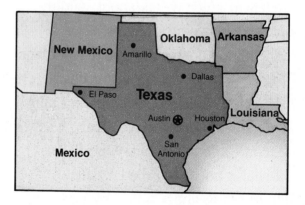

Summary ◆ Each word in the name of a street,
town, city, or state begins with a capital letter.

Guided Practice

Tell how to write each place name correctly.

1. fifth avenue **3.** savannah **5.** north carolina

2. red oaks **4.** wyoming **6.** market street

Practice

A. Write these place names correctly.

7. vermont
8. rock ridge
9. salt lake city
10. north shore drive
11. huntsville
12. greensboro
13. west virginia
14. santa fe
15. colorado
16. willow road

B. Write these sentences correctly. Remember to use a capital letter to begin each word in a place name.

17. I walked along hardy street.
18. This is the city named houston.
19. texas is a very large state.
20. The only state larger than texas is alaska.
21. My cousin has moved to san antonio.
22. He lives with his family on lamar road.
23. The capital city of texas is austin.
24. We drove on the lyndon baines johnson freeway.

C. Use a proper noun to complete each sentence.

25. I live in the town of _____ .
26. It is located in the state of _____ .
27. I am going to visit my cousins in _____ .
28. The bus made a left turn on _____ .
29. Someday I would like to visit _____ .

Apply • Think and Write

Creating Place Names ♦ Draw a map of a secret island. Write the name of each town, river, mountain, lake, and park.

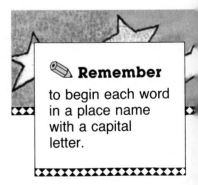

✎ **Remember**
to begin each word in a place name with a capital letter.

Tell about something strange that happened during each month of the year. Have most of the words begin with the same letter as the month does.

EXAMPLE: *Jack jogged to Juneau in January.*

4 Calendar Words

Look at the calendar for November. The names of the month and the days begin with capital letters.

Find each holiday and special day shown on the November calendar. How does each word in each name begin?

	Sunday	Monday	Tuesday	Wednesday	Thursday	Friday	Saturday
November					1	2	3
	4	5	Election Day 6	7	8	9	10
	Veterans Day 11	12	Robert Louis Stevenson's Birthday 13	14	15	16	Homemade Bread Day 17
	18	19	20	21	Thanksgiving Day 22	23	24

Summary ♦ The name of a day or month begins with a capital letter. Each word in the name of a holiday or special day begins with a capital letter.

Guided Practice

Find the names of days, months, holidays, and special days in these sentences. Tell how to write these names correctly.

1. Poet Robert Louis Stevenson was born in november.
2. Erica made a poster for election day.
3. The fourth thursday in november is thanksgiving day.
4. On veterans day my scout troop marched in a parade.
5. We baked bread on homemade bread day.

Practice

A. Find the names of days, months, holidays, and special days. Write these names correctly.

6. Many people enjoy parades on new year's day.
7. My friends and I look forward to february 2.
8. Everyone knows that is groundhog day!
9. On valentine's day many people wear red.
10. presidents' day is also celebrated in february.
11. april fools' day is never held in march or may.
12. We celebrate mother's day in may.
13. father's day is the third sunday in june.
14. Early in july we celebrate independence day.

B. Write each sentence. Use capital letters correctly.

15. The first monday in september is labor day.
16. We also observe native american day in september.
17. columbus day is also called discovery day.
18. october 15 is world poetry day.

C. Capitalize these holidays and special days. Use each one in a sentence.

19. new year's day
20. groundhog day
21. valentine's day
22. april fools' day
23. thanksgiving day

Apply ◆ Think and Write

Dictionary of Knowledge ◆ Look up *memory aid* in the Dictionary of Knowledge. Copy the sentence that helps you remember how to spell *December*.

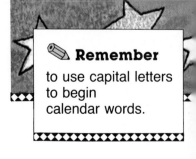

✎ **Remember**
to use capital letters to begin calendar words.

What do you think *rural* means in this sentence?
Tad's dad enjoys rural living, but he works in the city.

VOCABULARY ◆
Context Clues

Sometimes you hear or read words that are new to you. Often the words around a new word will give you clues to its meaning. A clue that helps you understand a new word is called a **context clue**.

Read the sentences below.

> She was <u>jubilant</u> when she heard the news. Her broad smile showed her happiness.

Notice that words in the second sentence help you understand *jubilant. Smile* and *happiness* are clues that *jubilant* means "happy" or "joyful."

Another kind of context clue is used in the sentence below.

> ■ Mr. Jones was a very <u>humane</u>, or kind, man.

Notice how the word *kind* gives you a clue to the meaning of the word *humane. Kind* has almost the same meaning as *humane.*

Building Your Vocabulary

What do the underlined words mean in these sentences?

1. The <u>artificial</u> flowers looked real to Anne.
2. The book was <u>ancient</u>. It was the oldest book Peter had ever seen.
3. Mr. Mulligan's speech was <u>drawn-out</u>. It was so long that many people fell asleep.

Practice

A. Read each sentence. Write what you think the underlined word means.

1. The weather was <u>turbulent</u>. The storm caused high winds and waves.
2. The ship <u>swayed</u>—it rocked back and forth in the waves.
3. I stood at the <u>bow</u>, or front, of the ship.
4. The crew <u>huddled</u> together. They kept close to each other to keep warm.
5. Afterward the sea was <u>tranquil</u>—calm and quiet.

B. Complete the paragraph below. Use context to help you choose the missing words.

It's going to be a beautiful ____ day for our picnic. We're going to play ____, and there will be ____ of ____ to eat and ____ to drink. I hope it won't be too ____, because there isn't ____ shade at the park.

Language Corner ◆ Mirror Words

In the words below, the second part mirrors the first part.

yo-yo	**tutu**
tom-tom	**bye-bye**

In this group of words, the second part is very much like the first part.

wishy-washy	**shipshape**
super-duper	**zigzag**

What is the meaning of each mirror word in this corner?

How to Revise Sentences with Proper Nouns

You have learned that proper nouns name particular persons, places, and things. Proper nouns give important information to your reader. Read the sentences below. Which one gives more exact details?

1. We saw a monkey at the zoo.
2. We saw an orangutan at the San Diego Zoo.

Each sentence gives information, but sentence **2** tells some very important details. Sentence **2** is a better, stronger sentence. Use proper nouns to add details to your writing.

The Grammar Game ♦ How quickly can you write two proper nouns to replace each common noun below?

teacher	holiday	poet
planet	athlete	river
city	neighbor	relative

Compare your list with a classmate's list. Did you write any of the same proper nouns?

Working Together

See how proper nouns can add details to your sentences. Work with your group on activities **A** and **B**.

A. Draw this "People Pizza." Each person in the group should use proper nouns to add the information on each slice.

B. Each group member should complete the paragraph. (Don't let anyone see what you wrote!) Then mix up the papers. Can the group figure out who wrote each paper?

I was born on ____. My middle name is ____. I live on ____ in the town of ____. ____ is one of my best friends.

In Your Group

♦ Ask questions.
♦ Record everyone's information.
♦ Keep everyone on the subject.
♦ Help the group finish on time.

WRITERS' CORNER ♦ Exact Information

When you choose nouns, think about the kind of information you want to give. What do you want your reader to know?

GENERAL INFORMATION: A doctor lives next door.
EXACT INFORMATION: A veterinarian lives next door.
DIFFERENT EXACT: Dr. Rivera lives next door.

Read what you wrote for the Writer's Warm-Up. Did you use nouns in your writing? Are their meanings clear?

MOUNTAIN POOL
oil on canvas by Robert Scott Duncanson
National Museum of American Art,
Smithsonian Institution, Gift of Dr. Richard Frates.

USING LANGUAGE
TO
CREATE

=== **PART TWO** ===

Literature *Poetry*

A Reason for Writing Creating

CREATIVE
Writing

FINE ARTS ◆ Look at the painting at the left. What do you see? Where do you think the place is? Imagine that you could step into the picture. What will you do at that place? Will you hike? Swim? Fish? Pretend you visited this place. Write a postcard to a friend. Tell your friend about the special place you visited.

CREATIVE THINKING ♦
A Strategy for Creating

A QUESTION WHEEL

Poets create new ways of saying things. Sometimes poets speak to things as if they were persons. Later you will be a poet. In the poem you write, you will speak to something.

What would you ask the wind? Here is part of a poem by David McCord. Find out what *he* asked the wind.

> Out of the morning,
> Washed in the blue,
> Wind I-am-blowing,
> *Where* are you?

Do you ever wonder about things? Poets often do. So do other people. When you wonder, you ask questions. It is a good way to think and to learn.

Learning the Strategy

What can you learn by asking questions? Suppose you start to do a math problem. You can't finish it. You wonder what to do next. How can you get help? Suppose you meet a new friend. You don't know very much about your new friend. What do you wonder? How can you find out?

Asking questions is a good way to find things out. A question wheel can help you think of questions. Write the name of something in the middle. Write questions about it around the outside. One question may help you think of others. Fill the wheel with questions. Here is a question wheel for your new friend. What else might you ask?

Using the Strategy

A. Is there a clock you can see right now? If not, imagine a clock. What do you wonder about that clock? What would you like to ask it? Make a question wheel. In the middle write *clock* or draw one. Fill your wheel with questions you would ask the clock.

B. Later you will read some poems. One is about a caterpillar. One is about a bee. One is about an owl. Choose one of these animals. Make a question wheel. In the middle write *What can I say to (your animal)?*

Fill the wheel with things you would say to it. Then read the poems. See what a poet said to your animal.

Applying the Strategy

- How did you decide what to ask the clock?
- What questions have you asked in school today? What did you find out?

LITERATURE

Most poets like to write about the world around them. Sometimes they like to talk to things like bugs and trees. Listen to how these poets talk to things that cannot answer them. What surprising things do you hear the poets say?

Little bird flitting,
twittering, trying to fly . . .
my, aren't you busy!

—*Basho*

The Wind

Wind in the garden,
Wind on the hill,
Wind I-am-blowing,
Never be still.

Wind I-am-blowing,
I love you the best:
Out of the morning,
Into the west.

Out of the morning,
Washed in the blue,
Wind I-am-blowing,
Where are you?

—*David McCord*

Caterpillar,
Caterpillar,
Soon
Soon
Soon

Caterpillar,
Caterpillar,
Out
Of your
Cocoon

Fly to Minnesota,
Fly to North Dakota,
Fly to Tallahassee,
Fly to Rome.

Fly to California,
Fly to Philadelphia,
Fly to Appalachia,
Fly to Nome.

Fly to Cincinnati,
Fly to Pensacola,
Fly to Walla Walla,
And then fly home.
—Eve Merriam

Move Over

Big
burly
bumblebee
buzzing
through the grass,
move over.

Black and
yellow
clover rover,
let me pass.

Fat and
furry
rumblebee
loud on the
wing,
let me
hurry
past
your sting.
—Lilian Moore

To a Firefly

Flitting white-fire insect,
waving white-fire bug,
give me light before I go to sleep!
Come, little dancing white-fire bug,
come, little flitting white-fire beast,
light me with your bright white flame,
your little candle!

—*Chippewa Algonquin*

Lulu, Lulu,
I've a Lilo

Owl, owl,	Lulu, lulu,
I've a secret.	I've a lilo.
And I am to blame.	And I am to blame.
I lost my brand-new handkerchief.	I lost my brand-new solosolo.
Isn't that a shame?	Isn't that a shame?
But you can't tell my secret, owl.	But you can't tell my lilo, lulu.
You don't know my name.	You don't know my name.

—*Charlotte Pomerantz*

 ## Reader's Response

Which poem was your favorite? Tell why.

Poetry

Responding to Literature

1. Would you like to talk to a bumblebee or to the wind? What would you say? Draw a picture. Show yourself with something you would like to talk to. Add a speech balloon. Write in it the words you would say.

2. Listen as your teacher rereads the poem about the caterpillar. Pretend you are jumping rope. Can you jump to the beat of the poem?

3. A big burly bumblebee buzzes. Choose an insect and write its name. Make a sentence about the insect. Use words that begin with the same beginning sound. Read your sentence aloud.

Writing to Learn

Think and Question ◆ Choose your favorite insect and ask it some questions. Make a question wheel like this one. Fill your wheel with questions.

(your favorite insect)

Question Wheel

Write ◆ Select your favorite question. Write what you think your insect's answer would be.

Close your eyes and picture yourself talking to a little firefly. Then take turns telling what you pictured and the first thing you said.

SPEAKING and LISTENING ◆
Poetry

Leo likes listening to Patti read her favorite poem about a caterpillar. He likes imagining his own pictures for the poem as he listens.

Good poems make good pictures for active readers and listeners, like Patti and Leo. You can be active readers and listeners, too, if you follow these guidelines.

Reading a Poem Aloud	1. Choose a poem you like. 2. Practice reading your poem aloud. Will you use the same voice for a soft wind and a furry caterpillar? 3. Imagine your own pictures for the poem as you read it. 4. Look for places to pause or stop in the poem. Watch for commas, end marks, and the ends of verses.
Being an Active Listener	1. Imagine your own pictures for the poem as you listen. 2. Try to picture yourself saying the poem, too. 3. Listen for clues to help you remember the poem. Listen for rhymes or repeated words and sentences.

Summary ◆ When you listen to a poem, be an active listener by imagining your own pictures. Listen for clues to help you remember the words.

Guided Practice

Play an echo game. One person reads each line below. Everyone else listens with closed eyes, then repeats the line.

1. A big, fat bumblebee came buzzing, buzzing after me.
2. A firefly flew by like a little lighted candle.
3. A caterpillar grew wings and flew to California.

Practice

A. Listen as your teacher reads aloud the poem "Move Over" from page 133. Imagine your own picture for the poem as you listen. Then draw the picture you imagined. Are you in the picture, too?

B. With a partner, take turns reading and listening to these verses from David McCord's poem "The Wind." The listener must repeat each line without looking at the words. After your turn, answer this question: What clues helped you remember the poem?

Wind in the garden,	Wind I-am-blowing,
Wind on the hill,	I love you the best:
Wind I-am-blowing,	Out of the morning,
Never be still.	Into the west.

Apply ♦ **Think and Write**

Dictionary of Knowledge ♦ Read about the firefly and the bumblebee in the Dictionary of Knowledge. Then talk with a partner about how the firefly and the bumblebee are alike and different.

✎ **Remember**
to imagine pictures as you listen to poetry.

GETTING STARTED

Do you know a verse about Humpty Dumpty? Do you know "One, two, buckle my shoe"? Say these verses aloud together. What other rhyming verses can you say?

WRITING ◆
Couplets

Most of us like to hear rhyming sounds, like *snow* and *blow*, *funny* and *sunny*, *mountain* and *fountain*. When we hear them, it's as if we were hearing music. Listen for the rhyming words in this poem.

The Mirror

I look in the Mirror, and what do I see?
A little of you, and a lot of me!

—William Jay Smith

When two lines rhyme, one after the other, we call the two lines a couplet. You'll find this easy to remember if you know that the word *couple* means "two."

Sometimes poets write rhyming poems using more than one couplet. What are the rhyming words in this poem?

—from White Fields

In the winter time we go
Walking in the fields of snow;
Where there is no grass at all;
Where the top of every wall,
Every fence, and every tree,
Is as white as white can be. . . .

—James Stephens

The longer poem on the next page is made of many couplets. How many couplets can you find? How many different rhymes?

Three

We were just three,
Two loons and me.
They swam and fished,
I watched and wished,
That I, like them, might dive and play
In icy waters all the day.
I watched and wished. I could not reach
Where they were, till I tried their speech,
And something in me helped, so I
Could give their trembling sort of cry.
One loon looked up and answered me.
He understood that we were three.

—Elizabeth Coatsworth

> **Summary** ♦ A **couplet** is two lines that rhyme, one after the other. You can use couplets in rhyming poems.

Responding to Poetry

1. Elizabeth Coatsworth remembers a time when she saw two water birds and spoke to them. Tell of a time when you spoke to something. Tell how it seemed to answer you.

2. What happens when you look in a mirror? Draw a picture of "a lot" of you and "a little" of something else.

3. Pretend you are the grass or a tree, and snow is covering you. How do you feel?

Apply ♦ Think and Write

Creative Writing ♦ Write the first line of "The Mirror."
Write a rhyming line of your own to go with it.

> ✎ **Remember**
> that you can write a poem with one or more couplets.

GETTING STARTED

Read the four words below. Then think of two more words that rhyme with each one.

sun   feet   blue   star

WRITING ◆
Tercets

A poem that has three rhyming lines together is called a tercet. Listen to the rhyming sounds in this poem.

Winter Moon

How thin and sharp is the moon **tonight**!	**A**
How thin and sharp and ghostly **white**	**A**
Is the slim curved crook of the moon **tonight**!	**A**

—*Langston Hughes*

There is a special way to show rhyming patterns in poetry. The sound of each end word is given a letter name. In "Winter Moon" the letter A names the sound of the first end word, *tonight*. Other end sounds that rhyme with *tonight* are called A, too. So the rhyming sounds of *tonight*, *white*, and *tonight* make the pattern called AAA.

Very often a tercet has more than one rhyming sound. In this poem there are four different end sounds with different letter names. Which two sounds are repeated?

At Black Mark Farm

At Black Mark **Farm**	**A**
we always **pass**	**B**
the cows out eating up the **grass**.	**B**
And every **time**	**C**
I wonder **how**	**D**
the grass can taste good to a **cow**.	**D**

—*Myra Cohn Livingston*

What is the rhyming pattern in this poem?

Taking Turns

When sun goes **home**
behind the **trees,**
and locks her shutters **tight**—
then stars come **out**
with silver **keys**
to open up the **night.**

—*Norma Farber*

Summary ♦ A **tercet** is a group of three lines that may rhyme in different ways.

Responding to Poetry

1. Have you ever thought of stars as silver keys? Talk with your classmates about other things that stars might look like to you.

2. How many shapes and colors have you seen when the moon comes out? Draw a picture of yourself looking at the moon. What shapes and colors do you see?

3. If grass tastes good to a cow, then what tastes good to you? Help make a list of favorite foods. Then vote to find out which food your class likes best.

Apply ♦ Think and Write

Creative Writing ♦ Think of some rhyming words that would make a good tercet. Write them in a rhyming pattern.

✎ **Remember**
that you can write a poem with one or more tercets.

Focus on the Poet's Voice

Have you ever talked to a flower? A bird? An ant? Poets sometimes "talk" to things around them. They do this in their writing. They speak to things that cannot answer.

In the poem "Go Wind," Lilian Moore speaks to the wind. Notice what she tells the wind to do.

Go wind, blow
Push wind, swoosh.
  Shake things
  take things
  make things
      fly.

Ring things
Swing things
fling things
      high.

Go wind, blow
Push things—whee.
  No, wind, no.
  Not me—
  not *me*.

The poet tells the wind to blow things and push things. What would *you* tell the wind to do?

The Writer's Voice ♦ Some poets ask questions when they speak to things. In the poem below, what does the Japanese poet Issa ask the wild geese? Put the question in your own words.

Wild geese, o wild geese
were you little
fellows too . . . when
you flew away from home?

Working Together

A poet sometimes speaks to nature. A poet may ask questions of things that cannot answer. Poets sometimes use their imaginations to answer their own questions. One famous poem begins, "O wild West Wind. . . ." Work with your group on activities **A** and **B**.

A. Take turns suggesting things in nature that you would like to talk to. Share your thoughts about each others' suggestions. Agree on one of the things to spend more time discussing.

B. Have each person write a question to ask the thing your group chose in activity **A.** Then take turns reading the questions aloud for everyone. Ask a person in the group to pretend to be the thing and to give its answer.

In Your Group

♦ Give your ideas to the group.
♦ Encourage others to share ideas.
♦ Help people understand what to do.
♦ List the group's ideas.

THESAURUS CORNER ♦ Word Choice

Look up the following nouns in the Thesaurus. Use each noun in a sentence that speaks to a river. Your sentence can ask the river a question, give it advice, or tell it what to do. Next, check the synonyms for each noun. If you find a better word than the one you used, change your sentence.

end   noise   part
picture   trip

WRITING PROCESS
CREATING

Writing a Poem

Poets speak to many things like stars and flowers. A poet may ask a flower a question. A poet may tell a star a secret. Of course, a star or flower cannot answer.

Eve Merriam spoke to a caterpillar. David McCord spoke to the wind. Have you ever wished upon a star? Then you, too, have talked to something that cannot answer.

Know Your Purpose and Audience

What's **MY PURPOSE**

Now you will write a poem. Your purpose will be to speak to something that cannot answer.

Who's **MY AUDIENCE**

Your audience will be your classmates. Later you can have a poetry reading. You can also make a ''poetry tree.''

1 Prewriting

First choose a topic. What will you speak to? Then gather ideas. What might you say to your subject?

Choose Your Topic ♦ What thing would you like to talk to? Your bike? Your goldfish? Make a list of things that cannot talk back. Then circle your topic choice.

Think About It	**Talk About It**
It will help to list things that are important to you. For example, you might list your bike but not the fence it leans on. Your bike is something you want to talk to, but the fence is not. Then look at your list. What do you like best?	Work with a partner to make your lists. Your partner can help you decide what to include. Ask questions such as ''What would you say to your bike?'' If you have something to say, put that thing on your list.

Topic Ideas

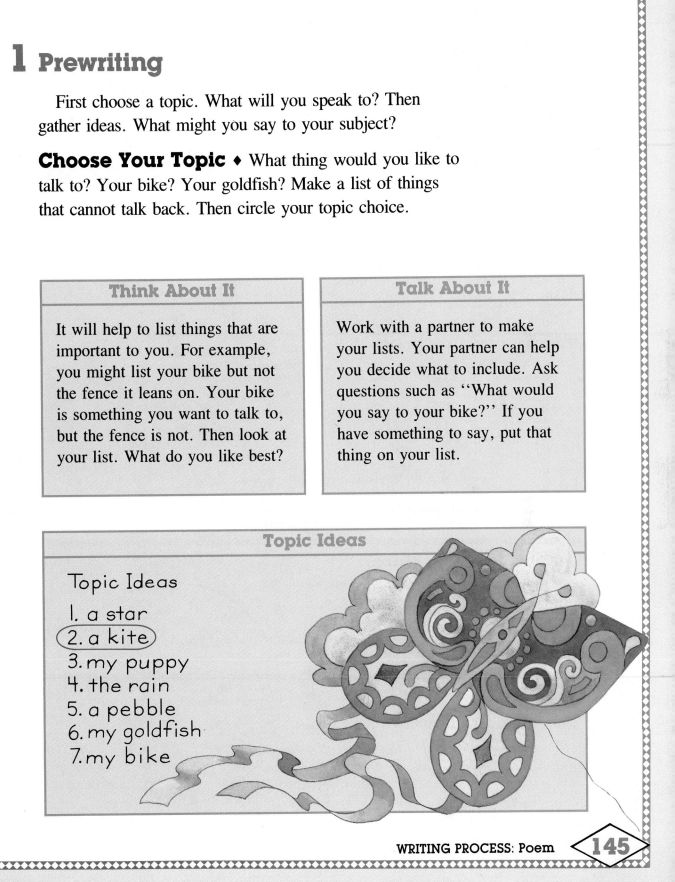

Topic Ideas
1. a star
2. a kite
3. my puppy
4. the rain
5. a pebble
6. my goldfish
7. my bike

Choose Your Strategy ♦ What could you say to the thing you chose? Here are two ways to get ideas. Read both. Then use the one you like better.

PREWRITING IDEAS

CHOICE ONE

Draw and Talk

What will you talk to in your poem? Draw a picture of it. Then talk to the picture. Jot down notes about what you say. Write any rhyming words you think of.

Model

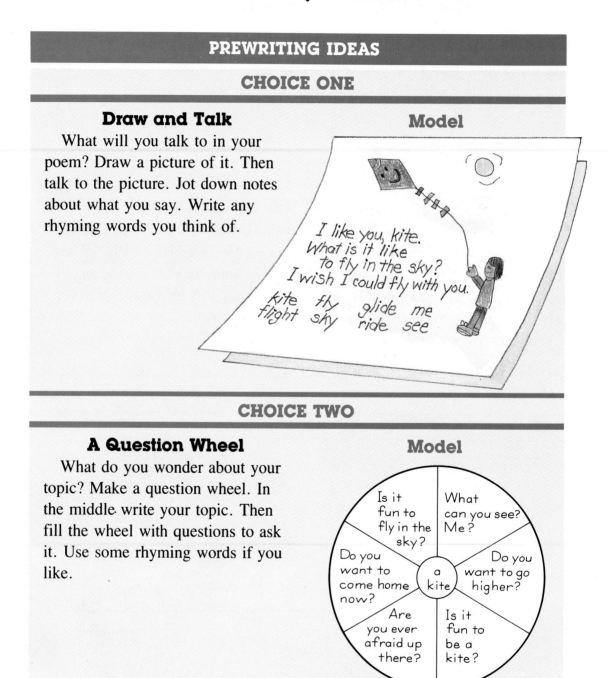

I like you, kite.
What is it like
to fly in the sky?
I wish I could fly with you.

kite   fly   glide   me
flight sky   ride   see

CHOICE TWO

A Question Wheel

What do you wonder about your topic? Make a question wheel. In the middle write your topic. Then fill the wheel with questions to ask it. Use some rhyming words if you like.

Model

Is it fun to fly in the sky?

What can you see? Me?

Do you want to come home now?

a kite

Do you want to go higher?

Are you ever afraid up there?

Is it fun to be a kite?

2 Writing

Now write your poem. Use your drawing or question wheel to help you. You might begin with a question or an "I wonder" sentence.

♦ Kite, what do you see when you fly in the sky?

♦ I wonder what it's like to fly.

You may write a couplet or a tercet if you like. You may also write without rhymes. You can change words later. For now, just let your ideas bubble out!

Sample First Draft ♦

I wonder, kite, what you would do

If I didn't hold on to you.

Would you be quick and fly up high

And not come back this month?

I want to now what you can see.

Can you see my house? can you see me?

I'd like to be a kite like you.

Then I could also fly and flutter!

3 Revising

Try this idea to help make your poem even better.

REVISING IDEA

FIRST Read to Yourself

Think about your purpose. Did you write a poem about a thing? Think of your audience. Will your classmates enjoy your poem? Circle any words you might like to change.

Focus: In your poem, did you speak to a thing? Is it a thing that cannot answer you?

THEN Share with a Partner

Ask a partner to read your poem aloud. Listen carefully. These guidelines may help you.

The Writer

Guidelines: Listen as your partner reads. Decide if you need to fix anything.

Sample questions:
- What was the best part?
- **Focus question:** What else could I ask this thing?

The Writer's Partner

Guidelines: Read the poem slowly and clearly. Give your honest ideas.

Sample responses
- The part I liked best was ____.
- Could you ask ____?

Revising Model ◆ This poem is being revised. The marks show changes the writer wants to make.

Quick is an overused word. Swift is more interesting.

The proper noun July added a detail to the poem.

> I wonder, kite, what you would do
>
> If I didn't hold on to you.
>
> ~~swift~~
> Would you be ~~quick~~ and fly up high
>
> until july
> And ~~not~~ come back ~~this month~~?
>
> I want to now what you can see.
>
> Can you see my house? can you
>
> see me?
> ~~Aren't you afraid that you might fall?~~
> ~~And do you ever miss me at all?~~
> I'd like to be a kite like you.
> ⋀
> —too
> Then I could ~~also~~ fly and flutter!

The writer's partner suggested these questions.

The writer wanted to end with a rhyming couplet.

Read the poem above. Read it the way the writer *wants* it to be. Then revise your own poem.

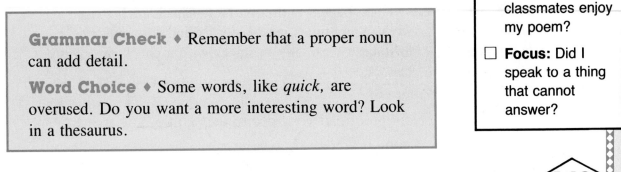

Grammar Check ◆ Remember that a proper noun can add detail.

Word Choice ◆ Some words, like *quick*, are overused. Do you want a more interesting word? Look in a thesaurus.

Revising Checklist

- ☐ **My purpose:** Did I write a poem about a thing?
- ☐ **My audience:** Will my classmates enjoy my poem?
- ☐ **Focus:** Did I speak to a thing that cannot answer?

4 Proofreading

Now check your poem. Fix any mistakes in spelling or capital letters.

Proofreading Model ♦ Here is the poem about a kite. Notice that mistakes have been fixed in red.

I wonder, kite, what you would do

If I didn't hold on to you.

swift
Would you be ~~quick~~ and fly up high

until july
And not come back ~~this month~~?

know
I want to (now) what you can see.

Can you see my house? can you
                              ＝

see me?
~~Aren't you afraid that you might fall?~~
~~And do you ever miss me at all?~~
I'd like to be a kite like you.
^

too
Then I could ~~also~~ fly and flutter!
                                    ^

PROOFREADING IDEA

Trading with a Partner

Trade papers with a partner. Check each other's work. Sometimes it is easier to find someone else's mistakes. Mark any mistakes with a check or a wavy line.

Now proofread your poem, add a title, and make a neat copy.

5 Publishing

Here are two ways to share your poem with others.

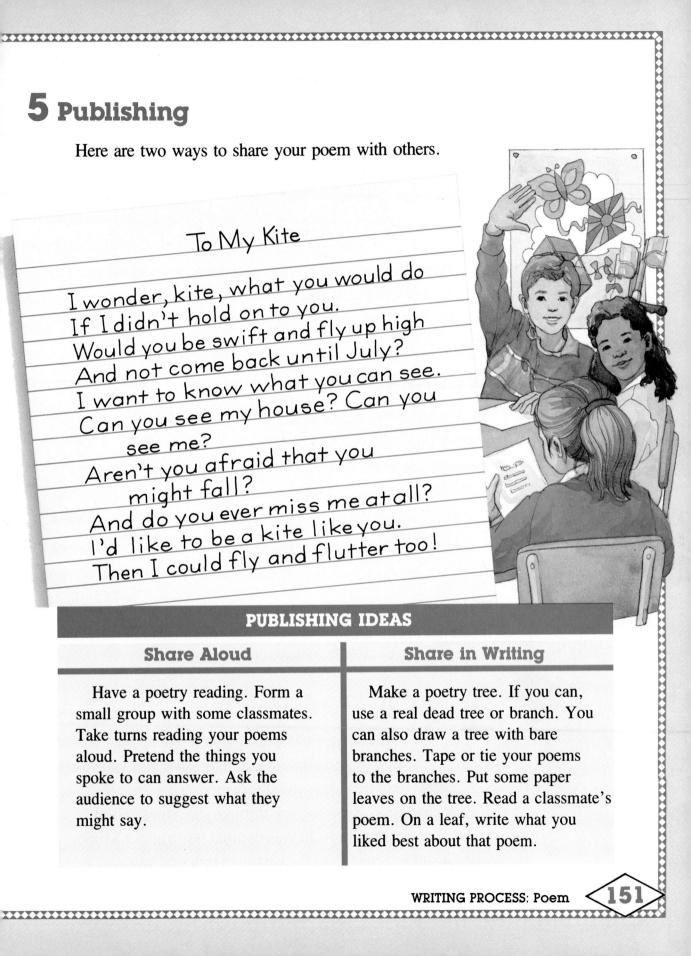

To My Kite

I wonder, kite, what you would do
If I didn't hold on to you.
Would you be swift and fly up high
And not come back until July?
I want to know what you can see.
Can you see my house? Can you
   see me?
Aren't you afraid that you
   might fall?
And do you ever miss me at all?
I'd like to be a kite like you.
Then I could fly and flutter too!

PUBLISHING IDEAS

Share Aloud

Have a poetry reading. Form a small group with some classmates. Take turns reading your poems aloud. Pretend the things you spoke to can answer. Ask the audience to suggest what they might say.

Share in Writing

Make a poetry tree. If you can, use a real dead tree or branch. You can also draw a tree with bare branches. Tape or tie your poems to the branches. Put some paper leaves on the tree. Read a classmate's poem. On a leaf, write what you liked best about that poem.

Writing Across the Curriculum Science

In this unit you wrote a poem about nature. You asked questions about it and answered some of them. Scientists wonder about nature, too. They also try to answer questions about it.

Writing to Learn

Think and Wonder ♦ Study the picture. Then make a question wheel. Think like a scientist. Write as many questions as you can about the beehive.

Question Wheel

Write ♦ Go to the library. Ask the librarian to help you find information about beehives. Can you find answers to any of your questions? Write one answer you found.

Writing in Your Journal

In the Writer's Warm-up you wrote about something in nature that interested you. As you read this unit, you discovered that nature is always changing. Browse back through the pages. Think about changes in nature. In your journal write about a time when a sudden change in the weather surprised you.

BOOKS TO ENJOY

Read More About It

Inside Turtle's Shell and Other Poems of the Field *by Joanne Ryder*

This collection of poems is about things you might find in meadows and fields. The poems follow a day from morning until night.

Sky Songs *by Myra Cohn Livingston*

Look at the sky each day to notice that it never looks exactly the same. Imagine the sky at sunrise and sunset. How does it look when it is going to snow or rain? Read this collection of poems about the changing sky.

SKY SONGS

Myra Cohn Livingston, *Poet*

Leonard Everett Fisher, *Painter*

Book Report Idea Recorded Report

Poetry is meant to be heard. Why not create a poetry book report for others to hear?

Tape a Book Report

Choose poems from your book. Speak slowly and clearly. Begin by giving the titles and the authors. Invite your classmates to listen to your recorded report.

Unit 3

Nouns   *pages 116–117*

A. Write the underlined nouns. Then write *common* or *proper* beside each noun.

1. Our <u>class</u> went sailing in <u>Boston Harbor</u>.
2. We saw the <u>Customs House</u> in the <u>city</u>.
3. It is a few <u>blocks</u> from <u>South Station</u>.
4. The <u>subway</u> goes from <u>Ashmont</u> to <u>Fresh Pond</u>.
5. Each <u>station</u> is decorated with <u>art</u>.
6. <u>Carmen</u> knows the <u>artist</u> for this <u>mural</u>.
7. <u>Morse School</u> is built of <u>bricks</u> and <u>glass</u>.

Capital Letters and Periods   *pages 118–123*

B. Write each name correctly.

8. mr walt disney
9. carmen miranda
10. dr milton i levine
11. roger clemens
12. miss mary poppins
13. dwight d eisenhower
14. judy garland
15. ms barbara jordan
16. oveta culp hobby
17. mrs martha washington

C. Write each sentence. Use capital letters correctly.

18. It is usually warmer in louisiana than in maine.
19. On valentine's day I got a card from toledo.
20. I found a dime on thanksgiving day.
21. It was on hancock road.
22. Next sunday our family is going to albuquerque.
23. We will visit you on washington's birthday.

Context Clues *pages 124–125*

D. Write what you think each underlined word means.

24. I will <u>store</u> my things in the attic.

25. You will <u>adore</u> this great movie.

26. We <u>inched</u> our way through the crowd.

27. This chair looks too new to be an <u>antique</u>.

28. If everyone is <u>prompt</u> we can start on time.

29. Let's <u>pause</u> here until Henry catches up.

Proofreading

E. Proofread for capitals and periods. Write each sentence correctly.

30. baseball player german gonzales went to minnesota

31. sugar ray leonard signed a boxing contract

32. phoebe mills won in gymnastics in houston, texas

33. dr harold daniels worked for a football player

34. george m cohan composed music

35. he did not want to buy the boston braves

36. the adams museum held a reunion

F. Proofread the sentences. Each sentence contains a mistake. Look for spelling errors, missing end marks, and possessive errors. Write each sentence correctly.

37. The dogs bark woke the baby.

38. Did Steven's father call me

39. I met my friend at the ball gave.

40. The puppies eyes are not open yet.

Shape a Noun

Use the clues below to figure out ten proper nouns.

1. a state: *h*, and three vowel letters
2. a country: *M*, *x*, *c*, and three vowels
3. an ocean: *P*, *c*, *f*, *c*, and three vowels
4. a city: *S*, *n*, *F*, *r*, *n*, *c*, *s*, *c*, and four vowels
5. a continent: *r*, *p*, and four vowels
6. a lake: *S*, *p*, *r*, *r*, and four vowels
7. a park: *Y*, *l*, *l*, *w*, *s*, *t*, *n*, and four vowels
8. a holiday: *L*, *b*, *r*, *D*, *y*, and three vowels
9. a nurse: *C*, *l*, *r*, *B*, *r*, *t*, *n*, and four vowels
10. a hero: *S*, *p*, *r*, *m*, *n*, and three vowels

Word Designs

Use capital letters to design a word. Design your name, the month you were born, your state, or your town. You may also design your favorite holiday or a club you belong to.

Ted   Arbor Day   Valentine's Day   Seaside

Unit 3 Extra Practice

1 Common Nouns and Proper Nouns

p. 116

A. Write *common* or *proper* for each noun.

1. Los Angeles
2. building
3. Gulf of Mexico
4. tree
5. school
6. Cozy Inn

B. Copy the underlined nouns from the sentences below. Write *common* beside each common noun. Write *proper* beside each proper noun.

7. Clara Barton was born in America.
8. She taught at a school in New Jersey.
9. She helped the soldiers who were injured.
10. Clara began the American Red Cross.
11. Our city named Barton Park after her.
12. In December there was a flood in Riverdale.
13. Many people needed help.
14. The workers served meals at Tracy Hospital.

C. Each sentence below has two nouns. Write them. Then write *common* or *proper* beside each noun.

EXAMPLE: **Stacy is a nurse.**

ANSWER: **Stacy, proper   nurse, common**

15. A nurse cares for people.
16. Amy Jones works at a hospital.
17. Some doctors visit schools.
18. The dentist checks the students.
19. Sara works at Cook School.

D. Write the nouns in these sentences. Write *common* or *proper* after each noun.

20. Ponce de León explored Florida.
21. Many Indians, or Native Americans, lived there.
22. The Spanish built homes there.
23. Soon other settlers built on the land.
24. Many people live in the state now.
25. A large town in Florida is Miami.
26. Miami Beach is a famous resort.
27. A large lake in the state is Okeechobee.
28. Seminole Indians live on a nearby reservation.
29. Walt Disney World is located near Orlando.
30. The Atlantic Ocean borders Florida.
31. On the western coast is the Gulf of Mexico.
32. The Florida Keys extend to Key West Island.
33. Visitors to Florida flock to the beaches.
34. The sunny climate grows many tropical fruits.
35. Alligators and flamingos thrive there, too.
36. Tropical plants include orchids and palms.

2 Names and Titles
p. 118

A. Write each name correctly.

1. debra e bowles
2. p f lupa
3. mr nathan p davis
4. miss l k bloom
5. rodney thomas lewis
6. ms c rice
7. rin tin tin
8. sue ann lang
9. harriet tubman
10. dr juanita diaz
11. sandy c gates
12. mrs brenda zak
13. ms gail ong
14. dr james r black
15. l r beck
16. trigger

B. Write each sentence correctly.

17. mrs nancy rose trains dogs.

18. We took our puppy named j j to her class.

19. I saw barbara tracy and her gray poodle.

20. Her dog is named smoky.

21. The trainer is mr k g benton.

22. He helped miss t payne with her collie.

23. The collie ran to dr evans.

24. The smallest dog belongs to ray brown.

25. His terrier is named tiny terry.

26. The spotted dog belongs to ms rachel wolfe.

27. My brother jerry likes books about dogs.

28. His favorite author is albert p terhune.

29. Have you met miss p adams?

30. She and craig ellis work at the pet shop.

31. She sold a puppy to c w shay.

32. mr and mrs wint had a party.

33. dr and mrs parker arrived early.

34. mr phillip t garret brought salad.

35. tammy b hanes brought her dog named skipper.

36. bob silvers cooked hamburgers.

37. linda jackson and c g ate them.

3 Place Names

p. 120

A. Write these place names correctly.

1. nevada
2. grand canyon drive
3. safford
4. denver
5. peach springs
6. lincoln avenue
7. colorado
8. san francisco
9. east balboa way
10. south dakota

B. Write these sentences correctly.

11. Kevin lives in new jersey.
12. He read about arizona, the forty-eighth state.
13. He learned about an empty town named jerome.
14. Every year a city named prescott has a rodeo.
15. The rodeo parade begins on main street.
16. My cousins live on north bell road in phoenix.
17. Phoenix and tucson are cities in arizona.
18. There is a museum near tucson.
19. A city called yuma is close to california.
20. There are copper mines near tucson and miami.
21. Florida also has a city named miami.
22. A big park in mesa is near university avenue.

C. Write the place names in the following sentences correctly.

23. A beautiful state is california.
24. The state stretches between oregon and mexico.
25. Near the border of mexico is san diego.
26. A large city is los angeles.
27. Many tourists visit the film studios in hollywood.
28. Colorful san francisco also attracts many tourists.
29. Visitors ride the cable cars on california street.
30. They also drive over san francisco bay on the golden gate bridge.
31. The views of the pacific ocean are spectacular.
32. Nearby is the wine country of napa valley.
33. The climate changes as we cross the sierra nevada.
34. Near the eastern border is reno, nevada.

4 Calendar Words

p. 122

A. Find the names of days, months, holidays, and special days. Write these names correctly.

1. Susan B. Anthony was born in february.
2. Sally made a poster for lincoln's birthday.
3. The last monday in may is memorial day.
4. On arbor day our class planted trees.
5. Every tuesday and thursday we go to the library.
6. Christine's party is next wednesday.
7. My little brother was born in may.
8. Calvin's birthday is on groundhog day.
9. Did you see the parade on thanksgiving day?
10. Every saturday Larry has a piano lesson.
11. Helen Keller was born in june.
12. Some schools open in august.
13. Banks are closed on washington's birthday.
14. In Norway mother's day is in february.
15. The first moon landing was in july of 1969.

B. Write each sentence correctly.

16. The first day of may is bird day in some states.
17. Our class made cards for valentine's day.
18. Our school opens the tuesday after labor day.
19. In Canada, thanksgiving day is in october.
20. Columbus day is also called discovery day.
21. New year's day was on saturday last year.
22. Groundhog day is the second day of february.
23. Flag day was on a tuesday in june.
24. The second monday in october was columbus day.
25. Thanksgiving is the fourth thursday of november.

UNIT FOUR

USING LANGUAGE TO
PERSUADE

PART ONE

Unit Theme *Pets*

Language Awareness Pronouns

PART TWO

Literature *Socks* by Beverly Cleary

A Reason for Writing Persuading

Writing IN YOUR JOURNAL

WRITER'S WARM-UP ◆ What pet would you pick if you could have your choice? Would your pet be a horse? Would it be a dog or a cat? Would it be an unusual pet? Write in your journal. Tell what you would like best about your pet. Tell its name and what it would do with you.

♦ **GETTING STARTED** ♦

You and your friends are having a pet show. Tell about the show. Use the following words: *I, you, she, he, it, me, her, him, we, you, they, us, them.*

1 Writing with Pronouns

You know that nouns name persons, places, and things. Sometimes other words are used instead of nouns.

1. The <u>puppy</u> runs to the <u>children</u>.
2. <u>It</u> runs to <u>them</u>.

In sentence **2** the words *it* and *them* are pronouns. The pronoun *it* takes the place of the noun *puppy*. The pronoun *them* takes the place of the noun *children*.

A singular pronoun takes the place of a noun that names one person, place, or thing. A plural pronoun takes the place of a noun that names more than one person, place, or thing.

Singular Pronouns	Plural Pronouns
I, you, she, he, it me, her, him	we, you, they us, them

Summary ♦ A **pronoun** takes the place of a noun or nouns.

Guided Practice

Name the pronoun in each sentence below.

1. We enjoy animals.
2. May I feed the fish?
3. Bill gives her a dog.
4. Show us the ducks, please.

Practice

A. Write the pronoun in each sentence.

5. Debby and I asked Mom for a pet duck.
6. "You cannot keep a duck in the house!" said Mom.
7. "Why not?" Debby asked her.
8. "Ducks are outdoor pets," Mom said to me.
9. "Maybe we can get some fish," thought Debby.

B. Choose the pronoun in ( ) to take the place of the underlined noun or nouns. Write each sentence.

10. Debby and Joseph wanted some fish. (She, They)
11. The children got a tank for the fish. (them, you)
12. Joseph put fresh water in the tank. (Us, He)
13. Debby helped Joe install a water pump. (him, them)
14. Debby said, "The tank is ready!" (She, They)

C. Use a pronoun to replace the underlined word or words below. Write each new sentence.

15. Bill likes small animals.
16. Hamsters and gerbils make wonderful pets.
17. Don and I like gerbils the best of all pets.
18. Mr. Russell gave Lois a small kitten.
19. The kitten is special to Lois and me.

Apply • Think and Write

From Your Writing ◆ Look for the nouns you used in the Writer's Warm-up. Can any of your nouns be replaced by pronouns?

> ✎ **Remember**
> that pronouns can take the place of nouns when the meaning is clear.

Describe imaginary pets, but don't name them.
EXAMPLES: *They jump six feet. It flies backwards.*
She has ten legs. He changes color.

2 Subject Pronouns

The subject of a sentence names someone or something. Sometimes pronouns take the place of words in the subject. Look at the underlined subjects below.

1. a. Mr. Tanaka has a shop.
   b. He has a shop.
2. a. Joey and I went there.
   b. We went there.
3. a. The shop sells pets.
   b. It sells pets.

In sentence **1a**, *Mr. Tanaka* is the subject of the sentence. In **1b** the pronoun *he* takes the place of *Mr. Tanaka*. In **2b** the pronoun *we* takes the place of *Joey and I*. What pronoun takes the place of *the shop* in sentence **3b**?

> **Summary** ♦ The words *I*, *you*, *she*, *he*, *it*, *we*, and *they* are **subject pronouns**. Use these pronouns to replace nouns in the subjects of your sentences.

Guided Practice

The subject is underlined in each sentence below. Tell if there are pronouns or nouns in the subjects.

1. She went to Mr. Tanaka's pet shop with Dad.
2. The store is on Main Street.
3. They have birds, kittens, puppies, and fish.

Practice

A. The subject is underlined in each sentence below. Write *pronoun* if the subject is a pronoun. Write *noun* if the subject has one or more nouns in it.

4. A <u>girl</u> asks Mr. Tanaka to show her the rabbits.
5. <u>He</u> carefully picks up a rabbit.
6. <u>It</u> feels soft and cuddly in the girl's arms.
7. <u>Carol and Ron</u> also pet the rabbit.
8. <u>They</u> want to buy a pet.

B. The subject of each sentence is underlined. Change the subject to a pronoun. Write the new sentence.

9. <u>Shirley</u> asks how to feed a pet rabbit.
10. <u>Rabbits</u> eat hay, grass, cabbage, and carrots.
11. <u>Mr. Tanaka</u> talks about the care of rabbits.
12. <u>Jake and I</u> need a cage for the rabbit.
13. <u>The cage</u> must be cleaned every day.

C. Complete each sentence by adding a subject pronoun. Use each pronoun only once. Write the new sentences.

We   I   They   She   It

14. ____ own a pet rabbit.
15. ____ often visits our classroom.
16. ____ fills the food and water dishes daily.
17. ____ buy rabbit food at Benson's pet store.
18. ____ order a special brand of rabbit food.

Apply · Think and Write

Pronouns in Sentences ◆ Write sentences about rabbits. Use pronouns in the subject of some sentences.

> ✏️ **Remember**
> that subject pronouns can replace nouns in the subject of sentences.

♦ GETTING STARTED ♦

Play the game "In Grandmother's Trunk." Name something you found there. Tell who it is for without naming the person. Use a pronoun instead.

EXAMPLE: *In Grandmother's trunk I found a red hat for you.*

3 Object Pronouns

Pronouns can take the place of words in the predicate of a sentence. These pronouns are object pronouns. Look at the underlined words below.

1. a. The bird is for <u>Paul</u>.
   b. The bird is for <u>him</u>.
2. a. Paul likes <u>birds</u>.
   b. Paul likes <u>them</u>.

3. a. Tom has <u>the cage</u>.
   b. Tom has <u>it</u>.
4. a. Show <u>Tom and me</u>.
   b. Show <u>us</u>.

In sentence **1b** the pronoun *him* takes the place of *Paul*. In sentence **2b** the pronoun *them* takes the place of *birds*. In sentence **3b** *it* takes the place of *the cage*. What pronoun takes the place of *Tom and me* in sentence **4b**?

> **Summary** ♦ The words *me, you, him, her, it, us,* and *them* are **object pronouns**. You can use object pronouns in the predicates of sentences.

Guided Practice

Name the pronoun in the predicate of each sentence.

1. Mr. Shea gave us a large fish tank.
2. Sheila cleaned it with soap and water.
3. Dad gave me some angelfish.

Practice

A. Write the pronoun in each sentence.

    4. Tom gets two buckets of water for us.

    5. Sheila pours it into the fish tank.

    6. Ben spills water on her.

    7. Sheila wants him to mop the floor.

    8. Tom helps them clean up.

B. Choose the correct pronoun. Write each sentence.

    9. Tom puts gravel in the tank for (her, she).

    10. The younger children watch (we, us) work.

    11. Mother reminds (them, they) to watch quietly.

    12. Mr. Tanaka gave (I, me) a tropical fish.

    13. I thanked (him, he) for the surprise.

C. Use one of the pronouns below for each underlined word or words. Write each new sentence.

    them   **it**   **us**   **him**   **her**

    14. Mr. Tanaka shows <u>Sheila</u> how to use the fish net.

    15. We asked <u>Mr. Tanaka</u> how to use the air pump.

    16. He told <u>Tom and me</u> when to clean the tank.

    17. The food for <u>the guppies</u> is on the blue shelf.

    18. We use <u>the blue shelf</u> for our pet supplies.

Apply ◆ Think and Write

Dictionary of Knowledge ◆ Read about guppies in the Dictionary of Knowledge. Write sentences telling how to keep guppies as pets. Use object pronouns in some of the sentences you write.

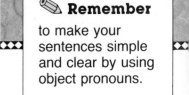

✏️ **Remember**
to make your sentences simple and clear by using object pronouns.

Say a silly phrase in which each word begins with the same letter. Start each phrase with *my*, *your*, *his*, *her*, *its*, *our*, or *their*.

EXAMPLES: *her huge hippopotamus, my muddy mittens*

4 Possessive Pronouns

Some pronouns show that something is owned. Read the sentences below.

> Dr. Kelly's office has a blue sign.
> Her office has a blue sign.

The possessive pronoun *her* shows that the office belongs to Dr. Kelly.

Study the possessive pronouns in the box below.

my	your	his	her
its	our	their	

Summary ◆ A **possessive pronoun** shows ownership. In your writing use possessive pronouns to take the place of nouns that show ownership.

Guided Practice

Name the possessive pronoun in each sentence.

1. Juan takes his cat to the veterinarian.
2. Her waiting room is full of pets and owners.
3. One puppy has its paw covered with tape.
4. Two poodles play with their ball.
5. The doctor keeps my sick duck.

Practice

A. Write the possessive pronoun in each sentence.

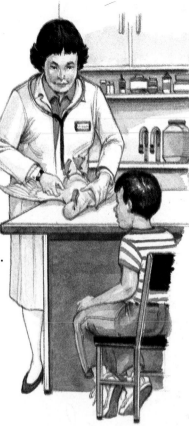

    6. The veterinarian said her name is Dr. Kelly.

    7. My duck is named Quackers.

    8. Quackers hurt his wing.

    9. "Your duck is not badly hurt," said Dr. Kelly.

   10. Our visit to the doctor was short.

B. Complete each sentence by adding a possessive pronoun.
Use each pronoun only once. Write the new sentences.

   her   their   my   his   its

   11. ____ dog hurt its paw.

   12. My dad drove ____ car to the doctor's office.

   13. ____ office is bright and cheerful.

   14. A bird got out of ____ cage!

   15. Both cats jumped on ____ hind legs.

C. Use a possessive pronoun to take the place of the
underlined noun in each sentence. Write the new sentence.

   16. Dr. Rita Kelly's office is near our home.

   17. The girls' kitten waited quietly.

   18. The dog's bark didn't mean anything.

   19. Gary's aunt has a pet shop.

   20. The animals' cages are bright and clean.

Apply ◆ Think and Write

Creative Writing ◆ Pretend that you own one of the pets
in this lesson. Write about your pet. Use possessive
pronouns in some of your sentences.

> ✎ **Remember**
> that you can add
> variety to your
> writing by using
> possessive pronouns.

Take turns completing these sentences. You could go on forever and ever!

_____ *and I saw a* _____.
The _____ *looked back at* _____ *and me.*

5 Using *I* and *me*

Read the sentences that Lana wrote.

■ **1.** I have two pets.   **2.** Oscar and Freddy play with me.

Lana used the pronouns *I* and *me* to talk about herself. She used *I* in the subject of sentence **1**. She used *me* in the predicate of sentence **2**.

3. Dan and I take care of our pets.
4. Freddy likes to play with Dan and me.

When Lana talked about herself and Dan, she named herself last. What pronouns did Lana use to name herself in sentences **3** and **4**?

Summary ◆ Use *I* in the subject of a sentence. Use a capital letter for the word *I*. Use *me* in the predicate of a sentence.

Guided Practice

Use *I* or *me* to complete each sentence.

1. _____ have a brother named Dan.
2. Dan and _____ are twins.
3. Dan goes to school with _____.
4. The teacher talked to Dan and _____.
5. He asked Dan and _____ to bring Freddy to school.

Practice

A. Use *I* or *me* to complete each sentence correctly. Write the pronoun you choose.

> **6.** Dan and ___ took Freddy to school.
> **7.** ___ held the aquarium on the bus.
> **8.** Dan helped ___ carry it across the street.
> **9.** ___ took the aquarium to my classroom.
> **10.** Freddy liked going to school with Dan and ___ .

B. Use the words *Dan and I* or *Dan and me* in each sentence. Write the sentences.

> **11.** The teacher asked ___ to tell about Freddy.
> **12.** First ___ displayed Freddy's aquarium.
> **13.** The children drew pictures of Freddy for ___ .
> **14.** ___ talked about Freddy's food.
> **15.** The children thanked ___ for bringing Freddy.

C. Decide which words below may be used to complete the sentences. Write the new sentences.

Dan and I   I and Dan   Dan and me   me and Dan

> **16.** ___ put soil and plants in the aquarium.
> **17.** The teacher gave ___ a sturdy cardboard box.
> **18.** ___ put Freddy's aquarium into the box.
> **19.** The late bus stopped for ___ .
> **20.** Mother asked ___ about Freddy's school visit.

Apply ◆ Think and Write

Creative Writing ◆ Pretend you are a pet shop owner. Write sentences about your work and business. Use *I* or *me* in each sentence.

✎ **Remember**
to use the pronouns *I* and *me* correctly.

VOCABULARY ◆
Homophones

When you write or speak, some of the words you use sound alike. In the sentence below, *son* and *sun* sound the same. They are not spelled alike, however, and they have different meanings.

■ His <u>son</u> watched the <u>sun</u> slowly rise.

Words that sound alike but have different meanings and spellings are called **homophones**. The words *son* and *sun* are homophones.

Spell the homophones in the sentences below. Do they have the same meanings?

The <u>knight</u> rode off into the <u>night</u>.
He was looking <u>for</u> <u>four</u> terrible dragons.

Building Your Vocabulary

Find the homophones in each sentence. Tell what each homophone means.

1. Nellie already knew the new student.
2. Dad will pick up our pizza in an hour.
3. "Oh," said the man, "do I really owe you that much?"
4. Ned knows his nose is sunburned.
5. Would you help me carry the wood?

Practice

A. Complete each sentence with a pair of homophones. Use each pair only once. (Hint: Four of your sentences will include a number word.)

1. Tim has ___ tickets ___ the basketball game.
2. Jill has ___ tickets ___ the same game.
3. Their team ___ only ___ game this year.
4. Thomas ___ the ball ___ the basket to win it.
5. Aaron ___ nearly ___ hot dogs at the game.

B. Choose the correct homophones to complete the rhyme.

Wanda said she saw last (week, weak)
A most enormous mountain (peak, peek).
It rose high up into the (heir, air)
And then just sort of ended (there, their).
White clouds went slowly sailing (buy, by)
Against a (pale, pail) blue summer sky.
She said, "I took (some, sum) pictures of it.
I hope you go. I (know, no) you'll love it!"

Language Corner ◆ Echo Words

Our language has many **echo words**. These are words that sound like the things they name. A cat *meows*. A cow *moos*. A bee *buzzes*.

What do these echo words make you think of?

**quack   neigh   hiss
honk   hee-haw**

How to Revise Sentences with Pronouns

You know that pronouns can be used instead of nouns in sentences. You can use pronouns instead of repeating the same noun too often. Read the sentences below. Which one sounds better to you?

1. Tommy's aunt invited Tommy to bring Tommy's best friend to the parade.
2. Tommy's aunt invited him to bring his best friend to the parade.

Sentence **1** uses the noun *Tommy* too often. The sentence sounds awkward. Sentence **2** is much smoother and easier to read. Look for chances to use pronouns in your writing.

The Grammar Game ♦ Check your pronoun power! Choose a noun from balloon **A** and write it. Which pronouns from balloon **B** can replace the noun you chose? Write them. Then start again with another noun.

A
Beth moon Jim's
Abe and Linda
Bill story Mom's

B
it her they
him you she
them his he

Working Together

Do activities **A** and **B** as a group. You will see how pronouns can make your sentences smoother.

A. Do these sentences sound familiar? Rewrite them. Use pronouns in place of the underlined words.

1. Mary had a little lamb. <u>The lamb's</u> fleece was white as snow.
2. Three little kittens lost <u>the kittens'</u> mittens, and <u>the kittens</u> began to cry.
3. Little Bo-Peep has lost <u>Bo-Peep's</u> sheep and can't tell where to find <u>the sheep</u>.

B. Write the paragraph below. Use pronouns instead of repeating the same nouns so often.

Mike has an unusual pet. Mike's pet is a tortoise. Mike keeps the tortoise in a tank. Mike and the tortoise are getting along fine!

In Your Group

- Listen to each other carefully.
- Show appreciation for people's ideas.
- Agree or disagree in a nice way.
- Help the group reach agreement.

WRITERS' CORNER ◆ Fuzzy Sentences

Sometimes using pronouns can confuse readers. In the fuzzy example, can you tell who talked about her trip?

Fuzzy: Amy called Sue. She talked about her trip.
Improved: Amy called Sue. Sue talked about her trip.

Read what you wrote for the Writer's Warm-up. Did you use pronouns in your writing? Are their meanings clear?

ADVENTURERS BETWEEN ADVENTURES
painting by Norman Rockwell

UNIT
FOUR

USING LANGUAGE
TO

PERSUADE

PART TWO

Literature *Socks* **by Beverly Cleary**
A Reason for Writing Persuading

CREATIVE
Writing

FINE ARTS ◆ Norman Rockwell painted the boy sleeping at the left. Where is the boy sleeping? What else do you see in the picture with him? What do you suppose the boy is dreaming? Is his dog in the dream? Is he dreaming about catching fish? Write a story that tells all about the boy's dream.

CREATIVE THINKING ♦
A Strategy for Persuading

A PREDICTION CHART

Characters in a story often try to persuade. That means they try to get someone else to do something. After this lesson you will read part of *Socks*. In this story two children have kittens for sale. They try to persuade people to buy them. Later you will do some writing to persuade.

Here is part of the story *Socks*. How are the children persuading people to buy a kitten? What are they saying?

> "He's the smartest kitten in the bunch," said George, his voice brimming with hope. . . .
> Socks struggled and mewed to be put down. Debbie would not let him go. "See," she said to the young couple, "he likes you."

How did George and Debbie think of what to say? They probably tried to make a prediction, or guess. They predicted what the couple would like about a kitten. George guessed they would like a smart kitten. Debbie predicted they would want a pet who liked them. Would you have made the same predictions?

Learning the Strategy

You often make predictions. Can you predict what a circus clown riding a unicycle might do? Sometimes you can predict several things that might happen. How many different things might the clown do? Suppose you ask your parents for a bike. What different things might they say?

How could predicting help you persuade them that you should have a bike?

Do any of your predictions ever come true? It can be fun to find out. A prediction chart can help. It might look like this.

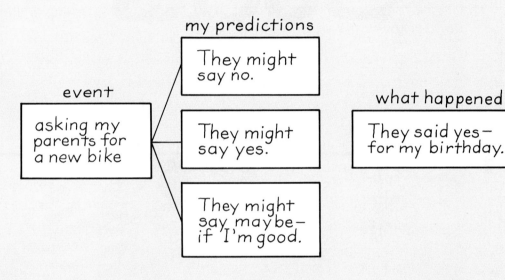

Using the Strategy

A. Make a prediction chart. Predict the next thing your teacher will say. Then write what your teacher really does say. Was anyone in the class right?

B. Think about George and Debbie trying to sell the kitten Socks. What do you predict will happen? Make a prediction chart. Fill in your predictions. After you read *Socks*, fill in what really happened in the story.

Applying the Strategy

- How did you decide what your teacher might say next?
- Can making a prediction ever help you? When? How?

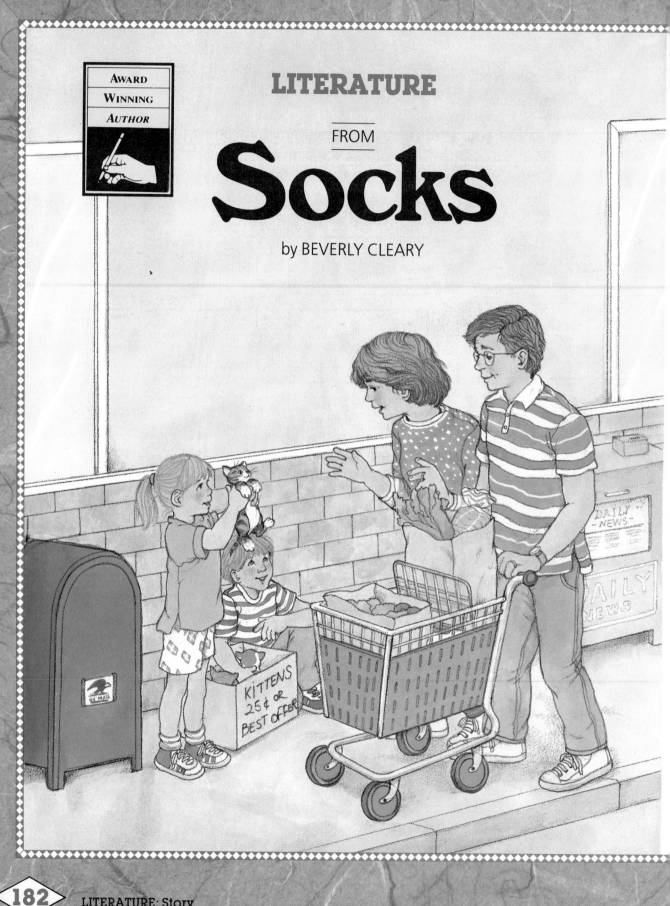

LITERATURE

FROM

Socks

by BEVERLY CLEARY

AWARD
WINNING
AUTHOR

KITTENS
25¢ OR
BEST OFFER

DAILY NEWS

DAILY NEWS

When the family cat had kittens, Debbie liked playing with them, especially the striped kitten with the white paws. She named him Socks. Yet Debbie's father thought that one family cat was plenty. So one summer morning, Debbie and her brother brought Socks and the other kittens to the supermarket. Debbie and George found a good spot near the door for selling their boxful of kittens.

All morning, Debbie and George tried to sell the kittens to shoppers. Yet Debbie wished she could keep Socks for herself. He was the smartest and best kitten of all, Debbie thought. That was why she kept hiding him from all the shoppers. She wanted to find just the right home for her favorite cat.

A young couple pushing a cart of groceries toward the parking lot paused to watch what was going on. Debbie, trusting their appearance, held Socks up for their inspection. "This is Socks," she said. "We named him Socks, because he looks like he's wearing white socks."

"He's the smartest kitten in the bunch," said George, his voice brimming with hope. If they sold one kitten, they could sell more, and he would be free to go the the library.

Unaware that his future was about to be decided, Socks struggled and mewed to be put down. Debbie would not let him go. "See," she said to the young couple, "he likes you."

"Look at his little paws and his little pointy tail," cried the young woman, whose name was Marilyn Bricker. "And look at his beautiful markings: those black stripes on his head and the black rings around his tail like the rings on a raccoon's tail and those little white socks. Oh Bill, we must take him. We need a cat to sleep in front of the fireplace this winter now that we have a house."

"He's a very smart kitten." George pressed for a sale. "He's housebroken, too."

"I always wanted a kitten when I was a kid," remarked Bill Bricker, "but my mother didn't like cats."

"Then you should have a kitten now," said his wife.

Debbie and George exchanged a look that wiped away their disagreements of the morning. They were about to sell a kitten.

Mr. Bricker reached into the pocket of his jeans for change. "Fifty cents is the best offer I can make," he said with a smile.

"Oh, that's all right." Debbie was willing to be generous. "Daddy said to give them away if we had to."

"Thank you," said George, as he accepted two twenty-five-cent pieces.

Debbie felt she should say something to make the transaction official. "Satisfaction guaranteed or your money—" She thought better of what she was about to say and instead handed the kitten to Mrs. Bricker. "Bye, Socks," she said. "Be a good kitten."

Library Link ♦ *You may wish to read* Socks *by Beverly Cleary to learn more about Socks and the Brickers.*

Reader's Response

Do you think Debbie and George will ever see Socks again? Tell why.

Socks

◆ Responding to Literature

1. Turn the story about Socks into a play. One way is a
    Readers Theatre. Different students read the parts of
    the characters in the story. A narrator reads all the lines
    that characters do not speak. Remember to read so that
    your audience can hear you.

2. What part of the story did you like best? Draw a picture
    that shows what you liked. Color the part of the picture
    that surrounds Socks.

3. How do you think Socks felt in the story? Pretend you
    are Socks. Say one thing to each of these characters:

    Mrs. Bricker   Mr. Bricker   Debbie   George

◆ Writing to Learn

Think and Predict ◆ What do you know about Socks's
new home? Do you think Socks will be happy there? Copy
the chart below. Add more information.

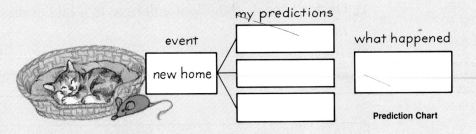

Prediction Chart

Write ◆ Write about Socks in this new home. Tell what you
think will happen.

Choose an animal and tell one thing you <u>know</u> about it:
Dogs bark. Then tell one thing you <u>think</u> about it: *Dogs are
the best pets.*

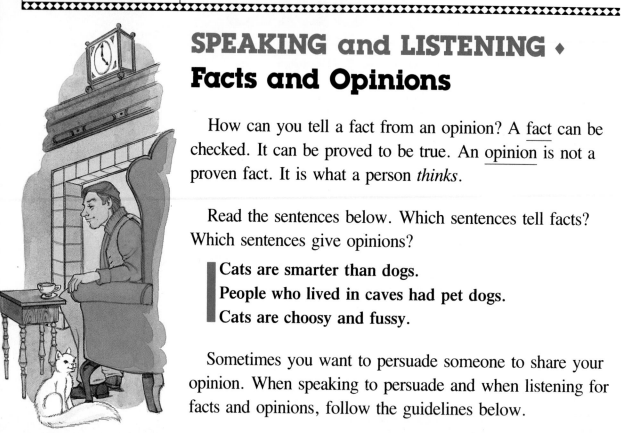

SPEAKING and LISTENING ♦
Facts and Opinions

How can you tell a fact from an opinion? A <u>fact</u> can be
checked. It can be proved to be true. An <u>opinion</u> is not a
proven fact. It is what a person *thinks*.

Read the sentences below. Which sentences tell facts?
Which sentences give opinions?

> **Cats are smarter than dogs.**
> **People who lived in caves had pet dogs.**
> **Cats are choosy and fussy.**

Sometimes you want to persuade someone to share your
opinion. When speaking to persuade and when listening for
facts and opinions, follow the guidelines below.

Telling Facts and Opinions	1. Clearly say what you think. Do not be shy. 2. Give facts and reasons for your opinion. 3. Respect other people's opinions. Be polite.
Being a Critical Listener	1. Decide if each statement you hear is a fact or an opinion. 2. Think about how facts could be checked or proved. 3. Respect opinions. They can be valuable, too.

> **Summary** ♦ A **fact** is true information about
> something. An **opinion** is what a person thinks about
> something.

Guided Practice

Tell whether each sentence is a fact or an opinion.

1. Cats are much smarter than dogs.
2. Guide dogs for the blind are trained in New Jersey.
3. All dogs are friendlier than cats.

Practice

A. Write *fact* or *opinion* for each sentence.

4. Nothing is more adorable than a beagle puppy.
5. Cats cannot bark, and dogs cannot purr.
6. Scientists know that dogs lived ten thousand years ago.
7. Cats are braver than dogs.
8. Cats helped to keep rats out of gold mines.
9. The Roman people secretly took cats into Europe.

B. Work with a partner. Take turns choosing from the questions below. Answer the question by giving your opinion. Try to persuade your listener to share your opinion.

10. Could someone your age take good care of a pet?
11. What kind of animal would make a good pet?
12. What kind of animal would not make a good pet?

Apply • Think and Write

Opinions of Others ♦ We all like to know our friends' opinions. First, complete this question: *What do you think about ____?* Then ask some friends to answer your question. Write the opinions of your friends.

> ✏️ **Remember**
> to give reasons
> for your opinions.

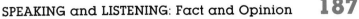

◆ GETTING STARTED ◆

In your opinion, which statement below is more true? Give reasons for your opinion.
All people need animals. All animals need people.

WRITING ◆
A Paragraph That Persuades

It was Be Kind to Animals Week. Ms. Pérez's class wanted to persuade people to help animals. The class members wrote persuasive paragraphs. They followed the guidelines given below. The paragraphs were displayed in the town library.

Writing a Persuasive Paragraph	1. In the first sentence, tell what you think needs to be done. State your opinion. 2. Support your opinion with facts or reasons. 3. Keep your readers in mind. Choose reasons that will appeal to them.

This is the paragraph Tony wrote. Did he follow the guidelines?

> Every dog should have a rabies shot. Rabies is a very serious disease. A dog cannot recover from rabies. Luckily, rabies can be prevented with a rabies shot. Protect your dog. It will not cost you anything. Take your dog to town hall this Saturday afternoon for a free shot.

Summary ◆ A **persuasive paragraph** gives an opinion. It also gives facts or reasons that support the opinion.

Guided Practice

Each sentence below gives an opinion. Give a fact or a reason that supports each opinion.

1. Dogs give companionship and love to their owners.
2. Dogs help their human friends.
3. Sometimes a dog can be your best friend.
4. Dogsled teams are useful in Alaska.

Practice

A. Each sentence below gives an opinion. Write a fact or a reason that supports each opinion.

5. A cat is a good pet if you live in an apartment.
6. Tropical fish make the best pets.
7. Dogs always make more noise than cats.
8. Hamsters are easy to care for.
9. A dog needs a place to run and play outdoors.

B. Write a paragraph. Use one of the opinions in **Practice A** as your topic sentence. Add sentences that give facts or reasons that support the opinion.

Apply • Think and Write

Dictionary of Knowledge ♦ Read about that beautiful animal from legends, the unicorn. Write a paragraph to persuade readers that a unicorn would or would not make a good pet.

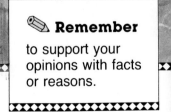

✎ **Remember**
to support your opinions with facts or reasons.

"We have ants, bunnies, canaries, and ducks," said the pet store owner. Can you add to the list?

WRITING ◆
Using Commas

A comma (,) is a special mark used in sentences. It tells you to stop for a moment between words. Read each sentence below aloud. Notice your voice at each comma.

> Jack, may I pet your new puppy?   Dinah, don't tease him.
> Yes, I think he will like you.   No, I'll pet him gently.

The underlined words are items in a series. Notice how commas are used in each series of three words.

> Ben, Jane, and Sarah played with the puppy yesterday.
> Should you call a puppy he, she, or it?

Commas help make ideas clear. A comma can change the meaning of a sentence. Notice the two sentences below.

> ■ No one can hold the puppy.   No, one can hold the puppy.

> **Summary** ◆ Use a **comma** after *yes* or *no* at the beginning of a sentence. Use a comma after the name of a person spoken to. Use commas to separate words in a series of three or more words.

Guided Practice

Tell where one or more commas belong in each sentence.

1. Mr. Soo can the puppy have milk?

2. Yes but not too much at a time.

3. Puppies need food water and exercise.

Practice

A. Write the sentences. Use commas where they are needed.

4. Kareem Daniel and Sara go to the library.
5. Mr. Ruben do you have a book about poodles?
6. Yes we got a new book last week.
7. Sara please show me your library card.
8. Do you want books about collies boxers and hounds?
9. No I just want books about collies.
10. Kareem the book about poodles is on that shelf.

B. Write a complete sentence to answer each question below. Begin the sentence with *Yes* or *No*. Don't forget the commas.

11. Do you know how to train a puppy?
12. Do you have a pet?
13. Is your favorite animal a kind of pet?

C. Add three words to each sentence. Use commas where they belong.

14. ___ ___ and ___ walked home. (boys' names)
15. They talked about ___ ___ and ___ . (pets)
16. My dog likes to eat ___ ___ and ___ . (foods)
17. Her fur is ___ ___ and ___ . (colors)
18. She can ___ ___ and ___ . (tricks)

Apply ◆ Think and Write

Using Commas ◆ Write three sentences about a pet. Tell about groups of things that go together. Example: *Hamsters like apples, carrots, and lettuce.*

✎ **Remember**

to use commas to separate items in a series of words.

Focus on Reasons

In the story *Socks,* Debbie and George want to persuade a young couple to buy a kitten. How do they go about it? Here are some of the things they say:

DEBBIE: ◆ The kitten is called Socks because his white feet look as if he is wearing socks.
◆ Socks likes the couple (based on a meow).
◆ Satisfaction is guaranteed (almost).

GEORGE: ◆ Socks is a very smart kitten.
◆ He is already housebroken.

Debbie and George give *reasons* to buy Socks. Debbie points out that Socks is special. He looks as if he is wearing white socks. When Socks mews, Debbie doesn't say, "Oh, he doesn't like being held." Instead, she says, "See, he likes you." Finally, she almost, but not quite, guarantees Socks.

George adds more reasons. Socks is smart—and he's housebroken! George and Debbie both choose reasons that appeal to the buyers.

The Writer's Voice ◆ In a story, you may find reasons that persuade a character to do something. What other stories besides *Socks* have you read that contain such reasons?

Working Together

Reasons will sometimes persuade a person to do something. As a group, discuss activities **A** and **B**.

A. Turn back to the selection from *Socks* and read it again. Then answer these questions within your group:

> **1.** Debbie and George have an easy time selling Socks to the Brickers. Why?
>
> **2.** What reasons does Marilyn Bricker have for wanting to buy a kitten? What reason might Bill have?
>
> **3.** Why did Debbie change her mind about giving a money-back guarantee?

Share your answers with those of other groups.

B. Suppose the Brickers had not wanted to buy a kitten. Have your group think of three reasons for not buying.

In Your Group

- Help others recall the story.
- Ask questions to get people talking.
- Agree or disagree in a friendly way.
- List the group's ideas.

THESAURUS CORNER ♦ Word Choice

Copy the sentences below. Use the Thesaurus to replace each word in dark type with a good synonym. Write a pronoun above each underlined word or words.

Jeremy **told** Susan that Jeremy wanted to buy a **small** calculator. Susan **laughed** and pointed to Susan's calculator. Susan said that the calculator was for sale. "I **like** doing arithmetic in my head," Susan gave as Susan's reason.

Writing an Advertisement

In the story *Socks*, Debbie and George sell a kitten. George says Socks is housebroken. Debbie says the kitten likes the Brickers. These reasons help to persuade the Brickers to buy Socks.

An advertisement is a good way to persuade. In an advertisement, you give reasons to buy something.

Know Your Purpose and Audience

In this lesson your purpose will be to write an advertisement. You will try to persuade readers to buy something.

Your audience will be your classmates. Later you can display your advertisement or read it aloud.

1 Prewriting

First you must decide what you want your readers to buy. Then think of reasons they might want to buy it.

Choose Your Topic ♦ Make a list of things you could sell. You might choose something you no longer need. Circle the thing you like as your topic.

Think About It

What will go on your list? You could include things you have outgrown. Is your baseball cap or your bike too small? Circle the item on your list that you like the best. It is easier to be persuasive about something you really like.

Talk About It

Your family might be able to help you with your list. Let them suggest things that you may not remember. Look over all your old toys. Are there any that are too young for you now? Also ask your friends for ideas.

Topic Ideas

For Sale
stickers
(bike)
soccer shoes
bird cage
games
baseball cap
old books
volleyball

Choose Your Strategy ♦ Here are two ways to plan your advertisement. Read both. Use the more helpful idea.

PREWRITING IDEAS

CHOICE ONE

A Good Points List

Make a "good points list." Write down the name of what you want to sell. List its good points. Is it fun? Does it work? Try to write at least five good points about it. Underline the three best points.

Model

Bike—Good Points
<u>cheap</u>
<u>new tires</u>
bell
kickstand
<u>new paint</u>

CHOICE TWO

A Prediction Chart

Make a prediction chart like this one. First, write what you plan to sell. Then predict questions that buyers might ask you. Last, write ideas for an advertisement that will answer the questions.

Model

what I will sell
my old bike

my predictions: what people might ask
Why buy an old bike?
Is it pretty?

advertisement ideas
costs less than a new bike
has new red paint

2 Writing

Read your good points list or prediction chart again. Begin writing by listing the best reason for buying your item. Here are two ways you could begin your advertisement.

- ♦ Here is news of a special ___.
- ♦ Think now about buying a ___.

As you write, think about what would persuade *you*. What reasons would make you buy your item? Include these reasons in your advertisement. Don't worry about making mistakes. You can make changes later.

Sample First Draft ♦

Think now about bying a bike. My bike is a real bargain. it has been well cared for. My mother and me fixed it all up last year. We put on a new coat of red paint. Then we put on new tires. It looks super! maybe it's right

3 Revising

Would you like to make changes to improve your advertisement? Here is an idea that will help you.

REVISING IDEA

FIRST Read to Yourself

Review your purpose. Did you write an advertisement? Think about your audience. Do you think your advertisement will persuade them to buy?

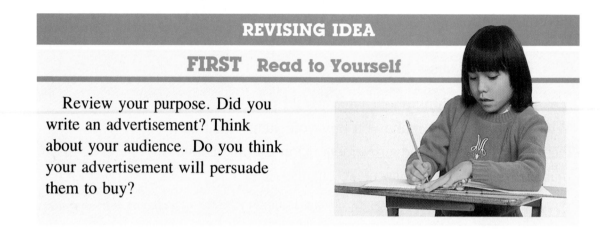

Focus: Did you give reasons why your item is a good buy? Put a caret (^) to show where you want to add a reason.

THEN Share with a Partner

Ask your partner to sit beside you. Read aloud as your partner reads silently. These ideas may help.

The Writer
Guidelines: Read slowly and clearly.
Sample questions:
• Do you have any questions about my item?
• **Focus question:** Can you think of reasons to add?

The Writer's Partner
Guidelines: Think about the writer's reasons. Remember you are trying to be helpful.
Sample responses:
• Can you tell me more about ____?
• A reason you could add is ____.

Revising Model ♦ Look at the advertisement that is being revised. Revising marks show changes the writer wants to make.

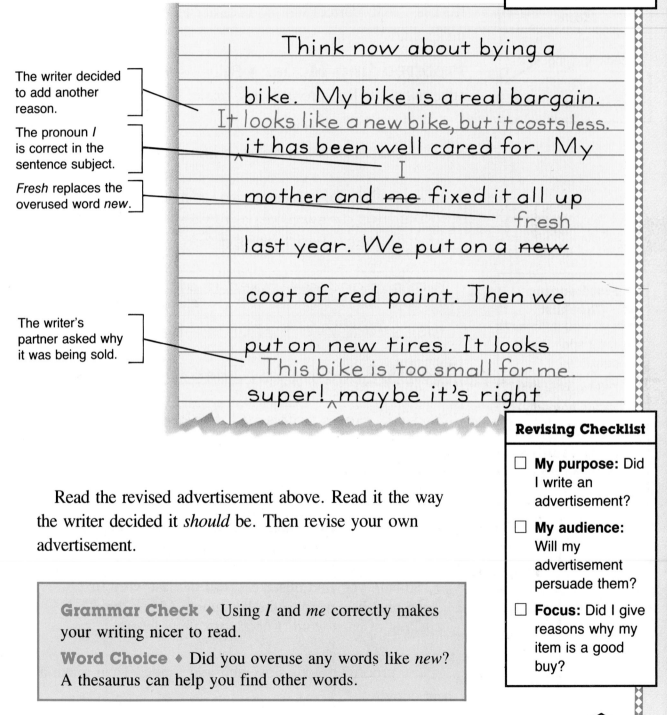

The writer decided to add another reason.

The pronoun *I* is correct in the sentence subject.

Fresh replaces the overused word *new*.

The writer's partner asked why it was being sold.

> Think now about bying a
>
> bike. My bike is a real bargain.
> It looks like a new bike, but it costs less.
> it has been well cared for. My
> ⋀ I
> mother and ~~me~~ fixed it all up
> fresh
> last year. We put on a ~~new~~
>
> coat of red paint. Then we
>
> put on new tires. It looks
> This bike is too small for me.
> super! ⋀ maybe it's right

Read the revised advertisement above. Read it the way the writer decided it *should* be. Then revise your own advertisement.

Grammar Check ♦ Using *I* and *me* correctly makes your writing nicer to read.

Word Choice ♦ Did you overuse any words like *new*? A thesaurus can help you find other words.

Revising Checklist

☐ **My purpose:** Did I write an advertisement?

☐ **My audience:** Will my advertisement persuade them?

☐ **Focus:** Did I give reasons why my item is a good buy?

4 Proofreading

When you proofread, you are being polite to your readers. Neat, correct writing is easier to read and understand.

Proofreading Model ♦ Below is the sample advertisement. Red proofreading marks have been added.

Proofreading Marks

check spelling ⬭

capital letter ＝

> Think now about ~~bying~~ *buying* a
>
> bike. My bike is a real bargain.
> I̲t looks like a new bike, but it costs less.
> ∧＝ it has been well cared for. My
>
> I
> mother and ~~me~~ fixed it all up
>   *fresh*
> last year. We put on a ~~new~~
>
> coat of red paint. Then we
>
> put on new tires. It looks
>   This bike is too small for me.
> super! ∧＝ maybe it's right

Proofreading Checklist

☐ Did I spell words correctly?

☐ Did I use capital letters correctly?

☐ Did I use correct marks at the end of sentences?

☐ Did I use my best handwriting?

PROOFREADING IDEA

Spelling Check

To help you find mistakes, read the last word first. Then read backward to the beginning. Check the spelling of each word. Check for capital letters.

Now proofread your story and add a title. Then make a neat copy.

5 Publishing

Is your advertisement really persuasive? Here are two ways to find out.

A Bargain Bike

Think now about buying a bike. My bike is a real bargain. It looks like a new bike, but it costs less. It has been well cared for. My mother and I fixed it all up last year. We put on a fresh coat of red paint. Then we put on new tires. It looks super! This bike is too small for me. Maybe it's right for you or someone you know.

PUBLISHING IDEAS

Share Aloud

Read your advertisement aloud. Ask classmates to listen for facts and opinions. Your opinion is that they should buy your item. Ask them to tell one supporting fact from your advertisement.

Share in Writing

Display the advertisements. Place a blank index card under each one. If you want to buy something, write your name. When there are several names on each card, count them. See how many ''buyers'' were persuaded.

CURRICULUM
• CONNECTION •

Writing Across the Curriculum Mathematics

In this unit you wrote an advertisement. You predicted questions people might ask about what you were selling. Mathematicians make different kinds of predictions. They call their predictions *estimates*.

Writing to Learn

Think and Analyze ♦ A collie pup weighs 1 pound when it is born. In the first year of its life, it will gain about 5 pounds a month. Estimate the weight of the dog when it is a year old. Write your estimate, or estimates, on a prediction chart.

Prediction Chart

Write ♦ Use your chart. Tell whether you would give a collie pup as a gift to a friend who lives in a small city apartment. Give reasons why you would or would not.

Writing in Your Journal

In the Writer's Warm-up you wrote about owning a pet. What did you learn in this unit about pets that you didn't know before? If you could have any pet in the world, which one would you choose? In your journal explain your choice.

Read More About It

Ribsy *by Beverly Cleary*
The author of *Socks* wrote a book about a dog named Ribsy. Ribsy belongs to Henry Huggins. One day Ribsy and Henry get separated. Find out what happens when a city dog gets lost in the country.

Mystery Cat *by Susan Saunders*
Hillary and Kelly Ann each adopt a cat. But who could guess they would both adopt the same cat! Unexpected adventures begin as they try to untangle the mess.

Book Report Idea Book Commercial

Commercials try to persuade you to buy certain products. For your next book report, try to ''sell'' your book.

Make a Book Poster
Use large paper. Make a catchy poster for your book. Write the title and the author's name in big letters. Try to convince others to give your book a try.

SPECIAL TODAY

Excellent book about your favorite kind of pet!! It will make you laugh!

Read

S O C K S

by Beverly Cleary

UNIT REVIEW

Unit 4

Pronouns   *pages 164–173*

A. Choose the correct pronoun in ( ) to complete each sentence. Write each sentence.

1. (We, Us) went down the Mississippi in a steamboat.
2. (She, Her) is called the *Delta Queen*.
3. Henry joined (we, us) at Cape Girardeau.
4. (Him, He) pointed out the levees beside the river.
5. People built (them, they) to protect the towns.
6. (Them, They) save the towns from floods.
7. The boat took Marguerite and (I, me) to the dock.
8. We watched (her, she) float away.

B. Write the possessive pronoun in each sentence.

9. Our town is near the river.
10. The scouts took their rafts downstream.
11. The river sometimes overflows its banks.
12. Bella says the river is her favorite place.
13. My family fishes on the west bank of the river.
14. Does your family like fish?

Homophones   *pages 174–175*

C. Write each sentence. Use the correct homophone in ( ).

15. A dog has (for, four) legs.
16. I have (won, one) nose.
17. Do you (no, know) what kind of bear that is?
18. (I, Eye) tied a rope around the tree.

Fact and Opinion   *pages 186–187*

D. Write *fact* if the sentence states a fact. Write *opinion* if
the sentence states an opinion.

19. Utah is the best state to visit.
20. It has the most interesting places of any state.
21. The Great Salt Lake is in Utah.
22. My friend moved to Utah.
23. You will enjoy visiting there.
24. Salt Lake City is the capital of Utah.

Commas   *pages 190–191*

E. Write each sentence. Use commas correctly.

25. Sandra please tell us about your surprise.
26. Felipe did you guess the surprise?
27. Yes I heard the kitten mewing.
28. Marta do you have a pet canary?
29. No it is a parakeet.
30. Lilia help me lift this cage.
31. Yes I will help you.

F. Write each sentence. Use commas where they are
needed.

32. Eli Andrew and I took a ferry.
33. I like boats trains airplanes and cars.
34. The map shows rivers bays and oceans.
35. Eli found strawberries blueberries and raspberries.
36. Andrew caught crabs shrimp and fish.

CUMULATIVE REVIEW

Sentences *pages 4–17*

A. Write *yes* if the word group is a sentence. Write *no* if the word group is not a sentence.

1. Many Indian tribes.
2. Lived on the plains.
3. They hunted for food.
4. Did not farm.
5. They lived in villages.
6. Spanish horses.

B. Write each group of words in sentence order.

7. useful Horses were.
8. difficult Hunting is.
9. stopped farming Tribes.
10. buffalo hunted They.
11. decorated Teepees were.
12. be can Tents moved.

C. Write each sentence correctly. Use a capital letter and put the correct mark at the end.

13. the Indians grew corn
14. it grew very tall
15. corn was a major crop
16. corn provided food
17. that stalk is very high
18. we cooked the corn
19. do you like popped corn
20. the corn cakes are great

D. Write *subject* if the subject is underlined. Write *predicate* if the predicate is underlined.

21. <u>Buffalo skins</u> were used for cooking pots.
22. <u>The Indians</u> put water in the skins.
23. They <u>put hot stones in the water.</u>
24. <u>The red-hot stones</u> heated the water.

Nouns   *pages 62–71, 116–117*

E. Write the noun in each pair of words.

25. tribe, write
26. pole, used
27. make, clothing
28. fire, cooking
29. buffalo, run

30. little, stone
31. cut, hair
32. corn, dry
33. cold, tree
34. trail, long

F. Write *singular* if the underlined noun is singular. Write *plural* if the underlined noun is plural.

35. The settlers moved West.
36. They brought food.
37. Many rode in wagons.
38. Some families walked.
39. They built log cabins.

40. Mr. Ross bought land.
41. Friends came to stay.
42. Towns were started.
43. A river was nearby.
44. They caught fish.

G. Write the plural form of each noun.

45. family
46. class
47. man
48. ranch
49. city
50. farmer

51. bench
52. wish
53. mat
54. fox
55. woman
56. crush

H. Write the possessive form of each noun.

57. cats
58. Phil
59. horses
60. tent

61. Mrs. Ming
62. truck
63. sky
64. settlers

65. children
66. scout
67. turtles
68. friend

I. Write the underlined nouns. Then write *common* or *proper* beside each noun.

69. Albert Einstein was a famous scientist.

70. He was born in Germany.

71. As a boy, Einstein read science books.

72. He enjoyed learning about space and time.

73. He worked in a laboratory.

74. Einstein won a Nobel Prize in 1921.

75. His birthday is March 14.

Capital Letters and Periods *pages 118–123*

J. Write each noun correctly.

76. mr robert lawson

77. charlotte zolotow

78. beatrix potter

79. miss emily dickinson

80. rachel field

81. maurice sendak

82. dr seuss

83. clara judson

84. charles m schulz

85. ezra jack keats

86. louisa may alcott

87. isaac b singer

K. Write each sentence. Use capital letters correctly.

88. The august moon hung over san francisco bay.

89. We will stay in california until labor day.

90. In september my sister starts college in omaha.

91. My brother lives on franklin street in alexandria.

92. We visited the smoky mountains last june.

93. On the fourth of july, we were in chattanooga.

94. My birthday is next tuesday, on memorial day.

95. Cousin emily is coming from oklahoma for new year's day.

Pronouns *pages 164–173*

L. Choose the correct pronoun in ( ) to complete each sentence. Write each sentence.

   96. Skip showed (I, me) his pet parrot.
   97. (We, Us) watched it clean its feathers.
   98. Skip's sister told (we, us) about parrots' beaks.
   99. Parrots use (they, them) to hold food.
   100. (She, her) said the lower beak is hollow.
   101. Skip said the parrot pinched (he, him) once.

M. Write the possessive pronoun in each sentence.

   102. I sold my bike to Tim.
   103. His dad paid for the bike.
   104. Tim's family lives on our street.
   105. I go to their house sometimes.
   106. Tim's sister asked me to her birthday party.

Commas *pages 190–191*

N. Write each sentence. Use commas correctly.

   107. Terry can you go swimming with me?
   108. No I have to cut the grass.
   109. Carmen do you like this bike?
   110. Yes that's the one I plan to buy.

O. Write each sentence. Add commas where they are needed.

   111. Becky invited Dean Lynn and Rick to her party.
   112. They ate talked and sang ''Happy Birthday.''
   113. Her mother told them stories jokes and riddles.
   114. Becky received books games and puzzles.

Unit 4 Challenge

A Pronoun Crossword

Copy the crossword graph. Then complete the puzzle. (Hint: One word is used more than once.)

Across

3. a subject pronoun
6. both a subject pronoun and an object pronoun
8. a possessive pronoun
9. an object pronoun
10. a possessive pronoun
11. a possessive pronoun
12. a subject pronoun

Down

1. a subject pronoun
2. both an object pronoun and a possessive pronoun
4. an object pronoun
5. a possessive pronoun
6. both a subject pronoun and an object pronoun
7. a possessive pronoun
11. an object pronoun

A "Me" Poem

Sometimes I play tennis.
Aunt Sarah visits me.
Mr. Ho and I go fishing.

Write a "Me" Poem. Use the letters of your first name.

Unit 4 Extra Practice

1 Writing with Pronouns
p. 164

A. Write each sentence. Underline the pronoun.

1. We used tools.
2. Teri gave me a saw.
3. She used a hammer.
4. You bring the nails.
5. I have the wood.
6. The birds watched us.

B. Write the pronoun in each sentence.

7. Many machines help us work.
8. Craig and I raised the flag at school.
9. We used a pulley on the flagpole.
10. He moved some heavy books with a lever.
11. The wooden board lifted them easily.
12. Nora showed me some new tools.
13. She likes to build things.
14. I would rather paint.
15. You can buy paint at the store.
16. The clerk smiled at us.

C. Choose the pronoun in ( ) to take the place of the underlined word or words. Write each sentence.

EXAMPLE: Kenny watched Rosa and Steve. (her, them)
ANSWER: Kenny watched them.

17. The boy carried a box. (Us, He)
18. The girl pulled a wagon. (She, We)
19. The wagon had four wheels. (Them, It)
20. Rosa had to wait for Maseo. (him, them)
21. The wheels made the work easier. (They, She)
22. Kenny and Steve rode in the wagon. (It, They)

2 Subject Pronouns

p. 166

A. The subject is underlined in each sentence below. Write *pronoun* if the subject is a pronoun. Write *noun* if the subject has a noun in it.

1. <u>I</u> walked by the restaurant with Dale.
2. <u>The restaurant</u> is on Front Street.
3. <u>Tamika</u> ate lunch there on Saturday.
4. <u>They</u> fix delicious sandwiches.
5. <u>She</u> had a tuna fish sandwich with lettuce.
6. <u>Tim</u> has tea there in the afternoon.
7. <u>The Soup Shop</u> is bright and cheerful.
8. <u>I</u> ate tomato soup with rice yesterday.
9. <u>You</u> should taste the chicken soup.
10. <u>The vegetables</u> are delicious.
11. <u>We</u> like the onion soup best.

B. Change the subject of each sentence to a pronoun. Write each new sentence.

EXAMPLE: **The restaurant is always crowded.**
ANSWER: **It is always crowded.**

12. The customers wait near the door.
13. Mrs. Harris also serves omelets.
14. Ben likes the omelet with cheese.
15. Students eat there often.
16. The meals are tasty and not expensive.
17. Dad always orders the chili.
18. The chili is hot and spicy.
19. Marty and I want beef stew today.
20. Mom ate a bran muffin.
21. The muffin was fresh and warm.

3 Object Pronouns

p. 168

A. Write the pronoun in each sentence.

1. Mr. Costa gave me some stamps.
2. Emily Costa wrote a letter to him.
3. Emily sent it from Portugal.
4. The teacher wants to see them.
5. Maybe Mr. Costa will save stamps for you.
6. The librarian showed me a special book.
7. Luís asked him about famous stamp collectors.
8. Some United States Presidents saved them.
9. Did Mr. Kwan tell you about a large collection?
10. The Queen of England owns it.

B. Use one of the pronouns below for each underlined word or words. Write each new sentence.

her	it	us	them	him

11. My uncle has collected <u>stamps</u> for years.
12. He showed <u>Brett and me</u> a strange stamp.
13. The picture was upside down on <u>the stamp</u>.
14. I asked <u>Uncle Ray</u> about valuable stamps.
15. He gave <u>Sally</u> two stamps from Japan.
16. She studied <u>the watermarks</u> carefully.
17. Mom gave <u>John</u> a red stamp for his collection.
18. She could see the silk in <u>the paper</u>.
19. He will show <u>the album</u> at school.
20. Give <u>Marla</u> the stamps with <u>pictures of ships</u>.
21. Those stamps are for <u>Pat</u>.
22. Lois also saves <u>stamps</u>.
23. Rick has <u>an album</u>.
24. Rick is helping <u>Todd and me</u> with <u>our albums</u>.

4 Possessive Pronouns

p. 170

A. Write the possessive pronoun in each sentence.

1. Barry and his family live in an apartment.
2. There are six floors in our building.
3. Your house is near the school.
4. That is my sister's mobile home.
5. Her kitchen is very tiny.
6. There are many old houses in our town.
7. I like my cousins' wind chime.
8. The wind chime hangs from their roof.
9. Your house has a big fireplace.
10. Its bricks are red and black.

B. Copy each sentence pair. Use a possessive pronoun to complete the second sentence in each pair.

EXAMPLE: **Ricardo has cousins in California. ____ cousins live in San Francisco.**

ANSWER: **Ricardo has cousins in California. His cousins live in San Francisco.**

11. Claudia and Steve live on Bay Street. ____ street is hilly.
12. I received a postcard from San Francisco. ____ card showed colorful houses.
13. Steve drew a picture of houses in San Francisco. ____ picture showed a house with a tower.
14. Ruth and I will visit San Francisco. ____ plane leaves on Tuesday.
15. Ruth likes bright colors. ____ house is red.
16. Marla's house has a bright red roof. ____ house overlooks San Francisco Bay.

5 Using *I* and *Me*

p. 172

A. Use *I* or *me* to complete each sentence correctly. Write the pronoun you choose.

1. Last week my cousin Norman called ____ .
2. ____ wish my cousins lived closer.
3. ____ would like to visit them in Texas.
4. Uncle Leo would take Norman and ____ to a ranch.
5. My cousin and ____ might ride horses.
6. ____ have a twin brother.
7. Chuck and ____ wear the same size.
8. Aunt Bea sent sweaters to Chuck and ____ .
9. Chuck told ____ to choose one.
10. ____ picked the one with blue stripes.
11. ____ also have a sister.
12. Sally is very special to ____ .
13. Sally and ____ share many secrets.
14. Chuck won't tell secrets to ____ .

B. Choose the correct word or group of words in ( ) to complete each sentence. Write each sentence.

15. Uncle Bob gave ____ a very old book.
    (Jill and I, I and Jill, Jill and me, me and Jill)
16. ____ read about the Bobbsey twins.
    (Jill and I, I and Jill, Jill and me, Me and Jill)
17. ____ thought Flossie and Freddie were funny.
    (Me, I)
18. Jill drew a picture of them for ____ . (me, I)
19. Flossie and Freddie Bobbsey look like ____ !
    (me and Jill, Jill and me, I and Jill, Jill and I)

USING LANGUAGE
TO

IMAGINE

=== **PART ONE** ===

Unit Theme *The World of Make-Believe*

Language Awareness Verbs

=== **PART TWO** ===

Literature "The Sleeping Prince" retold by Alison Lurie

A Reason for Writing Imagining

Writing
IN YOUR JOURNAL

WRITER'S WARM-UP ◆ In the world of make-believe, just about anything can happen. What make-believe stories do you like? What do you like best about these stories? Maybe you like having three wishes. Maybe you like talking animals or magical things that happen. Write in your journal about make-believe stories. Tell what you like best about them.

1 Writing with Verbs

Do you remember Cinderella? Read the sentences below. Notice the underlined words.

> Cinderella sews her stepsisters' gowns.
> Her stepsisters wear beautiful clothes.
> The two sisters dance at the ball.

Words like *sews, wear*, and *dance* are verbs. A verb tells what someone or something does. Verbs show action.

The verbs are underlined in the sentences below. What action does each verb show? Can you make up another sentence with the same verb?

> The stepsisters spill food on the floor.
> Cinderella cleans the floor.

Summary ◆ A word that shows action is a **verb**. Use a word that shows action in every sentence.

Guided Practice

Name the verb in each sentence.

1. Cinderella gets a bucket of water.
2. She finds the soap.
3. The stepsisters watch Cinderella.

Practice

A. Write the verb in each sentence.

4. The two stepsisters receive an invitation.
5. Cinderella helps her sisters with their dresses.
6. Her sisters go to the ball.
7. Cinderella weeps in a corner of the kitchen.
8. A fairy godmother talks to Cinderella.

B. If the underlined word in the sentence is a verb, write *verb*. If it is not a verb, write *not a verb*.

9. The fairy godmother <u>changes</u> a pumpkin into a gold coach.
10. She <u>touches</u> six mice with her magic wand.
11. Six gray <u>horses</u> appear before their eyes.
12. The coach <u>takes</u> Cinderella to the prince's ball.
13. Cinderella and the <u>prince</u> dance at the ball.

C. Write the sentences. Use a verb to complete each sentence.

14. Suddenly the clock ___ twelve.
15. Cinderella ___ from the ball.
16. She ___ one glass slipper.
17. The prince ___ everywhere for Cinderella.
18. Cinderella and the prince ___ and live happily ever after.

Apply • Think and Write

From Your Writing ♦ Read what you wrote for the Writer's Warm-up. Underline the action verbs you used.

> ✎ **Remember**
> that every sentence needs a verb.

What does a pig do? *A pig wallows in the mud.*
What do pigs do? *Pigs slurp food.*

2 Verbs in the Present

A verb in the present time shows action that happens now. A verb in the present must agree with the subject of the sentence.

> One pig **builds** a house of straw.
> The three **pigs** run from the wolf.

The verb *builds* is used with the singular noun *pig*. A singular noun names one person, place, or thing. Verbs in the present time that are used with singular nouns end in *-s* or *-es*.

The verb *run* is used with the plural noun *pigs*. A plural noun names more than one person, place, or thing. Verbs in the present time that are used with plural nouns do not add *-s* or *-es*.

> **Summary** ◆ A verb in the **present time** shows action that happens now. A present-time verb needs to agree with its subject.

Guided Practice

Choose the correct verb to complete each sentence.

1. One pig (build, builds) a house of brick.
2. The wolf (blow, blows) down two houses.
3. All three pigs (live, lives) in the brick house.

Practice

A. Write the correct verb in ( ) to complete each sentence.

4. Many fairy tales (use, uses) the number three.

5. Goldilocks (meet, meets) three bears.

6. A fish (give, gives) a fisherman three wishes.

7. Three fairies (spin, spins) yarn for a girl.

8. A father (send, sends) three sons to work.

B. Write each sentence with the correct form of the verb in
( ). Use the verbs in the present time.

9. The father ____ each son a present. (give)

10. One son ____ a rooster to an island. (take)

11. People ____ the rooster is wonderful. (think)

12. A man on the island ____ a donkey. (ride)

13. The donkey ____ a heavy load for a woman. (pull)

C. Complete the sentences below, using each verb only
once. Write each completed sentence.

run   receives   gives   chases   lives

14. One boy ____ a cat from his father.

15. The cat ____ with the king.

16. Mice ____ through the king's palace.

17. The cat ____ all the mice.

18. The king ____ the cat away.

Apply • Think and Write

Fairy-Tale Sentences ♦ Write sentences about your
favorite fairy tale. Be sure to use verbs in the present time.

✎ **Remember**
to be sure that
each verb you use
agrees with
its subject.

What does Joe the Giant do?
> EXAMPLE: *He eats an enormous breakfast.*

What do the giants, Joe and Jill, do?
> EXAMPLE: *They climb a huge beanstalk.*

3 Using Pronouns and Verbs That Agree

Sometimes a pronoun is used in the subject of a sentence. Read the sentences below.

> He wants the hen's eggs.
> She plays a golden harp.
> It shines in the sunlight.

Notice the verbs *wants*, *plays*, and *shines*. Verbs in the present time used with *he, she,* or *it* end in *-s* or *-es*.

Read each of the following sentences.

> I wish for a pot of gold.   You need good luck.
> We sell silver coins.   They bring good fortune.

Notice that verbs in the present time used with *I, you, we,* or *they* do not add *-s* or *-es*.

> **Summary** ♦ A verb in the present time must agree with the pronoun used in the subject of a sentence.

Guided Practice

Choose the correct verb to complete each sentence.

1. They (live, lives) in a cottage in the woods.
2. She (hear, hears) the birds singing.
3. It (make, makes) them feel happy.

Practice

A. Write the correct verb in ( ) to complete each sentence.

    4. She (like, likes) her son named Jack.

    5. You (know, knows) about their troubles.

    6. "It (appear, appears) we have no money," she said.

    7. He (take, takes) the cow's milk to market.

    8. They (sell, sells) some milk every day.

B. Use verbs in the present time in the sentences below.
Write each sentence with the correct form of the verb in ( ).

    9. Mother ____ about a business. (talk)

    10. She ____ her hands with worry. (wring)

    11. "We ____ to earn money," she says. (need)

    12. He ____ his mother to cheer up. (tell)

    13. "I ____ we must sell the cow," she says. (think)

C. Use a verb in the present time to complete each
sentence. Write the sentences.

    14. They ____ some magic beans.

    15. He ____ the beanstalk.

    16. "I ____ the bag of gold," thinks Jack.

    17. "We'll ____ the golden eggs," says mother.

    18. You ____ how the story ends.

Apply • Think and Write

Fairy-Tale Sentences ◆ Write sentences in the present
time about Little Red Riding Hood. Use pronouns as the
subjects of some of your sentences.

✎ **Remember**
that the verbs
you use need to
agree with their
subjects.

GETTING STARTED

Yesterday I went to Grandma's house. I talked to Tommy and I painted a picture.
What did you do yesterday?

4 Verbs in the Past

Read the sentences below. The underlined words are verbs in the past time. They tell about actions that already happened.

> The writer <u>remembered</u> his childhood.
> He <u>showed</u> his stories to friends.

Most verbs in the past time end in *-ed*.

Look at the verbs in the sentences below. Which verb shows action that is happening now? Which verb shows action that already happened?

> Marcus <u>mails</u> a story to his friend.
> Marcus <u>mailed</u> a story to his friend.

Summary ◆ A verb in the **past time** shows action that already happened. Most verbs in the past time end in *-ed*.

Guided Practice

Find the verb in each sentence below. Tell if it is in the present time or the past time.

1. The author picks up his pen.
2. He opened a new package of paper.
3. Then he looked for his notes.

Practice

A. If the verb is in the present time, write *present*. If the verb is in the past time, write *past*.

4. Hans Christian Andersen remembered his boyhood.
5. He lived in a small fishing village.
6. He traveled to Copenhagen to begin his career.
7. Today people look at his books with pleasure.
8. His writing inspires both children and adults.

B. Use verbs in the past time in the sentences below. Write each sentence with the correct form of the verb in ( ).

9. As a boy, Hans ____ many songs. (learn)
10. Books and music ____ his bookshelf. (fill)
11. Hans ____ in the woods. (walk)
12. Hans ____ his puppet theater. (enjoy)
13. He ____ stories for his puppets. (invent)

C. Use each verb in the past time to complete a sentence. Write the sentences.

work   publish   like   discover   present

14. With his puppets he ____ plays.
15. Hans ____ as a singer in a boys' choir.
16. A director of the Royal Theater ____ Hans.
17. Hans ____ his talent for writing.
18. Then he ____ a book of fairy tales.

Apply • Think and Write

Writing About the Past ♦ Write sentences about things you liked to do when you were six years old.

> ✎ **Remember**
> that verbs in the past time tell about events that already happened.

What do the animals do at the park?

EXAMPLES: *The duck swims in the pond.*
The birds sing with delight.
The frog watches the grasshopper.

5 Spelling Verbs in the Present

Verbs in the present time used with singular nouns end in -*s* or -*es*. Read the sentences below. What letter has been added to each verb?

■ **The duck floats on the water. It swims along the shore.**

Sometimes -*es* is added to verbs in the present time. Add -*es* to verbs that end in *s, ss, x, ch,* or *sh*.

| **The duck passes a goose.** | **Mother fixes a nest.** |
| **She watches her babies.** | **She rushes to help.** |

When a verb ends in a consonant and *y*, change the *y* to *i* and add -*es*. Look at the examples below.

■ **cry, cries** **hurry, hurries**

> **Summary** ◆ Some verbs in the present time end in -*s* or -*es*. The spelling of some verbs changes when -*es* is added.

Guided Practice

Use the verb in ( ) to complete each sentence. Spell the correct present-time form of the verb.

1. Taro ____ home. (rush)

2. Jon ____ now. (relax)

3. Kari ____ me. (call)

4. Molly ____ the dog. (dry)

5. Luis ____ a cat. (touch)

6. Miki ____ a frog. (carry)

Practice

A. Write each verb below. Then write the form that ends in -*s* or -*es*.

7. read   **11.** scratch   **15.** like

8. wish   **12.** mix   **16.** fry

9. marry   **13.** hurry   **17.** catch

10. fuss   **14.** guess   **18.** push

B. Use verbs in the present time in the sentences below. Write each sentence with the correct form of the verb in ( ).

19. The mother duck ____ her eggs. (hatch)

20. A duckling ____ to come out of the shell. (try)

21. The ugly duckling ____ in the pond. (splash)

22. The pig ____ at the ugly duckling. (laugh)

C. Use verbs in the present time to complete the sentences below. Write each complete sentence.

23. The duckling ____ away.

24. He ____ some wild ducks.

25. Later the ugly duckling ____ to a cottage.

26. A beautiful white bird ____ by the pond.

Apply · Think and Write

Dictionary of Knowledge ♦ Read about the Grimm brothers. Jakob and Wilhelm Grimm are famous for the fairy tales they wrote. The stories had been told aloud for many years. Write sentences telling why you would like to read their stories.

> ✏️ **Remember**
> to make sure you spell each present-time verb correctly.

6 Spelling Verbs in the Past

Verbs in the past time tell about actions that already happened. Many past-time verbs end in *-ed*. Look at the past-time verb in each sentence below.

> The king <u>named</u> the baby girl Snow White.
> The queen <u>rocked</u> her in a cradle.

Sometimes the spelling of a verb changes when *-ed* is added. Look at these examples.

> ■ dry, dr<u>ied</u>   hop, hop<u>ped</u>

The verb *dry* ends in a consonant and *y*. The *y* is changed to *i* before *-ed* is added. The verb *hop* ends in one vowel and one consonant. The final consonant is doubled before *-ed* is added.

Summary ◆ Most verbs in the past time end in *-ed*. The spelling of some verbs changes when *-ed* is added.

Guided Practice

Spell the past-time form of each verb below.

1. step   **3.** try   **5.** study
2. hug   **4.** hum   **6.** walk

Practice

A. Write each sentence. Use the form of the verb in ( ) that tells about past time.

    7. Snow White ____ in a castle. (live)

    8. One day the queen ____ with the mirror. (chat)

    9. She ____ out, ''Who is fairest of them all?'' (cry)

    10. The mirror ____, ''Snow White.'' (reply)

    11. The queen ____ Snow White to leave. (order)

B. Each underlined verb is in the present time. Change each verb to the past time. Write each new sentence.

    12. Snow White <u>raps</u> on the door of a cottage.

    13. In the cottage <u>dwell</u> seven dwarfs.

    14. The queen <u>prepares</u> a bad apple for Snow White.

    15. An old woman <u>carries</u> the apple to Snow White.

    16. Snow White <u>drops</u> to the floor after the first bite.

C. Use the verbs below in the past time to complete the sentences. Write the sentences.

marry   kiss   hurry   fear   plan

    17. All the dwarfs ____ Snow White was dead.

    18. They ____ out to find her.

    19. The prince ____ Snow White and broke the spell.

    20. Snow White and the prince ____ a wedding.

    21. They ____ and lived happily ever after.

Apply • Think and Write

A Story Ending ♦ Think about your favorite fairy tale. Write a new ending for the story. Be sure to use verbs in the past time.

> ✎ **Remember**
> to make sure you spell each verb in the past time correctly.

◆ GETTING STARTED ◆

See if you can "undo" these words by adding the letters *un*: *lock, curl, apple, fold, buckle, walk, latch, leash*. Which words would not let you "undo" them?

VOCABULARY ◆
Prefixes

Look at how the words below are built.

> re + tell = retell
> un + cover = uncover

A **base word** is the simplest form of a word. The words *tell* and *cover* are base words. The word parts *re-* and *un-* are called prefixes. A **prefix** is a letter or letters added to the beginning of a word. A prefix changes the meaning of a word.

Look at the chart below to find out the meanings of the prefixes *re-* and *un-*.

Prefix	Meaning	Example
re-	again	repaint
un-	the opposite of	unsnap

Building Your Vocabulary

Each word below has a prefix. Tell what each word means.

1. uncover	**4.** reheat	**7.** refill
2. unhook	**5.** unbox	**8.** replay
3. reread	**6.** reappear	**9.** unseal

Practice

A. Read the meanings below. Then write a word that has
the prefix *un-* or *re-* for each meaning.

EXAMPLE: **opposite of wrap**
ANSWER: **unwrap**

1. opposite of tie   **4.** write again

2. heat again   **5.** opposite of paid

3. opposite of zip   **6.** make again

B. Rewrite the story. Add a prefix to each word in ( ).

Once there were two squirrels named Undo and
Redo. Undo was always messing things up. Every
morning, Undo would (make) all the beds. Then he
would (fold) all of the clothes and (buckle) all of
the shoes.

Redo was always doing things again. He (painted)
their little nest every afternoon. He (read) his books at
least three times and (wrote) all his letters. Undo and
Redo made a good pair, because everything that Undo
(did) Redo (did)!

Language Corner ◆ Tongue Twisters

Are you good at saying
tongue twisters? Try saying
this one five times fast: *She
sells seashells by the
seashore.* Here is another:
Toy boat.

Make up some tongue
twisters of your own. Use
words that begin with the same
sounds.

How to Revise Sentences with Verbs

In this unit you have learned about using verbs in sentences. Choosing exact verbs can make your sentences interesting. Exact verbs also give different information to readers. What difference does changing the verb make in these sentences?

1. The elf talked to the giant.
2. The elf whispered to the giant.

Both sentences tell you that the elf talked to the giant. But sentence **2** tells you exactly how the elf talked. Now read sentence **3**. Changing the verb again gives a different picture of the conversation.

■ 3. The elf shouted to the giant.

The Grammar Game ◆ Go on a verb adventure! Write two exact verbs for each word below. Write them as quickly as you can.

look	like	find
eat	jump	walk
cook	laugh	rain

Working Together

See how using exact verbs can improve your writing. Work with your group on activities **A** and **B**.

A. Choose an exact verb to replace the underlined verb in each sentence. Can you write the sentences again, choosing different exact verbs?

1. At Silly Zoo, green kangaroos <u>move</u> happily.
2. Polka-dot elephants <u>move</u> slowly along.
3. Pink ponies <u>move</u> across velvet pastures.
4. Smiling snakes <u>move</u> around the purple trees.

B. Complete the paragraph below. Use an exact verb of the group's choice for each sentence.

On Fridays, Mr. and Mrs. Jack Sprat ___ to market. They ___ vegetables and bacon. Then they ___ home and ___ lunch. They ___ everything on the platter!

In Your Group

♦ Give your ideas to the group.
♦ Encourage others to share ideas.
♦ Look at others when they talk.
♦ Thank people for their ideas.

EXACT VERBS

stomp	gallop
leap	crawl
slither	hop
trot	ramble

WRITERS' CORNER ♦ Overused Verbs

Choosing exact verbs will help you avoid using the same words too often.

EXAMPLE: I did the dishes. Then I did my homework. Finally I did the crossword puzzle.

IMPROVED: I dried the dishes. Then I finished my homework. Finally I worked on the crossword puzzle.

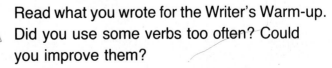

Read what you wrote for the Writer's Warm-up. Did you use some verbs too often? Could you improve them?

Illustration by Mercer Mayer
From *Beauty and the Beast* by Marianna Mayer

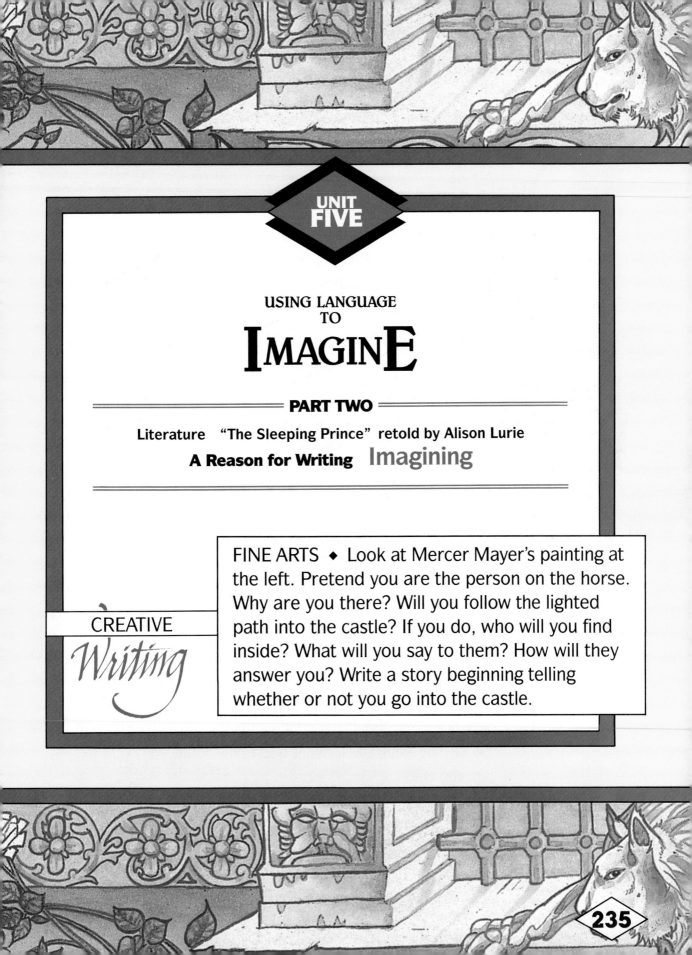

UNIT FIVE

USING LANGUAGE TO

IMAGINE

=== **PART TWO** ===

Literature "The Sleeping Prince" retold by Alison Lurie

A Reason for Writing Imagining

CREATIVE
Writing

FINE ARTS ◆ Look at Mercer Mayer's painting at the left. Pretend you are the person on the horse. Why are you there? Will you follow the lighted path into the castle? If you do, who will you find inside? What will you say to them? How will they answer you? Write a story beginning telling whether or not you go into the castle.

CREATIVE THINKING ◆
A Strategy for Imagining

A QUESTION WHEEL

Imagining can be a way of pretending or making believe. One kind of imaginary story is a fairy tale. After this lesson you will read one called "The Sleeping Prince." Later you will write a fairy tale of your own.

In "The Sleeping Prince," a bird sings. Can you tell that the bird is imaginary? How? Here is what it sings.

> Gold and white and red,
> The Prince sleeps in his bed. . . .
> White and red and gold,
> He shall sleep till time is old.

Do you wonder what the song means? Do you wonder what will happen? Wondering is a good way to find things out.

Learning the Strategy

When you wonder, you ask questions. For example, suppose there will be a school pet show. What questions might you ask your teacher about it? Think about magic shows and magic mirrors and magic carpets. Do you have any questions about magic? Imagine that the fire chief will be visiting your class. What questions would you want to ask the chief?

A question wheel can help you think of questions. Write the name of something in the middle. Write questions about it around the outside. One question may help you think of others. Fill the wheel with questions. Here is a question wheel for the fire chief. What questions would you add?

The Fire Chief's Job
- Why are you visiting our school?
- Where do you work?
- What is the hardest part of your job?
- What do you like about your job?

Using the Strategy

A. What do you know about dinosaurs? What would you like to know? Make a question wheel. In the middle write *dinosaurs* or draw one. Then fill your wheel with questions about dinosaurs. Can your teacher answer some of your questions? Where do you think you could find more answers?

B. Read the bird's song from "The Sleeping Prince" again. What do you think it means? Can you guess what is "gold and white and red"? Make a question wheel. Write *"The Sleeping Prince"* in the middle. Fill the wheel with questions about the story. Then read the story to find the answers.

Applying the Strategy

♦ How did you think up the questions for your wheel?
♦ When might it be important for you to ask questions?

THE SLEEPING PRINCE

Retold by Alison Lurie

Once upon a time there lived a king and queen
who had one daughter whom they loved dearly.
Now on a day in winter, when the countryside was
covered with snow, she was sitting at her window
sewing. As she sewed she pricked her finger, and a
drop of red blood fell on the sill in the golden
sunlight. And a bird in a tree outside sang:

> "Gold and white and red,
> The Prince sleeps in his bed."

The princess was struck by these words, and
called out, "Pray, little bird, sing again!" And the
bird sang:

> "White and red and gold,
> He shall sleep till time is old."

The princess cried, "Ah, little bird, sing again!"
And the bird sang:

> "Red and gold and white,
> He wakes on St. John's Night."

"But what does your song mean?" asked the
princess. So the bird told her that in a castle far, far

away, and further still, there dwelt the noblest and handsomest prince in the world, with skin as white as snow and lips as red as blood and hair as golden as the sun. A spell had been cast over him, so that he fell into a deep sleep from which he could wake only once a year, on St. John's Night. And thus it would be until the end of time. But if a maiden were to watch beside his bed, so that he might see her when he woke, then the spell would be broken.

"And where is this castle?" asked the Princess.

"I do not know," said the bird, "except that it is far, far away, and further still, so that to get there you must wear out a pair of iron shoes."

Days passed, and the princess could not forget the song the bird had sung. At last she said to herself that she must and would go to find the Sleeping Prince, and free him from the spell. But as she knew that her father and mother would never consent to let her make such a journey, she said nothing to them. She had a pair of iron shoes made, and as soon as they were ready, late one night, she put them on and left the palace.

The princess walked on and on, far and farther. She walked into a great, dark forest. She walked in scorching sun and pouring rain. She walked until her clothes grew ragged and her iron shoes wore thin. Still, she kept searching for the castle of the Sleeping Prince. She would not rest until she found it.

On her journey the princess stopped three times to ask the way to the prince's castle. Each time she came to a cottage in the woods. Each time an old woman invited her in for supper. Each time the princess had to hide when the old woman's son came home. You see, each old woman was the mother of a great, angry Wind who would have harmed the princess. Surely one of these Winds blowing over the earth could tell his mother the way to the castle. Surely the princess could overhear the Winds' words from her hiding place.

Yet the first old woman's son, the East Wind, did not know the way to the castle of the Sleeping Prince. The West Wind said the same. Only the last one, the North Wind, knew the path the princess should follow. The path outside his door led straight to the castle gate.

The North Wind also knew something else worth hearing. Two sleeping lions guarded the gate to the castle and ate anyone who tried to pass through. There was only one way to enter the castle, the North Wind said. You must pick two white roses growing by the North Wind's door. If you threw these roses at the lions, they would lie down and let you pass.

As soon as it was light the next morning the princess set out, taking with her two white roses from the bush by the North Wind's door. She walked on and on, far, far, and further still. The sun scorched her and the rain wetted her and the snow chilled her. At last she looked down, and saw that her iron shoes were worn quite through. She looked up, and saw before her the towers of a castle.

Soon she came to the gate, and saw the two great lions guarding it. When they caught sight of the princess they began to growl and paw the ground and show their teeth, so that she wanted to run away. Yet all the same she went on. Just as the lions began to spring at her she threw the white roses at them; and at once they became tame, and began to purr and rub themselves against her like kittens. The gates opened for the princess, and she walked barefoot into the castle.

Inside she found many rooms, all of them furnished as magnificently as any prince could desire. But what was most strange was that everyone and everything in the castle was asleep, and try as she might the princess could not wake them. The servants were asleep in the hall, the cook and maids in the kitchen, the gardener in the garden, the groom and the horses in the stable, the cows in the barn, the chickens and ducks in the poultry yard, and even the flies on the wall.

The princess searched through all the rooms of the castle, and at last she came to a bedchamber

hung with curtains of silver, and on the bed asleep lay the handsomest prince in the world. His skin was white as snow, his lips as red as blood, and his hair golden as the sun.

The princess could not wake him, so she sat down beside his bed. Just as evening fell, a table covered with the most delicious supper appeared before her; and when she had eaten, it vanished. All night long she watched by the sleeping prince. At dawn the table appeared again, and vanished when she had eaten just as before.

The days passed, and the weeks, and the months. Still the princess sat every night by the side of the sleeping prince, waiting for him to wake. At last it came to be St. John's Eve, but she did not know it, for she had lost count of time on her long journey.

At midnight the clock in the tallest tower, which had until then been silent, began to strike. On the stroke of twelve the prince yawned, opened his eyes, and saw the princess sitting beside his bed, barefoot and in rags like a beggar maid.

"At last, the spell has been broken!" he cried.

Now there was a noise and clamor of voices downstairs, a neighing and mooing and clucking and quacking, as everyone in the castle awoke from their long sleep: the servants in the hall, the cook and maids in the kitchen, the gardener in the garden, the groom and the horses in the stable, the cows in the barn, the chickens and ducks in the poultry yard,

and even the flies on the wall. But the prince paid
no heed to any of this, for he was gazing at the princess.

"Whoever you may be, my life belongs to you,"
he said. "Will you marry me?"

The princess looked into his eyes, and saw that
he was as good and brave as he was beautiful. "With
all my heart," she said.

And so they were married with great ceremony
and feasting that lasted for three days. Then the
prince and princess mounted on the two fastest
horses in his stable, and rode to the castle of the
king and queen, who were overcome with joy to see
their daughter again. As for the prince, though he
was surprised to discover that his wife was not a
beggar maid after all, he was not happier, for he
already loved her more than all the world.

Library Link ♦ *If you liked this story, you may wish to
read* Clever Gretchen and Other Forgotten Folktales, *retold
by Alison Lurie.*

Reader's Response

Do you think the princess made the right decision to travel
alone to look for the prince?

THE SLEEPING PRINCE

◆ Responding to Literature

1. What was your favorite part of the story? Retell it for your classmates. Then listen to the parts your classmates chose to tell.

2. Imagine that you are the bird or the North Wind's mother. Tell how the princess looked to you when you saw her for the first time.

3. The words *gold*, *white*, and *red* were used often in the story. Write the three words in any order. Write a second rhyming line about the story.

◆ Writing to Learn

Think and Question ◆ What do you wonder about the prince and the princess? Make a question wheel like this one. Fill your wheel with questions.

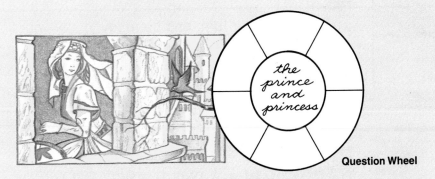

Question Wheel

Write ◆ Choose your favorite question to answer. Write about what might happen to the prince and princess.

◆ GETTING STARTED ◆

Choose something to act out without words.
EXAMPLES: washing windows, riding a horse, fishing

SPEAKING and LISTENING ◆
Acting Out a Fairy Tale

Would you like to turn a story into a play? A play is a story that is acted out by people. It is fun to act out a story. The actors, or players, become story characters. Sometimes a play has a narrator. The narrator reads whatever the characters do not say.

To act out a story, you need to prepare. First, choose a story. Then identify the characters. What will they say? What will they do? Next, decide who will play each part. Do you need a narrator for your play? Choose someone for this part if you do.

Saying Your Lines	1. Speak with expression. Show how your character feels. 2. Use your body, too, to show how your character feels. 3. Say only your character's words. Do not say "he said," for example.
Being an Active Listener	1. Listen for your turn, and be ready to say your line. 2. Be polite. Do not whisper or talk while others speak. 3. Listen to the parts of the other players and watch their actions.

Summary ◆ A **play** is a story that is acted out by people. The actors become story characters. When you act, show how the story character feels. Use your face, voice, and body.

Guided Practice

Practice saying these lines with feeling. You may wish to use motions to add to the feeling.

1. PRINCESS: Ah, little bird, sing again!
2. OLD WOMAN: Oh, my son, don't be angry!
3. PRINCE: At last, the spell has been broken!
4. PRINCE: Whoever you may be, my life belongs to you. Will you marry me?
5. PRINCESS: With all my heart.

Practice

A. Act out each part below. Use your face and body to show how you feel. Say how you feel, too.

6. QUEEN: while sewing, pricks her finger
7. PRINCESS: puts on her iron shoes and walks
8. LION: growls and threatens the princess
9. LION: becomes tame and purrs at the princess
10. SERVANT: awakes from the long sleep

B. Use the story of "The Sleeping Prince" and act it out as a play. Remember to follow the guidelines in this lesson.

Apply ◆ Think and Write

Words for a Character ◆ Choose a character from "The Three Bears." Write something the character might say that is not in the story. For example, what might Baby Bear say about Goldilocks? "Someone read all of the books on my bookshelf."

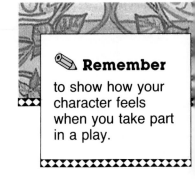

✎ **Remember**
to show how your character feels when you take part in a play.

The princess must cross a river of flames. On the other shore is a terrifying dragon. She has one wish. What should she wish?

WRITING ◆
Story Problems

When you write a story, you invent a main character, or hero. Next you invent a problem your hero must solve. But how will your hero solve that problem? That also is up to you. You must think of a solution.

If your story is a fairy tale, your job is easier. Why? You can use make-believe. Look at how some problems are solved in "The Sleeping Prince."

PROBLEM: Two lions spring at the princess.
SOLUTION: Make-believe! She throws two white roses at the lions. At once they become tame.

PROBLEM: The princess waits for months. Still the prince does not wake up.
SOLUTION: Make-believe! On Saint John's Eve the clock strikes midnight. The prince yawns and opens his eyes!

Summary ◆ In a story the main character has a problem to solve. The problem is solved by make-believe in a fairy tale.

Guided Practice

In "The Sleeping Prince" the princess faced problems. They are listed below. Now you be the author. Invent a new way to solve each problem. You, too, can use make-believe.

1. Two fierce lions guard the castle gate.
2. As she waits at the castle, she gets hungry.
3. She waits and waits, but the prince sleeps.

Practice

A. Here are some problems for a story hero. Write a way to solve each one. You may use make-believe.

4. Your hero is locked in a castle tower.
5. Your hero faces a grumbling giant.

B. Make up a story problem like the ones in **Practice A**. Write a sentence that tells what the problem is. You may begin like this: My hero is ____ .

Apply ◆ Think and Write

Dictionary of Knowledge ◆ Read about Hans Christian Andersen. Think about one of the stories he wrote. Who was the hero of the story? Write a paragraph about the hero's problem.

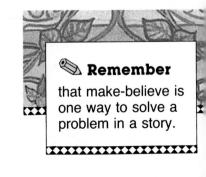

✏️ **Remember**
that make-believe is one way to solve a problem in a story.

Focus on Fairy Tales

A fairy tale often begins with "Once upon a time. . . ." It tells of magic and adventure. It may have princes and princesses, giants and elves, witches and wizards. The people you meet in fairy tales are not the kind of people you meet in everyday life!

Many fairy tales have a hero and a heroine.

HERO: The hero may be a prince. Sometimes he is on an important mission, but not always. In the story you read earlier, the handsome prince is asleep.

HEROINE: The heroine is a princess. She has the important mission in the story—to rescue the sleeping prince.

In a fairy tale, the world of magic mixes with the world we know. Anything can happen! Some things seem real. Others are make-believe.

The hero and heroine of a fairy tale face difficulties. But they win out in the end, and everyone lives happily ever after.

The Writer's Voice ◆ In "The Sleeping Prince," the princess waits months for everyone to wake up. Put yourself in her place. Would you have waited? What would you have done?

Working Together

Fairy tales have magic and make-believe. They also have people, places, or events that could be real. As a group, do activities **A** and **B**.

A. With your group decide which of these things could really happen.

   1. As the princess sewed, she pricked her finger.
   2. The bird sang, "White and red and gold. . . ."
   3. Two white roses made the lions become tame.
   4. Each night the princess sat beside the prince's bed.
   5. After she had eaten her meal, the table vanished.

B. Help your group look for real and make-believe. With your group, make a chart like the one below for "The Sleeping Prince." Try to find five real and five make-believe events in the story.

Real	*Make-believe*
1. The countryside was covered with snow.	**1.** A spell had been cast over the prince.

In Your Group

- Encourage others to share ideas.
- Keep the group on the subject.
- Look at others when they talk.
- Record the group's ideas.

THESAURUS CORNER ◆ Word Choice

Look up the verb *tell* in the Thesaurus. Think about what you might say if you were telling a fairy tale. Write five sentences about telling the story. Use a different synonym for *tell* in each sentence.

WRITING PROCESS
IMAGING

Writing a Fairy Tale

Many make-believe things happen in fairy tales. For example, in "The Sleeping Prince" the wind speaks. Food magically appears on a table. These things can't happen except in fairy tales. That's one reason why fairy tales are fun to write!

Know Your Purpose and Audience

What's MY PURPOSE

In this lesson you will write a fairy tale. Your purpose will be to tell a story about a fairy-tale character.

Who's MY AUDIENCE

Your audience will be a younger child. Later you can act out your story. You can also make a bottle puppet of the character in your story.

1 Prewriting

First choose a fairy-tale character. Then use a plan to get story ideas.

Choose Your Topic ♦ Who will be the main character in your fairy tale? Make a list of possible characters. Circle the name that is your favorite.

Think About It	Talk About It
You might start by thinking about your favorite fairy-tale characters. Are they smart? Are they funny or brave? What names will you put on your list? You can choose a character you know or make up a new one.	Your classmates can help you remember the names of characters. Tell each other your favorite fairy tales. That will help you remember the characters. Often your classmates will know stories that you forgot.

Topic Ideas

Fairy-Tale Characters
Prince Charming
Goldilocks
Jack and the Beanstalk
Cinderella

Choose Your Strategy ♦ Here are two plans for getting story ideas. Use the plan you like better.

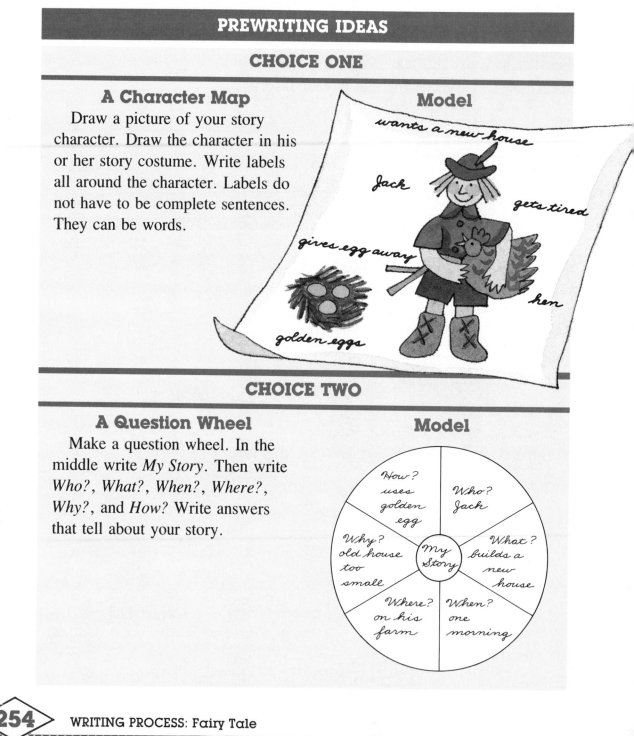

PREWRITING IDEAS

CHOICE ONE

A Character Map

Draw a picture of your story character. Draw the character in his or her story costume. Write labels all around the character. Labels do not have to be complete sentences. They can be words.

Model

wants a new house

Jack

gets tired

gives egg away

hen

golden eggs

CHOICE TWO

A Question Wheel

Make a question wheel. In the middle write *My Story*. Then write *Who?*, *What?*, *When?*, *Where?*, *Why?*, and *How?* Write answers that tell about your story.

Model

How? uses golden egg

Who? Jack

Why? old house too small

My Story

What? builds a new house

Where? on his farm

When? one morning

2 Writing

Look at your character map or question wheel. Then begin your story. How can you begin? Here are two ways.

♦ Once upon a time ____.

♦ Early one morning ____.

As you write, think about your character. What will your character do first? Then what will happen? How will the fairy tale end? Keep writing till your story is done. Don't worry about mistakes. You can fix them later.

Sample First Draft ♦

Early one morning Jack decided to bild a new house. Jack worked hard. after a while he got too tired. He had one part left to finish. Then Jack had an idea. He took a golden egg from his magic hen. He hands it to a carpenter. The carpenter made the house.

3 Revising

Now you have written your fairy tale. Would you like to make it better? This idea may help you.

REVISING IDEA

FIRST Read to Yourself

Think about your purpose. Did you write a fairy tale? Think about your audience. Will a younger child enjoy it? Then decide which part *you* like best.

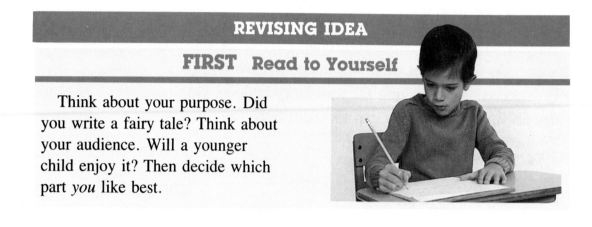

Focus: Is your story make-believe?

THEN Share with a Partner

Read your story to a partner. Then ask your partner for ideas. These guidelines may help.

The Writer

Guidelines: Read slowly. Listen to your partner's ideas.

Sample questions:
- Which part of my story did you like best?
- **Focus question:** How did you know my story was make-believe?

The Writer's Partner

Guidelines: Listen to the story carefully. Give your ideas in a kind way.

Sample responses:
- The part I liked best was _____.
- Could you tell why _____?

Revising Model ♦ The fairy tale below is being revised. The marks show the writer's changes.

The writer's partner wanted to know why.

This verb should be in the past time.

The word *constructed* is more exact than *made*.

The writer wanted a better fairy-tale ending.

> Early one morning Jack
>
> *build*
> decided to bild a new house.
> ∧His old house was too small.
> Jack worked hard. after a
>
> while he got too tired. He had
>
> one part left to finish. Then
>
> Jack had an idea. He took a
>
> golden egg from his magic hen.
> *handed*
> He hands it to a carpenter. The
> *constructed*
> carpenter made the house.
> ∧Jack lived happily in his
> house ever after.

Read the story above. Read it the way the writer thinks it *should* be. Then revise your own fairy tale.

Grammar Check ♦ Do you want your story to be easy to read? Then make sure all the verbs are in the same time.

Word Choice ♦ Is there a better word for a word like *made*? A thesaurus can help you find more exact words.

Revising Checklist

☐ **My purpose:** Did I write a fairy tale?

☐ **My audience:** Will a younger child enjoy my fairy tale?

☐ **Focus:** Is my story make-believe?

4 Proofreading

Proofreading makes your writing neat and correct. It is a way of being polite to your readers.

Proofreading Model ♦ Here is the tale about Jack's house. Red proofreading marks have been added.

Proofreading Marks
check spelling ⬭
capital letter =
indent paragraph ¶

Early one morning Jack
                    build
decided to (bild) a new house.
∧His old house was too small.
    Jack worked hard. ̲after a
while he got too tired. He had
one part left to finish.¶ Then
Jack had an idea. He took a
golden egg from his magic hen.
        handed
He hands it to a carpenter. The
        constructed
carpenter made the house.
    Jack lived happily in his
∧house ever after.

Proofreading Checklist

☐ Did I spell words correctly?

☐ Did I indent paragraphs?

☐ Did I use capital letters correctly?

☐ Did I use correct marks at the end of sentences?

☐ Did I use my best handwriting?

PROOFREADING IDEA

Handwriting Check

Make sure that you write each letter correctly. Did you dot every *i*? Did you cross every *t*?

Now proofread your fairy tale and add a title. Then make a neat copy.

5 Publishing

Now it's time to share your fairy tale with an audience.
Below are two ideas you might try.

Jack and the Magic Hen

Early one morning Jack decided to build a new house. His old house was too small.

Jack worked hard. After a while he got too tired. He had one part left to finish.

Then Jack had an idea. He took a golden egg from his magic hen. He handed it to a carpenter. The carpenter constructed the house.

Jack lived happily in his house ever after.

PUBLISHING IDEAS

Share Aloud	Share in Writing
Practice telling your story. If you like, have friends help you act it out. Then visit a younger child or a younger class. Dress like your story character. Tell or act out your story. Ask members of your audience what part they liked best.	Make a bottle puppet of your story character. Glue a ball onto the neck of a clean plastic bottle. Then paint a face on it. Make clothes and hair from paper, cloth, and yarn. Read other classmates' fairy tales. Guess which puppet goes with which story.

Writing Across the Curriculum Music

In this unit you wrote a fairy tale. You asked questions to help get ideas for your story. Asking questions can help people write songs, too.

Writing to Learn

Think and Wonder ♦ Imagine you are singing "Twinkle, Twinkle, Little Star." As you sing, you are looking at a star in the sky. How many questions could you ask the star? Fill a question wheel with star questions.

Question Wheel

Write ♦ Look at your question wheel. Then write some new words for "Twinkle, Twinkle, Little Star." Write a question you could sing to the star.

Writing in Your Journal

In the Writer's Warm-up you wrote about the world of make-believe. Look back through this unit. What new things did you learn about fairy tales? In your journal write about what you learned.

BOOKS TO ENJOY

◆ Read More About It

The Wonderful Wizard of Oz
by L. Frank Baum
This classic tale of Dorothy's adventures in the Land of Oz was first published in 1900. You will enjoy the special details the author used.

The Weaving of a Dream
by Marilee Heyer
A poor widow weaves dreams into a precious cloth. But fairies steal it away. What will happen when her sons try to recover it?

◆ Book Report Idea   Silhouette Report

Show what the story made you think.

Create a Silhouette
Ask a friend to trace the shadow of your head from the side. Pretend the head stands for your imagination. Combine sentences, words, and pictures to describe the make-believe world of your book. Don't forget to give the title and author.

UNIT REVIEW

Unit 5

Verbs   *pages 218–229*

A. Write each sentence. Use the correct present-time form of the verb in ( ).

1. Jeannine _____ butterflies. (collect)
2. She _____ a lot about them. (know)
3. Most butterflies _____ in the daytime. (fly)
4. Some insects _____ with their feet. (taste)
5. A firefly often _____ in the dark. (glow)
6. Some insects _____ only one pair of wings. (use)
7. The other pair _____ the insect balance. (help)
8. Some mosquitoes _____ disease. (carry)
9. The dragonfly _____ other insects. (kill)

B. Write each sentence. Use the correct past-time form of the verb in ( ).

10. Marie Curie _____ in Poland. (live)
11. Later she _____ to France. (move)
12. She _____ science there.. (study)
13. She and her husband _____ together. (work)
14. They _____ radium. (discover)
15. The doctors _____ to help sick people. (try)
16. Marie Curie _____ two Nobel Prizes. (receive)
17. One day she _____ for a visit. (stop)
18. We _____ into the room to greet her. (step)

Prefixes   *pages 230–231*

C. Write a word that has the prefix *un-* or *re-* for each meaning below.

19. the opposite of do
20. make new again
21. the opposite of changed
22. order again
23. the opposite of fold
24. measure again

25. the opposite of opened
26. tell again
27. the opposite of tie
28. pay again
29. the opposite of screw
30. wind again

Real and Make-Believe   *pages 248–249*

D. Write *real* or *make-believe* for each story described below.

31. The cat opened the door and asked me the time.
32. I took the cat downstairs to the kitchen.
33. I looked in the refrigerator for a piece of fish.
34. Anyone who eats the fish will swim like a seal.
35. The cat ate the fish and washed its whiskers.
36. I sat down and watched the evening news.
37. The chipmunk answered the phone.
38. The cat played the violin.

E. Change each make-believe story below to a real story.

EXAMPLE: The ant balanced a ball on its nose.
The seal balanced a ball on its nose.

39. My cat called me upstairs.
40. I saw a giant peek around the corner.
41. The rabbit plowed the garden.
42. The trumpet danced around the room.
43. Her bear unlocked the door and waited inside.

LANGUAGE PUZZLERS

Unit 5 Challenge

A Holiday Game

Play this game about holidays and special days. Add each item in **Column B** to an item from **Column A**. (Hint: Subjects and verbs must agree.)

Column A	Column B
1. Mother's Day	comes in January.
2. Presidents' Day	play tricks on people.
3. Thanksgiving	wave on the Fourth of July.
4. Halloween	comes in November.
5. American flags	falls on October 31.
6. Martin Luther King Day	honors Washington and Lincoln.
7. On April Fools' Day we	honors mothers.

Verbs in Code

Ten verbs are written in code below. Can you figure them out? (Hint: 1 = a and 2 = b.)

1. 7-18-1-2-2-5-4
2. 4-18-9-5-19
3. 1-20-20-1-3-8-5-19
4. 18-5-12-9-5-4
5. 7-18-9-16-16-5-4
6. 6-12-9-16-16-5-4
7. 18-5-12-1-24-5-19
8. 3-18-9-5-4

21-14-19-3-18-1-13-2-12-5
#13-5

Unit 5 Extra Practice

1 Writing with Verbs
p. 218

A. Write the verb in each sentence.

1. Heidi skates on the frozen lake.
2. Chad climbs the hill with his sled.
3. The dog runs up the hill with Chad.
4. Two boys build a snow family.
5. Katy throws a snowball at the tree.
6. Pierre carries his new skates.
7. My friends play ice hockey.
8. The team practices every day after school.
9. Edgar and Jay bring the equipment.
10. Rod scores a goal in almost every game.

B. If the underlined word in the sentence is a verb, write *verb*. If the underlined word is not a verb, write *not a verb*.

11. Peggy and Jack ride in an old-fashioned sleigh.
12. A pony pulls the sleigh around the city park.
13. Peggy holds the pony's reins.
14. The pony trots along in the snow.
15. Two dogs chase after the sleigh.

C. Write the sentences. Use a verb to complete each sentence.

16. Conrad ___ his snowshoes.
17. The girls ___ new mittens.
18. A squirrel ___ up the tree.
19. Wesley ___ three deer.
20. A bird ___ over the frozen lake.

2 Verbs in the Present

p. 220

A. Write the sentences. Choose the correct verb in ( ) to complete each sentence.

1. My friends (raise, raises) gerbils.
2. Gerbils (come, comes) from China.
3. Cory (clean, cleans) their cage often.
4. Dot (drink, drinks) from a water bottle.

B. Use verbs in the present time in the sentences below. Write each sentence with the correct form of the verb in ( ).

EXAMPLE: Mona ___ pets in the shop. (see)
ANSWER: Mona sees pets in the shop.

5. Some gerbils ___ tricks. (know)
6. One gerbil ___ on the boy's shoe. (sit)
7. Another gerbil ___ inside the wheel. (climb)
8. Rusty and Dusty ___ in paper bags. (hide)
9. The pets ___ salt from a block. (lick)
10. Their front teeth ___ all the time. (grow)
11. A gerbil ___ on hard foods. (chew)

3 Using Pronouns and Verbs That Agree

p. 222

A. Write the correct verb to complete each sentence.

1. We (help, helps) our city stay clean.
2. You (sweep, sweeps) the sidewalk.
3. She (bring, brings) bottles back to the store.
4. They (plant, plants) beautiful flowers.

266 Extra Practice

B. Use verbs in the present time in the sentences below. Write each sentence with the correct form of the verb in ( ).

5. They ____ many ways to save materials. (find)
6. We ____ different kinds of things. (recycle)
7. He ____ his empty bottles. (return)
8. I ____ on both sides of my paper. (write)
9. We ____ paper bags several times. (use)
10. It ____ trees in the forest. (save)
11. They ____ broken windows. (replace)
12. You ____ the trash cans carefully. (cover)
13. We ____ to keep our town clean. (want)
14. I ____ my bicycle to school. (ride)
15. She ____ the bus to work. (take)

4 Verbs in the Past

p. 224

A. Use verbs in the past time in the sentences below. Write each sentence with the correct form of the verb in ( ).

EXAMPLE: **Some dinosaurs ____ on the land. (walk)**
ANSWER: **Some dinosaurs walked on the land.**

1. Dinosaurs ____ warm, moist places to live. (need)
2. Warm seas ____ most of the earth. (flood)
3. The earliest animals ____ in the sea. (remain)
4. Some reptiles ____ to the land. (crawl)
5. These creatures ____ from eggs. (hatch)
6. Flying reptiles ____ from the air. (hunt)
7. Then the earth ____ to change. (start)
8. The air and water temperatures ____ . (cool)
9. Dinosaurs ____ from the earth. (disappear)

B. If the verb is in the present time, write *present*. If the verb is in the past time, write *past*.

10. Workers in New Jersey discovered large bones.

11. They also uncovered some dinosaur teeth.

12. Dr. Leidy hunted for dinosaur bones in America.

13. Today people look at those bones in museums.

14. Scientists learn about early reptiles from bones.

15. My book shows pictures of giant lizards.

16. One dinosaur weighed thirty tons.

17. Its long body stretched seventy feet.

5 Spelling Verbs in the Present *p. 226*

A. Use verbs in the present time in the sentences below. Write each sentence with the correct form of the verb in ( ).

1. Gay _____ a puppet show for her friends. (prepare)

2. One puppet _____ a delicious meal. (fix)

3. He _____ eggs for the family. (fry)

4. The boy puppet _____ toy dishes. (wash)

5. His sister _____ them with a tiny towel. (dry)

6. Al _____ a story about a puppet family. (write)

7. Gert _____ in a swimming pool. (splash)

8. Bernie _____ the water with one toe. (try)

9. Then he _____ the pool on a raft. (cross)

10. The raft _____ near the edge. (float)

11. Polly _____ Bernie into the water. (push)

12. Miss Dimples _____ on a big towel. (relax)

13. Hopper _____ a beach ball to her. (toss)

14. Big Elmer _____ his feathers. (dry)

15. He _____ the beach ball in his beak. (carry)

B. Write each verb below. Then write the form that ends in -*s* or -*es*.

16.	read	**20.**	scratch
17.	wish	**21.**	mix
18.	fly	**22.**	hurry
19.	fuss	**23.**	guess

6 Spelling Verbs in the Past   *p. 228*

A. Write each sentence. Use the form of the verb in ( ) that tells about the past time.

1. We ___ the fitness course. (start)
2. Cathy ___ up and down the wooden steps. (skip)
3. I ___ carefully over logs. (hop)
4. Then we ___ to the next exercise. (hurry)
5. Our hearts and other muscles ___ hard. (work)

B. Each underlined verb is in the present time. Change each verb to the past time. Write the new sentence.

6. Fitness courses <u>start</u> in Europe.
7. Our city <u>plans</u> to build a free exercise trail.
8. People of all ages <u>try</u> the exercises.
9. Some folks <u>stop</u> at all the exercise signs.
10. Sometimes they <u>trip</u> on the logs.
11. At first I <u>worry</u> about not finishing the course.
12. I <u>rest</u> for a little while.
13. I <u>watch</u> a girl in a wheelchair.
14. She <u>pulls</u> herself up a ramp.
15. She <u>explains</u> how muscles and strength improve slowly with regular exercise.

USING LANGUAGE
TO
RESEARCH

PART ONE

Unit Theme   *Exploring the Wilderness*

Language Awareness   Verbs

PART TWO

Literature   *Sacagawea* by Wyatt Blassingame

A Reason for Writing   Researching

Writing
IN YOUR JOURNAL

WRITER'S WARM-UP ◆ What do you know about the wilderness? Can you imagine parts of the country where no one lives? Maybe you have gone hiking or camping deep in the woods. Try to imagine doing this with no cars, roads, maps, or signs. Write in your journal. Tell what you think about the wilderness.

Pretend that you explored the woods with your family yesterday. Use the words *came*, *did*, *went*, *had*, and *ran* to tell what you did on your outing.

EXAMPLE: *We came to the top of a hill.*

1 Verbs with Special Past Forms

You have learned that *-ed* is often added to verbs that show action that already happened. But some verbs change in other ways to show past time. Look at the chart below.

Verb	Present	Past
come	come, comes	came
do	do, does	did
go	go, goes	went
have	have, has	had
run	run, runs	ran

The sentences below show verbs in the past time.

Europeans <u>came</u> to America. Explorers <u>had</u> few maps.
They <u>did</u> a lot of hard work. They <u>went</u> on expeditions.

Summary ◆ Some verbs in the past time do not end in *-ed*. You will often use these past-time verbs.

Guided Practice

Tell the past-time form of the verb in ( ).

1. The horses ___ past the wagon. (run)
2. Four explorers ___ to the river on foot. (go)
3. They ___ to a mountain. (come)

Practice

A. Write *past* or *present* for each underlined verb.

    4. Big rivers <u>run</u> through the land.
    5. The Ohio River <u>goes</u> west to the Mississippi River.
    6. French explorers <u>came</u> to the Mississippi River.
    7. Then other settlers <u>did</u> the same thing.
    8. This map <u>has</u> the Missouri River outlined in red.

B. Choose the past-time form of the verb from the words in ( ). Write each complete sentence.

    9. The explorers ____ a good day for traveling. (have, had)
    10. The Appalachians ____ from north to south. (run, ran)
    11. Travelers ____ through a mountain pass. (go, went)
    12. Some people ____ by the Susquehanna River. (came, come)
    13. They ____ it on their own. (do, did)

C. Use the past-time form of the verb to take the place of each verb in ( ). Write the new paragraph.

    They (**14.** go) across the mountains. Then they (**15.** have) rivers and plains ahead of them. They (**16.** come) to the Mississippi. It (**17.** run) fast. The river was difficult to cross, but the explorers (**18.** do) it.

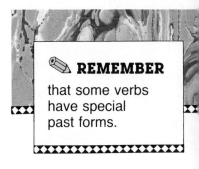

Apply • **Think and Write**

From Your Writing ♦ Write the action verbs you used in the Writer's Warm-up. Did you use any forms of *come, do, go, have,* or *run*?

273

Pretend you and your friend are explorers. Tell about yourselves. Use *am*, *is*, *are*, *was*, or *were* in your sentences.

EXAMPLES: *I am a camper. We are in a tent.*

2 The Verb *be*

Read the sentences. Notice the underlined verbs.

> Settlers moved to the wilderness.
> They lived in log cabins.

Verbs such as *moved* and *lived* show action. They tell what someone or something does or did.

Some verbs do not show action. Notice the underlined verbs in the sentences below.

> The horses were tired.   There are two boats ahead.
> One horse is sick.   I am in the last boat.
> A boat was in the river.

The verbs *am*, *is*, *are*, *was*, and *were* show being instead of action. These verbs tell what someone or something is or was.

> **Summary** ♦ A verb may show being. Use *am*, *is*, *are*, *was*, and *were* to tell what someone or something is or was.

Guided Practice

Name the verb that shows being in each sentence.

1. Explorers were brave.   **4.** The plains are broad.
2. Mountains are high.   **5.** The journey was hard.
3. The river is swift.   **6.** I am an explorer.

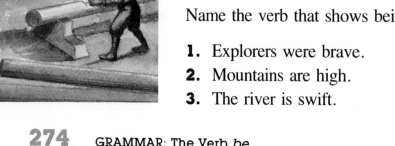

Practice

A. Write the verb that shows being in each sentence.

7. The journey was difficult.
8. Surveyors were in the wilderness.
9. This is the land of mountains.
10. Hunters are often mapmakers.
11. I am interested in old maps of the frontier.
12. This map is from the 1700s.

B. Copy each sentence. Draw one line under the verb if it shows being. Draw two lines under the verb if it shows action.

13. The Mississippi River borders several states.
14. The Arkansas River flows into the Mississippi.
15. Both of the rivers are long.
16. One river was muddy after the storm.
17. Some explorers wrote about their trips.
18. His story is in that journal.
19. I read part of the book.
20. Their adventures were interesting.

Apply ◆ Think and Write

Finding a New Place ◆ Write sentences about exploring a new place. The new place could be in your neighborhood or somewhere far away. Use the verbs *is*, *am*, *are*, *was*, and *were*.

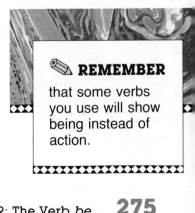

✎ **REMEMBER**
that some verbs you use will show being instead of action.

3 Using the Forms of *be*

The verbs *am*, *is*, *are*, *was*, and *were* are forms of the verb *be*. *Am*, *is*, and *are* tell about the present. *Was* and *were* tell about the past. When a form of *be* and the subject of the sentence are used together correctly, we say that they agree.

Using the Forms of *be*		
Subject	**Verb**	**Example**
I	am, was	I am an explorer. I was in the South.
singular nouns and *she*, *he*, *it*	is, was	A compass is useful. It was silver.
plural nouns and *we*, *you*, *they*	are, were	Canoes are light. They were in the water.

Summary ♦ The form of *be* that is used must agree with the subject of the sentence.

Guided Practice

Choose the correct form of the verb *be* in ( ).

1. De Soto (was, were) brave and courageous.
2. His men (was, were) strong.
3. They (am, are) famous for their explorations.

Practice

A. Write the correct form of the verb *be* in ( ).

   4. Florida (is, are) part of the United States.
   5. Many people (are, is) in the state of Florida.
   6. He (is, are) in the city of Orlando.
   7. The tourists (was, were) on the coast.
   8. I (was, were) on the eastern coast last year.
   9. I (am, is) in California this year.

B. Write each sentence. If the verb shows being in the present time, write *present*. If the verb shows being in the past time, write *past*.

   10. This is a map of De Soto's travels.
   11. His home was in Spain.
   12. De Soto's travels were in the Americas.
   13. We are in North America.
   14. I am in the United States of America.

C. Complete each sentence. Use *am, is,* or *are*.

   15. The explorers ____ in North Carolina.
   16. I ____ in Oklahoma today.
   17. The Mississippi River ____ a major waterway.
   18. I ____ eager to see the river.
   19. It ____ one of our longest rivers.

The Granger Collection

Apply ◆ **Think and Write**

Describing Your State ◆ Write sentences describing your state. Use the verbs *am, is, are, was,* and *were* in your writing.

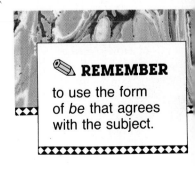

✎ **REMEMBER**
to use the form of *be* that agrees with the subject.

◆ GETTING ◆
STARTED

Pretend your family is moving. Tell what treasured belongings you and other family members have packed.
EXAMPLES: *I have packed my favorite books.*
Mom has packed her silver bracelet.

4 Main Verbs and Helping Verbs

A verb can be more than one word.

■ Many women **have explored** the wilderness.

The word *explored* is the main verb. The **main verb** is the most important verb in the sentence. The word *have* is a helping verb. A **helping verb** works with the main verb.

The verbs *have*, *has*, and *had* are often used as helping verbs. They help a main verb show action in the past time. When the helping verb is *have*, *has*, or *had*, the main verb often ends in *-ed*.

Read the sentence below. Which helping verb is used?

■ **The family has lived in a log cabin.**

> **Summary** ◆ A **helping verb** works with the main verb. A helping verb helps show action in the past time.

Guided Practice

Tell if a helping verb or a main verb is underlined.

1. The travelers have packed the wagons.
2. The men had washed the canvas.
3. The women had collected wood.
4. They have loaded the barrels of food.

Practice

A. Write the helping verb and the main verb in each sentence.

    5. Rebecca Woodson had moved to California.
    6. Her father has collected many farm tools.
    7. An older traveler has reported danger.
    8. Rebecca had expected some hard times.
    9. Many travelers have settled in the West.

B. Use the correct form of the verb in ( ). Write each sentence.

    10. They have ＿＿ in a wagon train. (travel)
    11. The children had ＿＿ wild gooseberries. (pick)
    12. Lodisa has ＿＿ a pie on hot stones. (bake)
    13. She had ＿＿ wolves nearby. (watch)
    14. Lodisa has ＿＿ the children. (protect)

C. Complete each sentence. Use *has* after a singular noun. Use *have* after a plural noun.

    15. The men and women ＿＿ talked about the journey.
    16. The oxen ＿＿ traveled through the woods.
    17. Caroline ＿＿ recalled pretty scenes.
    18. She ＿＿ reported about the animals.
    19. The travelers ＿＿ noticed many new things.

Apply • Think and Write

A Modern Trip ♦ Write sentences telling how you and your family prepared for a trip. Use the helping verbs *have*, *has*, or *had* in your sentences.

✏️ **REMEMBER**
that *have*, *has*, or *had* can help the main verb show past time.

♦ GETTING STARTED ♦

Make up rhymes about places you have visited and what you did, ate, or saw when you got there.

EXAMPLE: *I went to New York and ate roast pork.*

5 Using Irregular Verbs

You know that many verbs that show past time end in *-ed*. **Irregular verbs** do not add *-ed* to show action in the past. Verbs such as *do*, *go*, *eat*, *give*, and *see* change completely to show action in the past. They change again when they are used with *have*, *has*, or *had*.

Verb	Past	Past with *have*, *has*, or *had*
do	did	done
go	went	gone
eat	ate	eaten
give	gave	given
see	saw	seen

Tell which form of *see* is used with a helping verb below.

■ **Francisco Coronado had seen the Grand Canyon.**

> **Summary ♦** Some verbs change their form to show past time.

Guided Practice

Tell the correct past-time form of the verb in ( ).

1. Mexico (give) Coronado horses.
2. A guide had (go) to a Zuni village.
3. Coronado (see) the plains.

Practice

A. Write the correct past-time form of the verb in ( ).

   4. Coronado (see) herds of bison in Texas.
   5. He had (give) a description of them.
   6. The explorers (eat) bison meat.
   7. The Indians (do), too.
   8. They had (eat) meat before.

B. Choose the correct past-time verb in ( ). Write each sentence.

   9. Coronado's soldiers had (went, gone) over land.
   10. He had (gave, given) them directions.
   11. The soldiers (saw, seen) no gold.
   12. They had (saw, seen) the Zuni Indian villages.
   13. Later they (went, gone) to Kansas.

C. Change the underlined verb to the form shown in ( ). Write each sentence.

   14. In Kansas they do some trading. (past with *had*)
   15. The leaders give special directions. (past)
   16. The Indians eat with them. (past with *had*)
   17. They do many other things at the village. (past)
   18. They see new territory every day. (past)

Apply • Think and Write

Creating a Symbol ♦ Pretend that you have done a brave deed. Design a stamp in honor of yourself. Then write about your bravery. Try to use some of the past-time forms of the verbs from this lesson.

✏️ **REMEMBER**
to use the correct past forms of irregular verbs.

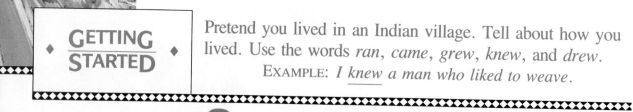

GETTING
STARTED

Pretend you lived in an Indian village. Tell about how you lived. Use the words *ran*, *came*, *grew*, *knew*, and *drew*.
EXAMPLE: *I knew a man who liked to weave.*

6 Using Irregular Verbs

You know that irregular verbs do not add *-ed* to show action in the past. Study the irregular verbs in the chart.

Verb	Past	Past with *have*, *has*, or *had*
run	ran	run
come	came	come
grow	grew	grown
know	knew	known
draw	drew	drawn

Read the sentences below. Which form of *know* is used without a helping verb?

> Meriwether Lewis <u>had come</u> from Ivy, Virginia.
> William Clark <u>knew</u> about the frontier.
> The men <u>had drawn</u> pictures of canoes.

Summary ♦ Irregular verbs have special past forms.

UNTITLED
engraving by F.C. Yohn
Historical Pictures Service, Chicago

Guided Practice

Tell the correct past-time form of the verb in ( ).

1. Lewis had (know) President Jefferson.
2. Lewis had (come) from Virginia.
3. The explorers (draw) sketches of the villages.

Practice

A. Write the past-time verb in each sentence. Some verbs have helping verbs. Write the helping verb, also.

4. The explorers had known about the Missouri River.
5. It ran through the territory.
6. The bear had grown six inches taller.
7. Clark drew pictures of the wildlife.
8. Lewis and Clark came to a Shoshone Indian village.

B. Use one of the past-time verbs below for each sentence. Write the sentences.

ran   knew   drawn   come   grew

9. Lewis ____ about the Shoshone Indians.
10. They had ____ through the Rocky Mountains.
11. Clark had ____ pictures in his journal.
12. Sacagawea ____ through the storm.
13. Wild berries ____ in the wilderness.

C. Write each sentence. Use the correct past-time form of the verb in ( ).

14. Lewis and Clark ____ to the frontier. (come)
15. The men had ____ each other before the trip. (know)
16. Sacagawea had ____ from the village. (run)
17. Clark ____ a map for the trip ahead. (draw)
18. Most of the trees had ____ tall. (grow)

UNTITLED
painting by Alfred Russell
The Bettmann Archive

Apply • Think and Write

Dictionary of Knowledge ♦ Read about the Shoshone Indians. Write about the daily lives of the people. Use past-time forms of *run* and *grow* in your sentences.

✎ **REMEMBER**

that some verbs change their form to show past time.

You and your family have settled on the frontier. What will you do for food and shelter? Start your sentences with *I'm*, *he's*, *she's*, *we're*, *I've*, or *we'll*.

7 Contractions

Look at the underlined words in these sentences.

■ **I have been reading.**   **I've learned about pioneers.**

The contraction *I've* is a shorter way to say *I have*. In a contraction an apostrophe (') shows where a letter or letters have been left out.

Pronoun + Verb = Contraction			
I + am = I'm	I + have = I've
he + is = he's	you + have = you've
she + is = she's	I + will = I'll
it + is = it's	you + will = you'll
they + are = they're	we + will = we'll
we + are = we're	

Summary ♦ A **contraction** is a shortened form of two words. Some contractions are formed from a pronoun and a verb.

Guided Practice

Name and spell contractions for the underlined words.

1. I will tell you about Robert Pulliam.
2. He is an early settler of Illinois.
3. It is eleven years after Lewis and Clark's expedition.

Practice

A. Write the contraction from each sentence.
Then write the two words that make up the contraction.

> **EXAMPLE:** We'll settle on the prairie.
> **ANSWER:** we'll, we will

4. I think you've heard of the Kickapoo Indians.
5. Pulliam said he's settling near their village.
6. They're collecting maple syrup today.
7. We're not surprised by Sugar Creek's name.
8. In the afternoon I'll make soap in a big tub.

B. Write each sentence. Use a contraction in place of the underlined words in each sentence.

9. It is a hard life for the Pulliams.
10. She is busy finding nuts and berries.
11. Today I have decided to go hunting.
12. We are hunting animals for fur.
13. We will trade the fur for tools.

C. Write a contraction for each of these word pairs.
Then use each contraction in a sentence.

14. I am	**17.** she is
15. they are	**18.** you have
16. you will	**19.** we will

Apply • Think and Write

Timed Writing ♦ Use these contractions to write as many
sentences as you can within ten minutes.

I'm   he's   she's   it's   we're   I'll   we'll

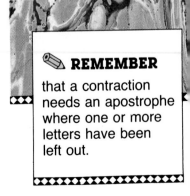

✎ **REMEMBER**
that a contraction
needs an apostrophe
where one or more
letters have been
left out.

Complete this rhyme.
If someone who reads is a reader,
And someone who leads is a leader,
Is someone who kneads bread a ____?

VOCABULARY ♦
Suffixes

Remember that a prefix is a letter or letters added to the beginning of a word: *un + wrap = unwrap*. Letters can also be added to the end of a word. A letter or letters added to the end of a word is a **suffix**. Look at the pairs of words below.

paint	act	own
painter	actor	owner

The second word in each pair ends with a suffix. The suffixes *-er* and *-or* may mean "someone who." A *painter* is someone who paints. An *actor* is someone who acts. What is an *owner*?

Each underlined word below ends with the suffix *-er*. What does each word mean?

Lewis and Clark were two famous explorers.
They were leaders of a trip up the Missouri River.

Building Your Vocabulary

Each word below has a suffix. Tell what the words mean and use them in sentences.

1. flyer
2. collector
3. visitor
4. player
5. dreamer
6. farmer

Practice

A. Read each meaning. Then write a word that fits the meaning and ends with the suffix *-er*.

-or

1. someone who cleans
2. someone who prints
3. someone who trains
4. someone who sings
5. someone who reports

6. someone who builds
7. someone who banks
8. someone who kicks
9. someone who walks
10. someone who travels

B. The pictures at the right show people at their jobs. Write the words that tell what they do. Use the suffixes to help you.

-er

C. Someone who skis is a *skier*. Write the words used to name people who do the things below.

11. boxes
13. hunts
15. sprints
12. climbs
14. speaks
16. jumps

-er

Language Corner ♦ Rare Words

Can you figure out what is unusual about the spelling of the words below?

aardvark   eel   llama

These words are even more unusual. Why?

raccoon   balloon   coffee

The underlined word below names a worker. It is <u>very</u> unusual. Why?

A <u>bookkeeper</u> takes care of business accounts.

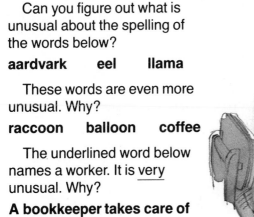

How to Revise Sentences with Verbs

You have been using verbs in the present time and in the past time. It is important to keep verbs in the same time when you write. Do you know why? The following paragraph will give you the answer.

Pam's grandparents lived on a farm. During summer vacation Pam helps with chores. She carried water from the well. She milks the cow. She worked hard and plays hard, too.

Some of the verbs tell about the past time, and some tell about the present time. Mixing times makes the paragraph hard to read and understand. Does it sound better this way?

Pam's grandparents lived on a farm. During summer vacation Pam helped with chores. She carried water from the well. She milked the cow. She worked hard and played hard, too.

The Grammar Game ♦ The time machine blew a fuse! Verbs from "then" and "now" are mixed up. Write a list of all the present-time verbs. Then write another list of all the past-time verbs.

danced	follows	write	went	hope
studies	looked	steal	grinned	was
burns	gave	sleeps	ran	try
saw	stare	borrowed	cries	grew

Working Together

Work with your group on activities **A** and **B**. Notice how keeping verbs in the same time makes writing easier to understand.

A. Change the time of the underlined verbs in the second sentences. Make these verbs tell about the same time as the first sentences.

1. We visited a museum. We <u>watch</u> a film.
2. People traveled by boat. The trip <u>is</u> long.
3. The boat finally arrived. Everyone <u>cheers</u>.
4. Friends waved hello. Relatives <u>hug</u>.
5. The travelers shared stories. Others <u>listen</u>.

B. Complete the paragraph with present-time verbs. Then write it again, using the same verbs in the past time.

Our class ___ picnics. Everyone ___ food to share. Leon ___ tacos. Beth ___ lemonade. Todd ___ the table. We all ___ too much!

WRITERS' CORNER ◆ Choppy Sentences

Choppy writing uses too many short sentences.

CHOPPY: I ran. I ran fast. I didn't want to miss the bus.

IMPROVED: I ran fast because I didn't want to miss the bus.

Read what you wrote for the Writer's Warm-up. Did you use too many short sentences? Can you improve them?

GREEN RIVER WYOMING
painting by Thomas Moran
Courtesy The Gerald Peters Gallery, Santa Fe.

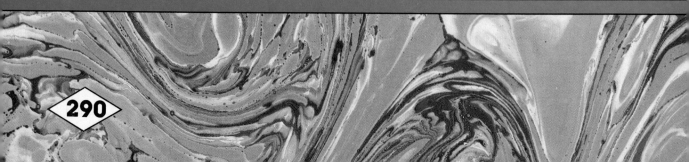

UNIT SIX

USING LANGUAGE TO

RESEARCH

=== **PART TWO** ===

Literature *Sacagawea* by Wyatt Blassingame

A Reason for Writing Researching

CREATIVE
Writing

FINE ARTS ◆ The painting at the left is called ''Green River Wyoming.'' What do you see in the painting? What interests you the most in the scene? What title would you have given the painting if you had done it? Write a new title for the painting. Make sure your new title tells what the painting means to you.

CRITICAL THINKING ♦
A Strategy for Researching

AN OBSERVATION CHART

Researching is gathering information. Sometimes a writer does research about a person's life. Then the writer may write a biography. A **biography** is a true story about a real person.

After this lesson you will read part of a biography. It is about Sacagawea, a Native American. Later you will write a short biography about someone.

Here is part of the biography of Sacagawea.

Sacagawea, with Little Pomp on her back, was in the largest boat. This was a big canoe with a sail, called the white pirogue. . . . Suddenly a great gust of wind hit the pirogue broadside. It made the boat lean far over. . . . Water began to pour into the boat.

The writer of *Sacagawea* did research. That means he observed, or studied, many details about Sacagawea. What details help you picture what happened in the pirogue?

Learning the Strategy

Observing details is often helpful. Suppose your pet gets lost. What details would you tell if you were writing an ad? Suppose you are making a map for a social studies project. On your map you plan to show interesting places in your community. What details must you know? How might you remember them?

An observation chart can help you remember details. Here is one you might make for your social studies map.

Silvertown	
Important Streets	Silver Street, Miner Road
Interesting Places	Coin Museum, old silver mine, Silvertown Park, old water mill

Using the Strategy

A. Think of a favorite item at home. It might be a game or something you like to wear. Make an observation chart about it. Write its name at the top. Write *Why I Like It* at the side. Then make up another heading for the side. It might be *Where It Came From* or *What I Do With It.* Write details for each heading.

B. Sacagawea travels in the wilderness. What do you think you would see, hear, or feel in the wilderness? Make an observation chart. At the top write *Wilderness.* At the side write *See, Hear,* and *Feel.* Record possible details. Then read Sacagawea's story. Did she see or hear what you recorded?

Applying the Strategy

♦ How does an observation chart help you notice details?
♦ When do you need to observe details at school?

LITERATURE

from
SACAGAWEA

by Wyatt Blassingame

About 200 years ago the land west of the Mississippi River was not yet part of the United States. In 1803, Captain Meriwether Lewis and Captain William Clark led a group of explorers to map the land. Pierre Cruzatte, part of the team, was a skilled boatman who spoke Indian languages. A family of three later joined the expedition. They were a Shoshone Indian woman named Sacagawea; her husband, Toussaint Charbonneau; and their baby son, Little Pomp.

Although Sacagawea was very young, she often helped the explorers find food or solve problems. She proved to be brave and strong. Here is a true story of Sacagawea's courage.

Boat Overturned!

It was early spring. High in the mountains the snow was just melting. The icy water flowed into the Missouri and flooded the great river. It made it difficult for the boats to fight their way upstream. But day after day the men kept on.

One day the wind blew harder than usual. There were big waves on the river. Sacagawea, with Little Pomp on her back, was in the largest boat. This was a big canoe with a sail, called the white pirogue. Charbonneau was steering. He could not swim and was afraid of the water. There were also two other men in the boat who could not swim. Cruzatte, a skilled boatman, was in the bow.

The boat held many valuable supplies, as Captain Lewis wrote later. *"Our papers, instruments, books, medicine, a great part of our merchandise, and in short almost every article . . . necessary to . . . insure the success of the enterprise."*

Suddenly a great gust of wind hit the pirogue broadside. It made the boat lean far over. Frightened, Charbonneau steered in the wrong direction. The pirogue rolled almost on its side. The passengers did not fall out, but water began to pour into the boat. Terrified,

Charbonneau began to jump crazily about. In another moment he would turn the boat over completely. Everyone and everything in it would be lost.

Both Lewis and Clark were on the riverbank at this time. They saw what was happening. They began to shout orders, but the boat was too far away for them to be heard. They thought about jumping into the river and swimming to help. But they knew the current was too strong. They would be swept downstream and drowned.

"If the boat goes all the way over," Clark muttered, "three men will drown. We will lose our most valuable supplies. We will have to turn back."

Then, to their amazement, they saw what was happening. In spite of the danger, Sacagawea was behaving with perfect calm. As the water poured into the boat, many of the supplies began to float. But before they could float away, the girl quickly gathered them up.

At the same time Cruzatte was ordering Charbonneau to be still. Then Cruzatte cut the sail away. With its weight gone, Cruzatte got the boat right side up. It was almost full of water, but the men managed to row it ashore. Sacagawea held the supplies safe in her arms.

Captain Clark began to laugh. "And we worried about bringing her," he said. "She certainly saved us this time."

Farther on they passed a river that flowed into the Missouri. They named it the Sacagawea in honor of her courage.

Library Link ♦ *If you want to learn more about Sacagawea and the Shoshones, read* Sacagawea *by Wyatt Blassingame.*

◆▷ Reader's Response

Do you think Sacagawea was brave? Why or why not?

SACAGAWEA

 ## Responding to Literature

1. What was your favorite part of the story? Tell what happened in that part.

2. If you had been in the boat with Sacagawea, how could you have helped?

3. Suppose you could go on a journey like this one. What supplies would you take? Make a list. Put a star beside the important items. Then compare lists with a classmate. What items are important on both lists?

Writing to Learn

Think and Record ♦ Lewis and Clark saw their white pirogue flood with water. Make an observation chart like this one. Record the details that they saw, heard, and felt.

The Pirogue Floods	
What I Saw	
What I Heard	
What I Felt	

Observation Chart

Write ♦ Imagine that you are Lewis or Clark. Write a page in your journal. Tell what you saw and how you felt.

GETTING STARTED

Play "In Other Words." One person tells about a travel experience. Another person repeats the information in his or her own words.

SPEAKING and LISTENING ◆
Remembering Information

In school you do a very important kind of listening. You listen to learn. Listening to learn takes effort. You need to understand and remember the information you hear. You need to be alert and pay attention. In other words, you need to be an <u>active</u> listener.

Here are some suggestions to help you listen for information. You can use them when you listen, both in and out of school.

Being an Active Listener	**1.** Get ready to listen. Sit up straight and look at the person who is speaking. **2.** Listen carefully. Think about what the person says. **3.** Listen for the main ideas. **4.** If you wish, jot down a word or two as you listen. Write words that help you remember the main ideas. This will help you understand what you heard. It will also help you remember the information. **5.** Sum up what the speaker says in your own words. If you cannot, you should ask questions about what was said.

Summary ◆ When you listen to learn information, pay attention. Then, in your own words, sum up what the speaker said.

Guided Practice

Listen as your teacher reads this paragraph. Then, in your own words, sum up what the paragraph says.

In spite of the danger, Sacagawea was behaving with perfect calm. As the water poured into the boat, many of the supplies began to float. But before they could float away, the girl quickly gathered them up.

Practice

A. Work with a partner. Take turns reading aloud the paragraphs below. You can read the first paragraph, and your partner can read the second paragraph. When you are the listener, sum up what you heard in your own words.

Sacagawea named her son Pomp. Pomp was a common name for a first son. The word meant "head" or "leader." Pomp also had a French name. Captain Clark playfully called Pomp "Pompey."

Sacagawea saw the tracks. She bent down to study them carefully. From the way the moccasins were made, she knew what tribe these Indians belonged to. "These are friendly Indians," she told Charbonneau, who told Captain Lewis.

B. Ask your partner some questions about Sacagawea.

Apply ♦ Think and Write

In Your Own Words ♦ What did you learn today in school? Write one thing you learned by listening.

✎ **Remember**
that listening carefully can help you understand and remember information.

GETTING STARTED

Play "Narrow That Topic." For example, name foods that begin with f, o, o, and d: *fig, onion, oyster, date*.

STUDY SKILLS ◆
Choosing a Topic

Suppose you want to write about a certain topic. It's a good idea to ask yourself some questions about your topic. Is the topic too big, or too broad? Are you sure it is small enough, or narrow enough, to manage?

Ben builds model boats. He wants to write about boats. Ben knows that *boats* is too broad a topic. He thinks the topic *wooden boats* is also too broad. Finally he decides to write about *houseboats*. That topic is narrow enough for Ben to do a good job.

> **Summary** ◆ Choose a topic that interests you. If the topic is too broad, you must narrow it down.

Guided Practice

Name the narrower topic in each pair.

1. weather, snow   **3.** biographies, books

2. sports, swimming   **4.** Rocky Mountains, Pikes Peak

Practice

A. Write *narrow* or *broad* for each topic below.

5. seasons
6. explorers
7. buffalo hides
8. kinds of houses
9. Bismarck, North Dakota
10. grasshoppers
11. Mississippi River
12. books

B. Write the narrowest topic from each group below.

13. famous people   Sacagawea   women
14. William Clark   explorers   heroes
15. shoes   clothing   moccasins
16. rivers   Missouri River   bodies of water
17. canoes   water transportation   boats
18. children   Pomp   babies
19. water   oceans   Pacific Ocean
20. land   Great Basin   desert

Apply • Think and Write

Narrow Topics ◆ Use what you learned in this lesson.
List a narrower topic for each broad topic below.

insects   cities   wild animals
fruits   workers   tame animals

✏️ **Remember**
to ask yourself
questions to help
narrow your topic.

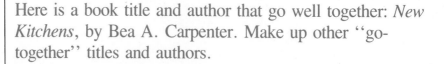

◆ GETTING ◆
STARTED

Here is a book title and author that go well together: *New Kitchens*, by Bea A. Carpenter. Make up other "go-together" titles and authors.

STUDY SKILLS ◆
Using the Library

Most libraries have special areas for children's books. Books of the same kind are grouped together. This makes them easier to find. The chart below describes some kinds of library books. Ask your librarian at school or at the public library where each kind is kept.

Fiction books

These are storybooks. The stories have been made up.

Nonfiction books

Nonfiction books give information about a subject. A **biography** is one kind of nonfiction book. Biographies tell true stories about the lives of real people.

Encyclopedias

An **encyclopedia** is a set of books that have information on many subjects. Entries in an encyclopedia are arranged in alphabetical order.

Other reference books

Reference books give information. Dictionaries and atlases are two kinds of reference books. A **dictionary** is a book of words. It gives their spellings and meanings. An **atlas** is a book of maps.

Summary ◆ A library has many kinds of books. Books of the same kind are grouped together.

Guided Practice

Identify each book below as fiction, nonfiction, or reference book.

1. a book about Sacagawea
2. a book of maps

3. a fairy tale
4. a mystery story

Practice

A. Read the book titles below. Write *fiction*, *nonfiction*, or *reference book* for each title.

5. *The Life of Geronimo*
6. *A Beginning Dictionary*
7. *Mystery at Red Rock*
8. *Explore the Grand Canyon*
9. *The Ugly Duckling*
10. *World Book Encyclopedia*

B. What kind of book would tell about each item below? Write *biography*, *atlas*, *dictionary*, or *encyclopedia*.

11. information about camels
12. the meaning of the word *trek*
13. maps of the fifty states
14. the full life story of Thomas Jefferson

Apply • Think and Write

A Reading Choice ♦ Look through some library books. Choose a fiction book, a nonfiction book, and a biography. Which book would you choose to read first? Tell why.

> ✎ **Remember**
> that a library has books of the same kind grouped together.

◆ GETTING ◆
STARTED

Think about something you did yesterday. In short groups of words, tell everything you remember about it. For example: *visited library, chose book, checked it out.*

WRITING ◆
Taking Notes in Your Own Words

Darla wanted information about Fort Mandan. That was where Sacagawea met Lewis and Clark. Darla read this paragraph in a book about explorers.

> The men used axes and handsaws. They cut down trees and trimmed off the branches. They built two rows of log cabins. Each cabin had one square room with no windows. Each had a stone fireplace for heat and cooking. Floors and ceilings were made of split logs. Mud filled the spaces between the logs.

Darla took notes about the information. She used her own words, and she wrote just enough to help her remember.

> Fort Mandan
> axes, saws—cut, trim trees
> log cabins—two rows
> one square room, no
>   windows
>
> fireplaces—for heat,
>   cooking
> split logs, ceiling,
>   floor
> mud between spaces

Summary ◆ To help you remember information you read, take notes in your own words.

Guided Practice

Read again the paragraph about Fort Mandan. Then close your book and think about what you read. Tell about the fort in your own words.

Practice

A. Read the paragraph. Then read the sentences and notes below it. Choose the better note for each sentence.

Everyone was busy inside the fort. Blacksmiths made small iron tools. These were traded with the Indians for food. Captain Clark was making maps. Some men prepared meat brought by hunters. Others made moccasins, shirts, or leggings from soft deerskins. Of course, someone always had to stand guard.

1. Everyone was busy inside the fort.
   busy fort   inside fort
2. Blacksmiths made small iron tools.
   small iron   blacksmiths made tools
3. These were traded with the Indians for food.
   tools traded for food   Indian foods used
4. Some men prepared meat brought by hunters.
   prepared meat   men hunted
5. Of course, someone always had to stand guard.
   someone stood   must always guard

B. Read the paragraph in **Practice A** again. Take notes in your own words.

Apply ◆ Think and Write

Dictionary of Knowledge ◆ Read about the desert named Great Basin. Take notes in your own words about why the desert is named Great Basin. Take notes about the location of the desert, too.

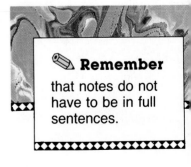

✎ **Remember**
that notes do not have to be in full sentences.

Focus on Facts

Sacagawea was a real person. She played an important role in American history. The story you read about her was part of a **biography.** A biography is the true story of a real person. It is built on facts.

When you write a biography, you must choose the facts that you use. You will find many facts about a famous person. There will probably be more facts than you need. Your choices are important. Here is an example showing some facts that the author of *Sacagawea* chose.

In spite of the danger, Sacagawea was behaving with perfect calm. As the water poured into the boat, many of the supplies began to float. But before they could float away, the girl quickly gathered them up.

The Writer's Voice ◆ In the example above, what reasons do you think the author used for choosing the facts given? Use the fact checklist below to help you answer this question. Which questions would you answer YES? Would you answer any of the questions NO?

♦ Is this fact important? Is it needed?
♦ Will this fact be interesting to readers?
♦ Does this fact show what the person was like?

Working Together

A biography uses facts to tell the story of a person's life. Work with your group on activities **A** and **B**.

A. Choose a well-known person to talk about. It could be someone from the past. It could be someone who is famous today. Make a list of things your group knows about this person. From the list, decide on three of the *most important* facts about the person.

B. As a group, go over your list from activity **A.** Do you have enough facts to write a short biography of this person? Make a list of questions about facts that you still need to find. List at least three questions even if you think you have enough facts already.

In Your Group

♦ Give your ideas to the group.
♦ Remind people to listen carefully.
♦ Agree or disagree in a nice way.
♦ List the group's ideas.

THESAURUS CORNER ♦ Word Choice

Find the entry for *trip* in the Thesaurus. Write the best synonym for *trip* in each of these sentences.

1. Sacagawea went with Lewis and Clark on their long **trip** to the west.
2. The **trip** down the Missouri River was dangerous.
3. Today a week in the Rockies can be a pleasant **trip.**

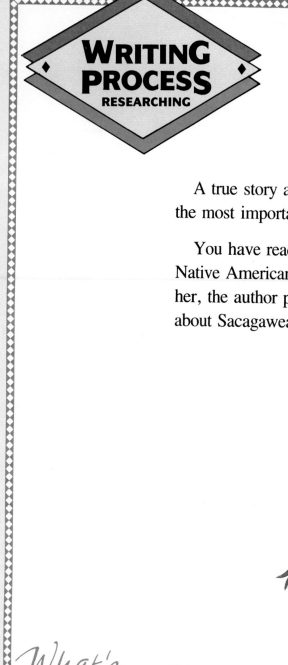

WRITING PROCESS
RESEARCHING

Writing About a Person

A true story about a real person is a biography. It tells the most important things about the person's life.

You have read a biography of Sacagawea. She was a Native American who lived long ago. Before writing about her, the author probably read about her. He found facts about Sacagawea. He used the facts to write a true story.

Know Your Purpose and Audience

MY PURPOSE

Now you will write a biography. Your purpose will be to write about a real person.

MY AUDIENCE

Your audience will be your classmates. Later you can read your biographies aloud. You and your classmates can also play a guessing game.

1 Prewriting

First choose a topic—a person to write about. Then find facts about that person.

Choose Your Topic ♦ Who would you like to write about? List the names of people you can find facts about. Then choose the one who interests you the most.

Think About It

Who will you choose? You might write about an American President. Think about an explorer or a dancer. Look for people in your social studies book. Then look at your list. What person can you picture clearly? That might be your choice.

Talk About It

Talk to your classmates about their choices. You might get an idea from a name you see on another person's list. You might also ask your librarian to help you find books about real people.

Topic Ideas

Real People to Write About
1. *Martin Luther King*
2. *Maria Tallchief*
3. *Christopher Columbus*
4. *Eleanor Roosevelt*
5. *Chief Crazy Horse*

Choose Your Strategy ♦ Here are two ways to gather facts. Read both. Try the way you like better.

PREWRITING IDEAS

CHOICE ONE

An Observation Chart

Make an observation chart. At the top, write the name of the person. At the side, write some questions about the person. Then read about the person. Look for answers to your questions. Write them in your observation chart.

Model

Maria Tallchief	
Where and when was she born?	*born in Oklahoma January 24, 1925*
Why is she famous?	*famous ballerina Native American*

CHOICE TWO

Note Cards

Read books about your person. Think about what you have learned. On cards, write notes in your own words. Then write the title and author of your book, or source.

Model

Topic   *Maria Tallchief Native American took dancing lessons became a famous ballerina*

Source   *Famous American Dancers by Juanita Lopez*

2 Writing

Put your observation chart or note cards in front of you. Then begin to write. Here are some ways to start.

♦ Maria Tallchief is a famous ballerina.
♦ Maria Tallchief was born on January 24, 1925.

Next write a paragraph about each main fact you found. End by telling how you feel about the person.

Sample First Draft ♦

Maria Tallchief was born on January 24, 1925, in Oklahoma. She is a Native american.

When she was little, she took lessons. She wanted to be a ballerina. She became a great and famous ballerina!

When she grew up, her dream comes true. She went to New York City to study ballay.

I like Maria Tallchief's story. It shows dreams can come true if you work hard.

3 Revising

Now you have written your biography. Would you like to make it better? Here is a way you can try.

REVISING IDEA

FIRST Read to Yourself

Think about your purpose. Did you write a biography? Think of your audience. Will your classmates enjoy it?

Focus: Have you told facts that your readers would like to know? Decide which fact *you* think is most interesting.

THEN Share with a Partner

Let a partner read your biography silently. Then talk about it. These guidelines may help.

The Writer

Guidelines: Ask your partner some questions. Then decide if you want to make any changes.

Sample questions:
- What did you like best?
- **Focus question:** What else would you like to know?

The Writer's Partner

Guidelines: Read carefully. Give your honest opinion.

Sample responses:
- I really like the part about ____.
- Can you tell more about ____?

WRITING PROCESS: Biography

Revising Model ♦ Here is a biography that is being revised. The marks show the writer's changes.

The writer added a fact about the lessons.

This fact was in the wrong order.

The writer's partner saw this verb in the wrong time.

Admire is a stronger word than *like*.

> Maria Tallchief was born on
>
> January 24, 1925, in Oklahoma. She
>
> is a Native american.
>
>   *dancing*
>
> When she was little, she took lessons.
>
> She wanted to be a ballerina. ~~She~~
>
> ~~became a great and famous ballerina!~~
>
> When she grew up, her dream
>
> *came*
>
> ~~comes~~ true. She went to New York
>
> City to study ballay.
>
>   *admire*
>
> I like Maria Tallchief's story. It shows
>
> dreams can come true if you work hard.

Read the biography above. Then revise your biography.

Grammar Check ♦ Keep all your verbs in the same time.

Word Choice ♦ A word such as *like* may be too weak. A thesaurus can help you find stronger words.

Revising Checklist

☐ **My purpose:** Did I write a biography about a real person?

☐ **My audience:** Will my class-mates enjoy it?

☐ **Focus:** Did I tell facts readers would like to know?

4 Proofreading

Before sharing your writing, check and fix mistakes.

Proofreading Model ♦ Here is the biography about Maria Tallchief. Red proofreading marks have been added.

Proofreading Marks

check spelling ⬭

capital letter =

indent paragraph ¶

¶ Maria Tallchief was born on January 24, 1925, in Oklahoma. She is a Native american.

When she was little, she took ^dancing^ lessons.

She wanted to be a ballerina. She became a great and famous ballerina!

When she grew up, her dream ~~comes~~ came true. She went to New York City to study ~~ballay~~ ballet.

^admire^ I like Maria Tallchief's story. It shows dreams can come true if you work hard.

Proofreading Checklist

☐ Did I spell words correctly?

☐ Did I indent paragraphs?

☐ Did I use capital letters correctly?

☐ Did I use correct marks at the end of sentences?

☐ Did I use my best handwriting?

PROOFREADING IDEA

Spelling Check

Cut a small window in a piece of paper. Move the window over your work to check one word at a time.

Now proofread your biography and add a title. Then make a neat copy.

5 Publishing

On a sheet of paper, write "Books I Read." List the books you read in alphabetical order. Add the list to your biography. Here are two ways to share your biography.

A Famous Ballerina

Maria Tallchief was born on January 24, 1925, in Oklahoma. She is a Native American.

When she was little, she took dancing lessons. She wanted to be a ballerina.

When she grew up, her dream came true. She went to New York City to study ballet.

I admire Maria Tallchief's story. It shows dreams can come true if you work hard. She became a great and famous ballerina!

PUBLISHING IDEAS

Share Aloud

Read your biography aloud. Ask your audience to listen for facts. At the end, ask classmates to name facts they heard.

Share in Writing

Make a cover for your biography. On it, write questions that your biography answers. Put all the biographies on a bulletin board. Try to answer the questions. Then read the biographies to find out the answers.

CURRICULUM ◆CONNECTION◆

Writing Across the Curriculum Social Studies

Recently you wrote a biography of a real person. An observation chart can help you record details about a person. People who study history often record details about historical figures. You can make an observation chart to discover what our first president was like.

Writing to Learn

Think and Observe ◆ George Washington was the first President of the United States. Look at this picture of him.

He is taking the oath of office. Pretend you can step into the picture. Make an observation chart. Write what you see, hear, and feel.

FIRST IN WAR, FIRST IN PEACE, AND FIRST IN THE HEARTS OF HIS COUNTRYMEN
Painting, Anonymous
Courtesy of the New York Historical Society, New York

Topic

Observation Chart

Write ◆ Use the information in your chart. Write about George Washington and the day he became President.

Writing in Your Journal

In the Writer's Warm-up you wrote about what it must have been like to explore a wilderness. Throughout this unit you learned about explorers. You read about some of the hardships of frontier life. In your journal write about the most interesting things you learned in this unit.

BOOKS TO ENJOY

Read More About It

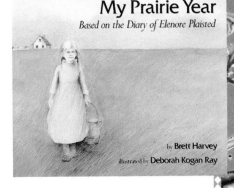

My Prairie Year *by Brett Harvey*
In 1889, a young girl named Elenore Plaisted
began a long trip with her family. They left
Maine to travel west. Elenore kept a diary.
The author is Elenore's granddaughter. She
used parts of the diary to write this book.

Children of the Wild West

by Russell Freedman
Photographers used to travel the wilderness,
too. They took pictures of pioneers, settlers,
and Indians. The author has used old photos
from the 1800s to show what it was like for
children in the rugged old days.

Book Report Idea Character Journal

Give a book report as though
you are a favorite character.

**Write a Character's
Journal** ◆ Pretend you are a
character in the book you
have read. Write a page of a
journal this character might
have kept. Tell about a
favorite part of the story.

UNIT REVIEW

Unit 6

Verbs   *pages 272–283*

A. Write each sentence. Use the correct form of the verb in ( ).

1. The last game (is, are) tonight.
2. Ted (went, gone) early for a good seat.
3. He (known, knew) it would be crowded.
4. The home team (was, were) winning.
5. Rick (ate, eaten) three hot dogs.
6. Dad (done, did), too.
7. One ball (came, come) right over us.
8. We (was, were) too surprised to catch it.

B. Write each sentence. Draw one line under the helping verb. Draw two lines under the main verb.

9. We have seen every home game.
10. Our team has played well.
11. They had hired a new coach.
12. The coach has helped the team members.
13. Their batting averages have improved.
14. The fans had hoped for more wins.

Contractions   *pages 284–285*

C. Write the contraction for each pair of words.

15. I am
16. you have
17. we will
18. he is
19. they are
20. you will

Suffixes *pages 286–287*

D. Write a word that has the suffix *-er* for each meaning.

21. someone who sings
22. someone who plays
23. someone who shouts
24. someone who follows
25. someone who walks
26. someone who reads
27. someone who builds
28. someone who trains

Narrowing a Topic *pages 300–301*

E. Write the narrowest topic from each group of topics.

29. people, cavemen, living things
30. hibernating animals, animals, brown bears
31. painters, Picasso, artists
32. western states, states, Oregon
33. dragonflies, insects, flying insects
34. my home, buildings, houses
35. pets, Max, animals
36. books, school books, dictionary

Library *pages 302–303*

F. Write *fiction, nonfiction,* or *reference book* for each title.

37. *Betsy Ross*
38. *A History of America*
39. *Nature Encyclopedia*
40. *The Mystery of Sam Hill*
41. *How to Build a Bike*
42. *Ben Franklin*
43. *The Elf's Party*
44. *The Woodland Indians*
45. *Dictionary of Slang*
46. *Elephant Jokes*
47. *George Washington*
48. *The Johnstown Flood*
49. *The Magical Machine*
50. *The World Atlas*
51. *Book of Knot Tying*
52. *The Life of Walt Disney*

Sentences   *pages 12–17*

A. Write each sentence. Draw one line under the subject. Draw two lines under the predicate.

    1. Owls are quiet.　**3.** Their eyes are big.

    2. They eat mice.　　**4.** They hunt at night.

Nouns   *pages 62–71, 116–117*

B. Write the plural form of each noun.

    5. owl　　**7.** feather　　**9.** patch　　**11.** berry

    6. beak　　**8.** city　　　**10.** branch　　**12.** wish

C. Write the possessive form of each noun.

    13. Gary　　**14.** eye　　**15.** birds　　**16.** children

D. Write *common* or *proper* for each noun.

    17. house　　**19.** claws　　**21.** London　　**23.** Maine

    18. April　　**20.** Tanya　　**22.** light　　**24.** rock

Capital Letters and Commas
pages 118–123, 190–191

E. Write each sentence. Use capital letters and commas correctly.

    25. Neil can you go to new york with us in june?

    26. Yes if I leave montana after memorial day.

    27. The bridge over the charles river was damaged in may.

    28. No valentine's day is on friday this year.

Pronouns   *pages 164–173*

F. Change the underlined word or words in each sentence to a pronoun. Write each new sentence.

29. <u>Ted and John</u> gave me a new camera.
30. I took some pictures of <u>Susan's</u> nephew.
31. <u>Tom</u> has made two statues.
32. One statue is in front of <u>Ted and Nancy's</u> house.
33. Tom gave it to <u>Ted and Nancy</u>.
34. <u>Tom's</u> other statue is in the park.

Verbs   *pages 218–229, 272–273, 278–283*

G. Write the correct present-time form of the verb in ( ). Then write the correct past-time form.

35. Tigger ＿＿ to have his ears tickled. (like)
36. He ＿＿ to get my attention. (meow)
37. Then he ＿＿ on my desk. (jump)
38. Tigger and Tish ＿＿ to sit on my lap. (try)
39. I ＿＿ to work all morning. (plan)
40. Tigger and Tish ＿＿ I would play. (wish)

H. Write each sentence. Draw one line under the helping verb. Draw two lines under the main verb.

41. Julian has eaten.   **43.** We have made salad.
42. He had cooked soup.   **44.** Marty has baked bread.

Contractions   *pages 284–285*

I. Write the contraction for each pair of words.

45. she will   **47.** you are   **49.** they are   **51.** we will
46. he is   **48.** we have   **50.** it is   **52.** you have

Hidden Verbs

Find the seven present-time forms of verbs in the puzzle. Write the past-time form for each.

b	i	s	h	a	s
d	g	o	a	r	e
g	d	r	u	n	z
c	o	m	e	x	b

Verb Gymnastics

The answer to each of the following is a past form of an irregular verb.

1. Write the name for a walking stick. Change the *n* to *m*.
2. Write the name for something you play. Change the *m* to *v*.
3. Write the name for something dogs like to eat. Change the *b* to *d*.
4. Write the name for a grown-up boy. Change the *m* to *r*.
5. Write a word that means "not old and not used." Add a *k*.
6. Write the name for a cat's foot. Change the *p* to *s*.
7. Write the name for a long dress. Add an *r* between the *g* and the *o*.
8. Write the word that means "not on time and not early." Drop the *l*.

Unit 6 Extra Practice

1 Verbs with Special Past Forms *p. 272*

A. Write each sentence. If the underlined verb is in the past time, write *past*. If the underlined verb is in the present time, write *present*.

1. Many people <u>go</u> to the Boston Marathon.
2. They <u>run</u> for hours.
3. We <u>came</u> to watch.
4. Our town <u>has</u> a mini-marathon.
5. Runners <u>go</u> from the high school to the park.
6. They <u>do</u> it to raise money for the hospital.
7. Last year everyone <u>ran</u> thirteen miles.
8. People <u>came</u> from many different places.

B. Write each sentence. Use the form of the verb in ( ) that tells about the past time.

9. The name for a long race ____ from Greece. (come)
10. A messenger ____ from a place called Marathon to Athens. (go)
11. He ____ it over two thousand years ago. (do)
12. He ____ with news of a Greek victory. (come)
13. The runner ____ about twenty-five miles. (run)
14. Early Olympic Games ____ marathon races. (have)
15. Those runners also ____ twenty-five miles. (run)
16. Beginning in 1908 the runners ____ more than twenty-six miles. (go)
17. Boston ____ its first marathon in 1897. (have)
18. A woman ____ for the first time in 1967. (run)

2 The Verb *be*

p. 274

A. Write the verb that shows being in each sentence.

1. March days are windy.
2. Yesterday was cloudy.
3. The clouds were puffy.
4. Spring days are here.
5. I was in the house.
6. Winter was dreary.
7. Today is sunny.
8. I am glad.

B. Write the sentence. Underline the verb that shows being in each sentence.

9. Kites were my friend Paco's favorite toys.
10. Last week his book report was about kites.
11. The book's author is Wyatt Brummit.
12. Kites are very popular.
13. I am a kite builder, too.

C. Copy each sentence. Draw one line under the verb if it shows being. Draw two lines under the verb if it shows action.

14. Early kites were very large leaves.
15. The string was a piece of vine.
16. Most kites are just for fun.
17. Some scientists use kites in their work.
18. Weather kites gather important information.
19. They show wind and air pressure.
20. Once a kite was in the air for seven days.
21. A very large kite weighed over nine tons.
22. Once over a thousand kites were on one line!
23. I am happy with one kite on a windy day.
24. My brother flies trick kites.
25. Two kites at once are plenty for him!

3 Using the Forms of *be*

p. 276

A. Write the correct form of the verb *be* in ( ).

1. I (am, is) interested in dolphins.
2. A dolphin (are, is) a small sea mammal.
3. Two dolphins (am, are) in our city zoo.
4. They (was, were) in a show at the zoo.
5. I (was, were) at the show last week.
6. The movie (was, were) about sea animals.
7. Dolphins (was, were) in the Pacific Ocean.
8. The water (am, is) warm in parts of the ocean.
9. A dolphin's nose (is, are) pointed.
10. Porpoises (are, is) smaller than dolphins.

B. Write each sentence. Use *am*, *is*, or *are*.

11. A dolphin ____ about six feet long.
12. I ____ smaller than a dolphin.
13. Dolphins and whales ____ mammals.
14. A dolphin's teeth ____ cone-shaped.
15. *Porpoise* ____ another name for dolphin.
16. Dolphins ____ friendly mammals.
17. They ____ helpful to people.

C. Write each sentence. If the verb shows being in the present time, write *present*. If the verb shows being in the past time, write *past*.

18. I am curious about sea animals.
19. My library book was about dolphins.
20. A school is a group of dolphins.
21. Dolphins are very intelligent.
22. They were always in schools!

4 Main Verbs and Helping Verbs

p. 278

A. Write *helping verb* or *main verb* for the underlined verb.

1. Trains have <u>carried</u> people and things.
2. Milk has <u>remained</u> cold in a refrigerator car.
3. Flatcars <u>have</u> delivered automobiles.
4. Early trains <u>had</u> used coal for power.
5. Workers had <u>shoveled</u> tons of coal.
6. Trains <u>have</u> changed in many ways.

B. Write the helping verb and the main verb in each sentence.

7. The museum has opened a display of trains.
8. Lono and I have returned several times.
9. He has wanted a book about old trains.
10. I had walked through the display before.
11. I have climbed on the engine car three times.
12. Lono has collected model trains for years.
13. His aunt had started the collection.
14. They have added pieces every year.
15. Lono has joined a model train club.
16. Many people have enjoyed this hobby.

C. Write each sentence. Use the correct form of the verb in ( ).

17. One kind of train has ____ underground. (travel)
18. America's first subway had ____ in 1897. (open)
19. Electricity has ____ subways since 1890. (power)
20. Many cities have ____ subway systems. (start)
21. One city has ____ its system the Metro. (call)

5 Using Irregular Verbs *p. 280*

A. Write the correct past-time form of the verb in ( ).

1. I have (go) home.
2. We (see) a play.
3. He had (do) the job.
4. They had (give) up.
5. She (eat) already.
6. You (do) it.

B. Write the correct past-time form of the verb in ( ).

7. Folks had ____ John Chapman plant seeds. (see)
8. He had ____ west around 1800. (go)
9. Johnny Appleseed ____ apple seeds to many people. (give)
10. They ____ him the name Johnny Appleseed. (give)
11. This pioneer ____ his work without pay. (do)
12. People have ____ apples from his trees. (eat)

C. Change the underlined verb to the form shown in ( ). Write each sentence.

EXAMPLE: I <u>see</u> many apple trees. (past with *have*)
ANSWER: I have seen many apple trees.

13. We <u>eat</u> homemade applesauce. (past)
14. I <u>do</u> all the peeling! (past)
15. Lena <u>goes</u> to the store for dried apples. (past)
16. She also <u>sees</u> apple pies for sale. (past)
17. You <u>eat</u> apple butter on toast. (past with *have*)
18. Sheila <u>gives</u> me apple juice. (past with *has*)
19. Rita <u>sees</u> another kind of apple. (past with *has*)
20. She <u>goes</u> to the Big Apple once. (past with *has*)
21. The people of New York <u>give</u> that nickname to their city. (past)

6 Using Irregular Verbs

p. 282

A. Write the correct past-time form of the verb in ( ).

1. I (run) to the barn.
2. I (know) the animals.
3. I (come) every day.
4. The pony had (grow).
5. It (come) to me.
6. I (draw) its picture.

B. Choose the correct past-time form of the verb in ( ). Write each sentence.

7. We (come, came) to my cousin's farm.
8. First I (run, ran) to the pond.
9. The ducklings (knew, known) how to swim.
10. The fawn has (grow, grown) quickly.
11. The colt (run, ran) fast.
12. The chicks have (come, came) over.
13. Sean had (drew, drawn) a funny picture of Billy.
14. In a picture Billy the goat had (grew, grown) a long white beard.

C. Write each sentence. Use the correct past-time form of the verb in ( ).

15. I have ____ often to the children's zoo. (come)
16. The zookeeper has ____ me for months. (know)
17. The fawn's wobbly legs have ____ . (grow)
18. It ____ away from me. (run)
19. An artist ____ to watch the animals. (come)
20. She ____ pictures of the spotted fawn. (draw)
21. Last time she had ____ the monkeys. (draw)
22. One shy monkey had ____ to its mother. (run)
23. Then it ____ to the artist. (come)
24. The monkey ____ the artist then. (know)

7 Contractions

p. 284

A. Write contractions for the underlined words.

1. <u>She is</u> hungry.
2. Now <u>they are</u> late.
3. I know <u>it is</u> ready.
4. <u>We will</u> help you.
5. <u>I will</u> wait for you.
6. <u>You have</u> done it now.

B. Write the contraction from each sentence. Then write the two words that make up the contraction.

EXAMPLE: **We're learning how to cook.**
ANSWER: **we're, we are**

7. Today we're having tacos for lunch.
8. First we'll buy beef, cheese, and lettuce.
9. I've never tasted tortillas before.
10. I think you've seen them at Elena's house.
11. She says they're made from corn.
12. When it's hot, a tortilla is delicious.
13. I'll help Melissa cook the beef.
14. Then she's going to grate the cheese.
15. Matt says he's cutting the lettuce and tomato.
16. I'm very hungry already!

C. Write each sentence. Use a contraction in place of the underlined words in each sentence.

17. <u>We are</u> cooking at school.
18. Tomorrow <u>we are</u> making a pot of chili.
19. You know that <u>it is</u> like a hot, spicy soup.
20. Monica, <u>you will</u> have to chop some onions.
21. Then <u>we will</u> serve corn bread, too.
22. <u>I am</u> sure it will taste just like Mom's!

UNIT SEVEN

USING LANGUAGE TO

DESCRIBE

PART ONE

Unit Theme *The Five Senses*

Language Awareness Adjectives

PART TWO

Literature *Through Grandpa's Eyes* by Patricia MacLachlan

A Reason for Writing Describing

Writing
IN YOUR JOURNAL

WRITER'S WARM-UP ◆ What do you know about your five senses? Have your senses ever warned you of danger? Think how many games depend on your senses. Could you play baseball if you couldn't feel the bat? See the ball? How many ways do you use your five senses? Write about your senses in your journal.

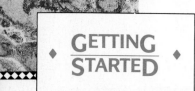

GETTING STARTED

Think of words that tell about an apple. What does an apple look like? How does it feel when you touch it? How does it smell or taste?

1 Writing with Adjectives

Remember that a noun names a person, place, or thing. Words that tell about nouns are called **adjectives**. An adjective may tell how something looks, feels, tastes, smells, or sounds. Notice the underlined adjective below.

■ Maria bit into a <u>sweet</u> apple.

The word *apple* is a noun. The word *sweet* is an adjective. *Sweet* tells how the apple smelled or tasted.

Find the adjectives that describe in this sentence.

■ Fred picked up shiny, smooth red apples.

The adjectives *shiny*, *smooth*, and *red* describe the apples. You can use adjectives to paint word pictures.

> **Summary** ◆ A word that describes a noun is an **adjective**. Use adjectives to make your writing more interesting.

Guided Practice

Name the adjective that describes each underlined noun.

1. I saw tiny <u>plants</u> floating on the pond.
2. The children rested on soft <u>beds</u>.
3. Molly listened carefully to the loud <u>noises</u>.

Practice

A. Read each sentence. Write the adjective that describes the underlined noun.

   4. Lilia and Cathy hiked along mysterious <u>trails</u>.
   5. They heard bubbly <u>streams</u> nearby.
   6. They saw golden <u>butterflies</u> in a meadow.
   7. Sharp <u>noises</u> made them turn around.
   8. Busy <u>chipmunks</u> were playing nearby.

B. Write each sentence. Use the bank of adjectives below to complete each sentence.

   cool   **sour**   **fresh**   **furry**   **noisy**

   9. Lilia saw the ____ raccoon with her eyes.
  10. She smelled the ____ air with her nose.
  11. She heard the ____ bees with her ears.
  12. Cathy felt the ____ water on her toes.
  13. They tasted ____ apples with their tongues.

C. Write each sentence. Add adjectives to complete each sentence.

  14. I eat ____ grapes.   **17.** I see ____ dogs.
  15. I hear ____ bells.   **18.** I feel ____ grass.
  16. I smell ____ roses.

Apply ◆ **Think and Write**

From Your Writing ◆ Read what you wrote for the Writer's Warm-up. Pick a sentence that is not very interesting. Write it again. Use adjectives to make your sentence more interesting.

> ✎ **Remember**
> that adjectives create word pictures for your reader.

I am going to Grandmother's house and I am taking *five fried fish*. What are you taking? Begin your answer with a number word, then add two more words that begin with the same sound.

2 Adjectives That Tell *How Many*

Read the sentences below. Which adjective in each sentence answers the question "How many?"

> You have **two** eyes.
> You only have **one** nose.

The word *some* tells how many, even though *some* does not tell an exact number. The underlined adjectives below tell *how many*. Which are number words? Which do not tell an exact number?

> five toes   few people
> ten fingers   some children

> **Summary** ♦ Some adjectives answer the question "How many?" Use adjectives that tell *how many* to add details to your writing.

Guided Practice

Name the adjectives that tell *how many*.

1. You hear sounds with both ears.
2. Your ear has many parts.
3. There are three bones in your middle ear.

Practice

A. Write each adjective that tells *how many*.

    4. I heard the six silly singers practicing.

    5. We saw five foolish fireflies flying overhead.

    6. I felt thirteen thin thimbles in the drawer.

    7. They tasted and enjoyed the ninety nice noodles.

    8. She smelled several special spices in the soup.

B. Use the number words below to complete the sentences.
Use each adjective only once.

    many   five   ten   one   two

    9. I have ＿＿ fingers on each hand.

  10. I have ＿＿ thumbs.

  11. My ＿＿ toes are cold.

  12. Each eye has ＿＿ eyelid.

  13. Each eyelid has ＿＿ tiny eyelashes.

C. Use a different adjective that tells *how many* to
complete each sentence. Write each sentence.

  14. I heard ＿＿ new bird songs this morning.

  15. Tena smelled ＿＿ kinds of red flowers.

  16. Chim felt ＿＿ different dark green leaves.

  17. Robert tasted ＿＿ fresh honey.

  18. Ellen saw ＿＿ tall giraffes.

Apply • Think and Write

See and Describe ◆ Write some sentences that describe
your favorite TV show. Use adjectives that tell *how many*.

✎ Remember
to use adjectives
that tell *how many*
to give details
to your reader.

◆ GETTING STARTED ◆

Careful Carlos, *Beautiful Belinda*, and *Funny Frieda* ride the bus. Make up similar names for other make-believe people who ride the bus.

3 Adjectives That Tell *What Kind*

Darling Domingo rode the bus. Read about his bus trip. Notice the underlined adjectives.

First the bus driver drove through a long, dark tunnel. Domingo could not see anything! Then the bus went on a bumpy road. Domingo bounced up and down on the hard seat. The blue bus took everyone to a large, wonderful park. Domingo got off the bus and ate two delicious sandwiches.

Remember that adjectives describe nouns. Some adjectives tell *what kind*. What kind of road did the bus go on? When you write, you may use describing adjectives to tell how things look, sound, feel, taste, or smell.

Summary ◆ Some adjectives answer the question ''What kind?'' You may use these describing adjectives to tell about size, shape, or color.

Guided Practice

Name the adjectives that tell *what kind*.

1. He heard loud sirens.
2. He smelled fragrant flowers in the park.
3. He saw a brown dog riding on a red truck.

Practice

A. Each sentence has two adjectives that describe the underlined noun. Write the adjectives.

  4. It was a cold, rainy <u>day</u>.
  5. Lars was wearing his bright, shiny <u>slicker</u>.
  6. Lars got on the crowded, late <u>bus</u>.
  7. He sat on the soft, squishy <u>seat</u> next to Pete.
  8. Pete shared his sweet, fresh <u>grapes</u> with Lars.

B. Write the paragraph. Use the adjectives below.

> **tall   busy   yellow   frisky   loud   small**

  The bus went past several (**9.**) buildings. Lars and Pete saw two (**10.**) dogs. One police officer blew her (**11.**) whistle. The cars and four (**12.**) buses stopped. Three (**13.**) children crossed the (**14.**) street.

C. Write adjectives that tell *what kind* for the sentences.

  15. Two buses went past a ____ car factory.
  16. Many ____ workers were making cars.
  17. Lars and Pete saw four ____ cars.
  18. Both hungry boys shared Pete's ____ apples.

  Can you also find the adjectives that tell *how many*?

Apply • Think and Write

A TV Commercial ♦ Write a TV commercial for your favorite food. Use adjectives that tell how the food looks, feels, tastes, and smells.

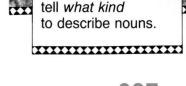

> ✏ **Remember**
> to use adjectives that tell *what kind* to describe nouns.

GETTING
STARTED

Play "I Spy with My Eye." Follow this example and find other things in your classroom to compare. *I spy a short red pencil. I spy a shorter blue pencil. The shortest pencil I spy is yellow.*

4 Adjectives That Compare

Adjectives describe nouns. One way they describe is by comparing persons, places, or things. Notice how the animals' eyes are compared in the sentences below.

> **1. A baby chick has small eyes.**
> **2. A grasshopper has smaller eyes than a baby chick.**
> **3. A ladybug has the smallest eyes of all three.**

When two nouns are compared, the *-er* form of the adjective is used. In sentence **2**, the eyes of the two animals are compared.

When three or more nouns are compared, the *-est* form of the adjective is used. In sentence **3**, the eyes of three animals are compared.

> **Summary** ♦ Use the *-er* form of an adjective to compare two persons, places, or things. Use the *-est* form of an adjective to compare three or more persons, places, or things.

Guided Practice

Name the missing adjective.

1. soft, softer, ____   **3.** green, greener, ____

2. loud, ____, loudest   **4.** ____, sweeter, sweetest

Practice

A. Write each sentence. Use the correct adjective in ( ).

5. Crabs have (harder, hardest) shells than shrimp.
6. The chameleon is not the (smaller, smallest) lizard.
7. That was the (swifter, swiftest) lizard of all.
8. A frog has (fewer, fewest) legs than a crab.
9. Dan's bullfrog is (older, oldest) than Karen's.

B. Add *-er* or *-est* to each adjective in ( ). Write each sentence.

10. A chameleon is (soft) than a crab.
11. The brown bullfrog was (tall) than the green one.
12. The crab is the (slow) animal on this beach.
13. The (fast) lizard at the zoo was gray and red.
14. That chameleon is (young) than my bullfrog.

C. Write each sentence. Use the adjectives below.

oddest   smallest   longer   slowest   smaller

15. This crab is ____ than a bullfrog.
16. That chameleon has the ____ eyes I've seen.
17. This is the ____ chameleon of all.
18. The ____ crab in the group reached the water last.
19. Jim's bullfrog is ____ than mine.

Apply ◆ Think and Write

Comparing Animals ◆ What is the fastest zoo animal? What is the strangest zoo animal? Is an elephant larger than a giraffe? Write sentences that answer these questions.

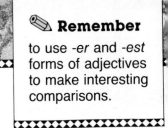

✎ **Remember**
to use *-er* and *-est* forms of adjectives to make interesting comparisons.

An alligator may eat an apple, an egg, or an octopus. What other things might an alligator eat?

5 Using *a*, *an*, and *the*

Articles are special adjectives that are used with nouns. Look at the underlined articles and the nouns that follow them in these sentences.

1. We went to the zoo to see the elephants.
2. Anita wanted to touch an elephant.
3. She heard a parrot chanting a rhyme.

Notice the article *the* in sentence **1**. *The* is used before both singular and plural nouns.

The articles *a* and *an* are used with singular nouns. Use *a* before words that begin with consonant sounds, such as *parrot* in sentence **3**. Use *an* before words that begin with vowel sounds, such as *elephant* in sentence **2**.

> **Summary** ♦ The words *a*, *an*, and *the* are a special kind of adjective. They are called **articles**.

Guided Practice

Tell which articles may be used before the nouns.

1. ____ monkey   4. ____ lizard   7. ____ chimpanzees
2. ____ elephants   5. ____ cats   8. ____ butterflies
3. ____ ostrich   6. ____ dog   9. ____ anteater

Practice

A. Choose the correct article in ( ) to complete each sentence. Write each sentence.

10. Anita cannot see (an, the) puppy.

11. Anita can hear (the, an) sounds of small paws.

12. She can touch (a, an) ear.

13. She can feel (a, an) tail wagging.

14. She can hug (a, an) ball of soft fur.

B. Use *a* or *an* to complete each sentence below.

15. Anita was reading ____ book with her fingers.

16. She listened carefully to ____ concert on TV.

17. She heard ____ song she liked very much.

18. Anita wore ____ apron when she helped in the kitchen.

19. She put ____ apple in her lunch box.

C. Think of two nouns to complete each sentence. Write each sentence.

20. Anita put the ____ on the ____.

21. She listened to a ____ on the ____.

22. I saw her with a ____ in the ____.

23. She found an ____ on the ____.

24. An ____ and a ____ are her favorite toys.

Apply ♦ **Think and Write**

Dictionary of Knowledge ♦ Read about the Braille Alphabet. People who use it depend on their sense of touch. Close your eyes and touch five objects. Write the names of the objects. Write *a* or *an* before each name.

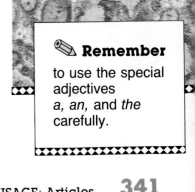

> ✎ **Remember**
> to use the special adjectives
> *a, an,* and *the* carefully.

♦ GETTING ♦
STARTED

What nursery rhyme does the following remind you of?
Jack and Jill marched up the slope
To pick up a bucket of water.
Remember the real rhyme. What words have been changed?

VOCABULARY ♦

Synonyms

Read the sentences below.

Matilda was a very <u>funny</u> cow.
Matilda was a very <u>comical</u> cow.
Matilda was a very <u>silly</u> cow.

The words *funny*, *comical*, and *silly* are synonyms.
Synonyms are words that have almost the same meaning.
The English language has many synonyms. What are some
other synonyms for *funny*?

It is important to choose the best words to say what you
mean. You can use a thesaurus or a dictionary to find just
the right word.

Building Your Vocabulary

Read each sentence. Name the synonym in ( ) for the
underlined word.

1. Jack is <u>nimble</u>. (sure-footed, slow)
2. Jack is <u>quick</u>. (happy, swift)
3. Jack <u>jumped</u> over the candlestick. (leaped, walked)
4. Humpty Dumpty had a <u>great</u> fall. (strange, big)

Practice

A. Read each sentence. Write the synonym in ( ) for the underlined word.

1. The lion let out a <u>terrible</u> roar. (awful, colorful)
2. Paula <u>peeked</u> around the door. (listened, looked)
3. It was a <u>chilly</u> day in October. (windy, cool)
4. An <u>ancient</u> house sat on the hill. (old, high)
5. It was a <u>moist</u>, foggy day. (wet, dark)
6. The lemon had a <u>sharp</u> taste. (sour, pointed)
7. The small animal felt <u>woolly</u>. (fuzzy, rough)
8. We heard a very <u>odd</u> sound. (new, strange)

B. Think of a synonym for each underlined word below. Then use the synonym to complete the sentence. If you need help, use the Thesaurus.

9. I used to have a <u>big</u> appetite. Now it's ____.
10. I used to be <u>good</u>. Now I'm ____.
11. I used to be <u>nice</u>. Now I'm ____.
12. I used to <u>jump</u> over puddles. Now I ____ over them.

Language Corner ♦ Word Histories

The word *muscle* comes from an ancient word that meant "little mouse." Bend your arm and feel the muscle move. Does it feel like a little mouse?

Guess what English word comes from the ancient word parts *syn*, meaning "like" or "together," and *nym*, meaning "name."

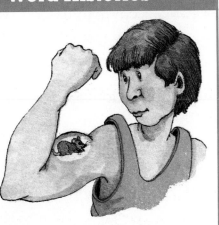

How to Expand Sentences with Adjectives

You know that adjectives are describing words. Adjectives add interest and details to sentences. You can choose adjectives that give readers a clear picture in their minds. Read the sentences below. Which one gives you a clearer picture?

1. The pony ate a carrot.
2. The frisky pony ate a crunchy carrot.

Both sentences tell about the pony. But sentence **2** gives more details. The adjectives *frisky* and *crunchy* make it easier to picture the pony enjoying a snack.

The Grammar Game ◆ Play adjective addition! Write one or two adjectives to describe each noun below. Choose adjectives that tell how things look, taste, feel, or sound. Write them as quickly as you can.

cat	pickle	treasure
moon	magician	ocean
bakery	accident	airplane
race	porcupine	city
lemonade	flower	garden
feet	music	bicycle

Working Together

See how using adjectives adds interest and details to your writing. Do activities **A** and **B** with your group.

A. Brainstorm! List as many different adjectives as you can for each sentence.

1. We go to a ___ school.
2. We eat ___ food.
3. We read ___ books.
4. We collect ___ coins.
5. We like ___ movies.
6. We ride in ___ cars.
7. We play ___ games.
8. We pick ___ flowers.

B. Read the verse below. Complete the verse with adjectives of the group's choice. Then write the verse again, using different adjectives. Notice how the second verse gives a different picture.

On that ___ night
We saw one ___ sight,
This ___ creature from Who-Knows-Where,
With ___ fingers and ___ hair!

WRITERS' CORNER ♦ Overused Adjectives

Some adjectives like *good* and *nice* are overused, or used too often.

OVERUSED: I saw a nice puppy. It had nice eyes.
IMPROVED: I saw a darling puppy. It had beautiful eyes.

Read what you wrote for the Writer's Warm-up. Did you overuse any adjectives? Can you replace them with more interesting words?

THE SOUTH LEDGES, APPLEDORE
oil on canvas by Childe Hassam
National Museum of American Art, Smithsonian Institution, Gift of John Gellatly.

USING LANGUAGE TO

DESCRIBE

═══ PART TWO ═══

Literature   *Through Grandpa's Eyes* by **Patrician MacLachlan**
A Reason for Writing Describing

CREATIVE
Writing

FINE ARTS ◆ The lady in this painting is enjoying one of her favorite places. She likes the smell of the salt water and the sound of the waves. What favorite place do you have? What do you see, hear, feel, or smell in your favorite place? Write a few lines of a poem about your favorite place.

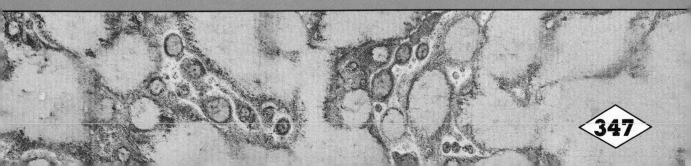

CRITICAL THINKING ◆
A Strategy for Describing

A VENN DIAGRAM

Describing is using details to paint word pictures. After this lesson you will read part of *Through Grandpa's Eyes*. This story is about John and his grandfather. John's grandfather is blind. In the story John describes how they wake up.

> In the morning, the sun pushes through the curtains into my eyes. I burrow down into the covers to get away, but the light follows me. . . .
>
> The sun wakes Grandpa differently. . . . He says it touches him, *warming* him awake.

John says he and Grandpa wake up in different ways. We can describe people by telling how they are different. We can also tell how they are alike.

◆ Learning the Strategy

You probably often notice how things are alike or different. This can be very useful. Suppose you are going to a new school. Would it help to know how it is like your old school? Would it help to know how it is different? Maybe you want a pet. How might you decide between a cat and a dog?

A Venn diagram is two circles that overlap. It shows how two things are alike and different. The Venn diagram on page 349 is about dogs and cats. The words in the

CRITICAL THINKING: Comparing/Contrasting

middle show how they are alike. The words on the outsides show how they are different. What ideas might you add?

Venn diagram:

Cats
different
Can stay indoors all the time
Smaller than most dogs
Wash themselves

alike
Like to be petted
Like to play
Need love
Need care
Are fun to own

Dogs
different
Must go outdoors every day
Bigger than most cats
Need baths

Using the Strategy

A. How is your school bag like a friend's school bag? How is it different? Make a Venn diagram. In the middle write how they are alike. On the outsides, write how each bag is different.

B. How might a young person and an older person be alike or different? Make a Venn diagram. Compare yourself to an older person. In the middle write how you are alike. On the outsides write how you are different. Then read to find out how John and his grandfather are alike or different.

Applying the Strategy

♦ Look at one Venn diagram you made. How did you decide what to put in each part?
♦ Have you ever noticed how two people are alike? Or different? Did you think it was interesting? Why?

LITERATURE

FROM

THROUGH GRANDPA'S
E Y E S

by Patricia MacLachlan

Of all the houses that I know, I like my grandpa's best. My friend Peter has a new glass house with pebble-path gardens that go nowhere. And Maggie lives next door in an old wooden house with rooms behind rooms, all with carved doors and brass doorknobs. They are fine houses. But Grandpa's house is my favorite. Because I see it through Grandpa's eyes.

Grandpa is blind. He doesn't see the house the way I do. He has his own way of seeing.

In the morning, the sun pushes through the curtains into my eyes. I burrow down into the covers to get away, but the light follows me. I give up, throw back the covers, and run to Grandpa's room.

The sun wakes Grandpa differently from the way it wakes me. He says it touches him, *warming* him awake. When I peek around the door, Grandpa is already up and doing his morning exercises. Bending and stretching by the bed. He stops and smiles because he hears me.

Illustrated by Deborah Ray

"Good morning, John."

"Where's Nana?" I ask him.

"Don't you know?" he says, bending and stretching. "Close your eyes, John, and look through my eyes."

I close my eyes. Down below, I hear the banging of pots and the sound of water running that I didn't hear before.

"Nana is in the kitchen, making breakfast," I say.

When I open my eyes again, I can see Grandpa nodding at me. He is tall with dark gray hair. And his eyes are sharp blue even though they are not sharp seeing.

Library Link ♦ *If you would like to read more about John and Grandpa, read* Through Grandpa's Eyes *by Patricia MacLachlan.*

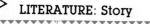

Reader's Response

❖❖❖

Would you like to visit Grandpa? Tell why or why not.

THROUGH
GRANDPA'S
E Y E S

Responding to Literature

1. John's favorite house is Grandpa's house. What is your favorite house? Tell why you like that house.

2. Grandpa "sees" with his ears. Close your eyes. Listen for one minute. Tell the things you heard. What information do you get from the sounds you hear?

3. The sun "warms" Grandpa awake. How do you wake up?

4. Older people often help us. Do you know an older person? How does that person help you?

Writing to Learn

Think and Compare ◆ Grandpa and John are alike and different in many ways. Copy the diagram below. Then add more details that tell how Grandpa and John are alike and different. How many can you add?

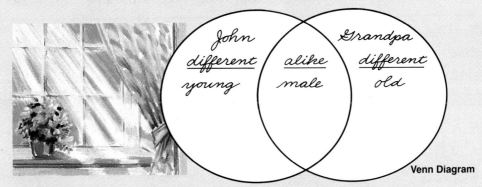

John
different
young

alike
male

Grandpa
different
old

Venn Diagram

Write ◆ Use the details to write one paragraph about John and Grandpa.

Describe an object in your classroom, but do not name it. Tell its color, shape, size, and sound if it makes one. Who will guess what it is?

SPEAKING and LISTENING ♦
An Oral Description

When you talk, do you say interesting things? Do people listen to what you say? Do they show interest? Do they want to hear more? In this lesson you will learn ways to make the things you say more interesting to other people.

Try using description when you speak. Tell what you see and hear. Give lively details. Have your listeners see and hear with you. Use the chart below as a guide.

Giving a Description	1. Use words that describe color, size, or shape. **Color:** rose, gold, sky-blue, lobster-red, pearly white **Size:** tiny, enormous, medium-sized, wide, small **Shape:** square, round, oval, pointed, curved, oblong 2. Use words that describe softness or loudness. quiet, low, faint, hushed, noisy, loud 3. Use words that sound like the sounds they name. bang, crash, moo, hiss, drip, honk, zip, sizzle
Being an Active Listener	1. Picture what is being described. 2. Listen for descriptive words. 3. Listen for sound-effect words.

Summary ♦ Use descriptive details to tell what you see and hear. Listen for descriptive details that other speakers give.

Guided Practice

Name words to describe each thing below. You may use words from the chart if you wish.

1. the sound of a car's horn
2. a sound heard in the country
3. the size, shape, and color of a balloon
4. a sound made by frying onions
5. the size, shape, and color of a robin's egg

Practice

A. In the book *Through Grandpa's Eyes,* John describes the sights, sounds, and smells of Grandpa's house. Think about what you see, hear, and smell when you wake up in the morning. Tell the class about it. Remember to use the guidelines for giving a description.

B. Listen as your classmates describe early morning sights, sounds, and smells. After each person speaks, write at least one descriptive word used by that person. Use the guidelines for being an active listener.

Apply • Think and Write

Describing Word Bank ◆ Make a list of descriptive words you especially like. Group together words that describe color, size, shape, or sound. You may think of more groups for your list. When you read or hear other descriptive words that you like, add them to your list. Soon you will have your own word bank.

✎ **Remember**
to listen for words that describe color, size, shape, and sound.

♦ GETTING STARTED ♦ Play a riddle game. Tell what you see, smell, hear, feel, and taste. *I see a field and smell peanuts. I feel the hot sun and hear the crowd roar. I taste a salty pretzel. Where am I?*

WRITING ♦
Using Your Senses to Describe

You have practiced describing things you see and hear. You have listened for words that describe color, shape, size, and sound. Now you will practice describing what you taste, smell, and touch. Use the chart below as a guide.

Use words that tell how something tastes, smells, or feels.

Tastes: salty, sweet, sour, spicy, bitter

Smells: smoky, sweet, musty, rotten

Feels: hot, sticky, sharp, icy, rough, smooth

If a taste or smell is hard to describe, just name the taste or smell.

Taste: the taste of vanilla, the taste of onion

Smell: the smell of mothballs, the smell of hay

Summary ♦ Writers describe what they see, hear, taste, smell, and touch. When you write a description, use your senses to tell details that describe.

Guided Practice

Describe each of these things.

1. the way sandpaper feels
2. how peanut butter tastes
3. the smells of springtime
4. how dough feels when you work with it

Practice

A. Write a sentence that describes the thing.

5. the taste of your favorite breakfast food
6. the smells of autumn
7. the way ice cubes feel
8. how rain feels when it falls on your face

B. In the book *Through Grandpa's Eyes,* Nana makes a sculpture of Grandpa's head. John says this:

> My eyes have already told me that it looks like Grandpa. But he shows me how to feel his face with my three middle fingers, and then the clay face.
> ''Pretend your fingers are water,'' he tells me.

Close your eyes now and try it. Feel your face with your three middle fingers. Can your fingers tell what your face looks like? Write three sentences that describe your face as ''seen'' by your sense of touch.

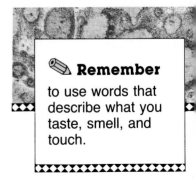

Apply ◆ Think and Write

Dictionary of Knowledge ◆ Read about Helen Keller. Then put yourself in her place. Write some sentences that tell what you would most like to see and hear.

> ✎ **Remember**
> to use words that describe what you taste, smell, and touch.

GETTING
STARTED

Choose one word to describe your classroom. Say the
word. Then give details that show why you chose that
word.

WRITING ◆
A Paragraph That Describes

When Amy read *Through Grandpa's Eyes,* she got an
idea. She would write a description of her grandma's
house. Amy started taking notes. She wrote what she saw,
heard, felt, smelled, and tasted. But there was one problem.
She had too many details. What should she do?

Amy needed a main idea for her description. She chose a
main idea and wrote the paragraph below. Notice that the
paragraph begins with a topic sentence that states the main
idea. Then the details follow the main idea.

My grandma's house is friendly. Warm sunshine pours
in the windows. Basker the cat lies in the sun. When she
hears me, she stretches on her little round rug. Then she
comes to greet me. She purrs happily as I scratch her
ears. The cozy smell of fresh-baked bread comes from
the kitchen. It tastes buttery and melts in my mouth. I
love Grandma's house!

Summary ◆ A paragraph can give a description.
Begin with a topic sentence that tells the main idea.
Then give details about the topic sentence. Paint a
picture in words for your reader.

Guided Practice

Read Amy's paragraph again. Tell its main idea. Then tell the details she sees, hears, smells, and tastes.

Practice

A. Choose an object you can look at right now. Write a topic sentence about the object. Then write four details that tell more about the object.

B. Think of something that makes a sound. Write a topic sentence about the thing you chose. Then write four details that tell more about it.

Apply ◆ **Think and Write**

A Descriptive Paragraph ◆ Write a paragraph that describes the scene shown in the picture.

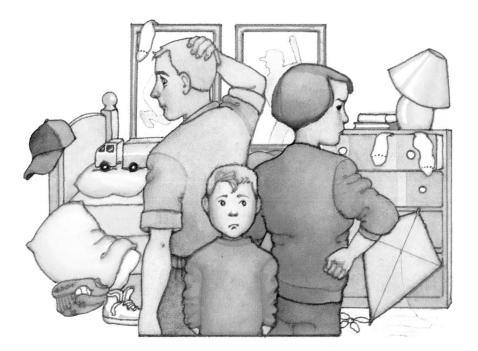

> ✎ **Remember**
> to choose a main idea and details for a paragraph that describes.

Focus on Descriptive Details

Think about *Through Grandpa's Eyes,* which you read earlier. Were you able to see through Grandpa's eyes as John did?

♦ Could you *feel* the sun warming you awake?
♦ Could you *hear* the banging of pots and the sound of water running?

Since Grandpa is blind, you see him through John's eyes.

♦ Did you *see* Grandpa as a tall man with dark gray hair and sharp blue eyes?

The author of this story makes her descriptions come to life. She lets you feel, hear, and see what is happening. How does she do this? The answer can be given in one word—details.

Details are small bits of information, but they are very important. They help you picture what you are reading. When you write, they are your tools. You use them to paint pictures with words.

The Writer's Voice ♦ Details can help a reader see, hear, feel, smell, or taste what is being described. Use Grandpa's method of seeing. Close your eyes right now. What can you hear? Feel? Smell?

Working Together

You can use all five senses to describe. Sometimes one sense—usually sight—is the main one in a description. As a group, work on activities **A** and **B**.

A. Choose three or four common objects to describe. One member of your group then closes his or her eyes (to be like Grandpa in the story). This person describes one of the objects without naming it. Others in the group identify the object. They can also add more details. This continues for all the objects. A different group member should describe each object.

B. Spend five minutes to observe your classroom. As a group, write down the details that would go in a description of it. Use these columns:

We see   We hear   We feel

Did you smell or taste anything? If so, list those details, too.

In Your Group

- ♦ Make sure everyone knows the directions.
- ♦ Ask others to talk.
- ♦ Look at others when they talk.
- ♦ Record the group's ideas.

THESAURUS CORNER ♦ Word Choice

Many of the words in the Thesaurus are adjectives. Write a description of your favorite room at home. Use at least five adjectives from the Thesaurus in your writing. (These do not have to be main entry words. They can be synonyms or antonyms.)

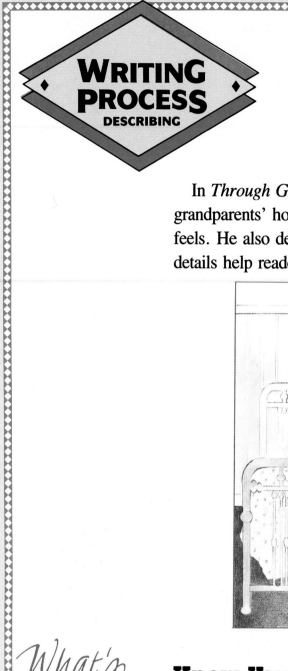

WRITING PROCESS
DESCRIBING

Writing a Description

In *Through Grandpa's Eyes*, John describes his grandparents' house. John tells what he sees, hears, and feels. He also describes what he smells and tastes. These details help readers feel as if they visited Grandpa's house.

MY PURPOSE

MY AUDIENCE

Know Your Purpose and Audience

In this lesson you will write a description. Your purpose will be to describe your favorite place.

Your audience will be your classmates. Later you and your classmates can read your descriptions aloud. You can also make a display box for them.

1 Prewriting

First you will need to choose your favorite place. Then you will need to gather details about it.

Choose Your Topic ♦ Think about some places you like. Make a list of your favorite places. Then circle the place you like the best.

Think About It

Which place will you choose? Draw a little picture of each place. You might like your room or your aunt's kitchen. Draw everything in your place that you can remember. Then decide. Draw yourself in your favorite place.

Talk About It

Talk to your friends about your favorite places. Think about places in your school, your home, or places where you play. You might get an idea from a place your friend lists.

Topic Ideas

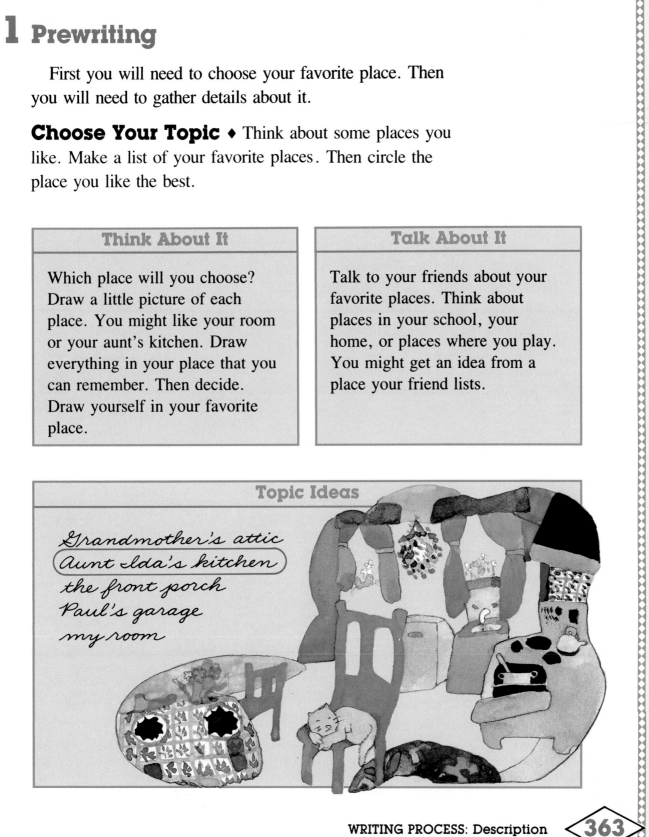

Grandmother's attic
(Aunt Ida's kitchen)
the front porch
Paul's garage
my room

Choose Your Strategy ♦ Here are two ways to remember details about your favorite place. Read both. Then decide which idea you will use.

PREWRITING IDEAS

CHOICE ONE

A Details List

Make a details list. Write *See*, *Hear*, *Smell*, *Taste*, and *Feel*. Then tell a partner about your favorite place. Tell what you see, hear, smell, taste, and feel in your favorite place. Write these details in your list.

Model

See	*red chairs*
Hear	*oven door*
Smell	*fresh bread*
Taste	*sweet butter*
Feel	*warm, happy*

CHOICE TWO

A Venn Diagram

Make a Venn diagram. Name one circle for your favorite place. Name the other circle for a similar place. Write details about each place. In the middle, list details that are alike. On the outsides, write details that are different. Decide why your favorite place is special.

Model

Aunt Ida's kitchen
different
colorful
warm

alike
good smells
good food

Our kitchen
different
mostly white
very neat

2 Writing

Read your details list or Venn diagram again. Let your list or diagram help you think about your favorite place. Picture it in your mind. Then begin writing your description. How can you begin? Here are two ways you might start.

♦ My favorite place is special because ____.

♦ I'm sure you would enjoy my favorite place ____.

The first sentence of your description should give your main idea. Add details that tell what is special about this place. Don't worry about mistakes. You can fix them later.

Sample First Draft ♦

My favorite place is Aunt
Ida's kitchen. It is very
colorfull. Lots of things are red
The walls and floor are white.
On weekends Aunt Ida cooks.
Then her kitchen gets warm.
It smells good, too. Last week
aunt Ida made me a rice
custard. Wasn't I lucky? I ate my
favorite food in my favorite place!

3 Revising

Now you have written your description. Do you want to make it better? This idea may help you.

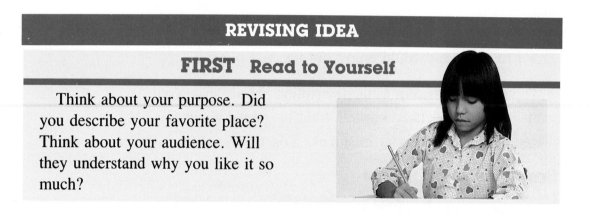

REVISING IDEA

FIRST Read to Yourself

Think about your purpose. Did you describe your favorite place? Think about your audience. Will they understand why you like it so much?

Focus: Did you tell what you see, hear, taste, smell, or feel? Put a caret (^) where you want to add a detail.

THEN Share with a Partner

Listen as your partner reads your description aloud. These guidelines may help you.

The Writer

Guidelines: Listen carefully. Ask your partner for ideas.

Sample questions:
- Can you imagine my favorite place?
- **Focus question:** Where could I add some details?

The Writer's Partner

Guidelines: Read aloud slowly and clearly. Try to give helpful ideas.

Sample responses:
- I liked the part where _____.
- Could you add more details about _____?

Revising Model ♦ Look at this description. The marks show changes the writer wants to make.

The writer's partner wanted to know more details.

Bakes is a more exact word than *cooks*.

The writer added a detail to describe the smell.

The adjective *delicious* added a detail.

> My favorite place is Aunt
> Ida's kitchen. It is very
> ~~The curtains and chairs~~
> colorfull. Lots of things are red.
> The walls and floor are white.
> _bakes_
> On weekends Aunt Ida ~~cooks~~.
> Then her kitchen gets warm.
> _sweet_
> It smells good, too. Last week
> _delicious_
> aunt Ida made me a ∧ rice
> custard. Wasn't I lucky? I ate my
> favorite food in my favorite

Read the description above. Read it the way the writer wants it to be. Then revise your own description.

Grammar Check ♦ Adjectives add details to your writing.

Word Choice ♦ Is there a more exact word for a word like *cooks*? A thesaurus can help you find exact words.

Revising Checklist

- ☐ **My purpose:** Did I describe my favorite place?
- ☐ **My audience:** Will my classmates understand why I like that place?
- ☐ **Focus:** Did I tell what I see, hear, taste, smell, or feel?

4 Proofreading

Try to fix mistakes. Neat, correct writing is easier to read and understand.

Proofreading Model ♦ Here is the description of Aunt Ida's kitchen. The new red marks are proofreading marks.

Proofreading Marks

check spelling ⬭

capital letter ═

indent paragraph ¶

My favorite place is Aunt Ida's kitchen. It is very ~~colorfull~~ colorful. The curtains and chairs Lots of things are red.

The walls and floor are white. On weekends Aunt Ida ~~cooks~~ *bakes.*

Then her kitchen gets warm. It smells sweet *~~good~~, too. Last week aunt Ida made me a* delicious *rice custard. Wasn't I lucky? I ate my favorite food in my favorite place!*

Proofreading Checklist

☐ Did I spell words correctly?

☐ Did I indent paragraphs?

☐ Did I use capital letters correctly?

☐ Did I use correct marks at the end of sentences?

☐ Did I use my best handwriting?

PROOFREADING IDEA

Spelling Check

Check one thing at a time. Read your work once for spelling mistakes. Then read it again for capital letters.

Now proofread your description, add a title, and make a neat copy.

5 Publishing

Now share your description with your classmates. Here are two ways to do it.

Aunt Ida's Kitchen

My favorite place is Aunt Ida's kitchen. It is very colorful. The curtains and chairs are red. The walls and floor are white.

On weekends Aunt Ida bakes. Then her kitchen gets warm. It smells sweet, too. Last week Aunt Ida made me a delicious rice custard. Wasn't I lucky? I ate my favorite food in my favorite place!

PUBLISHING IDEAS

Share Aloud

Read your description aloud to yourself. Practice until you do it smoothly. Then read your description aloud to the class. Ask your listeners to tell which details they liked best.

Share in Writing

Cover a large box with colored paper. Tape your descriptions to the box. During free time walk all around the box. Read the descriptions. Draw a picture of your favorite one.

Writing Across the Curriculum   Health

In this unit you described your favorite place. When you describe, you sometimes compare things. When you decide what to eat, you compare things, too. You decide which food looks, smells, and will taste better to you. A Venn diagram is useful for comparing things.

Writing to Learn

Think and Compare ◆ Look at the pictures below. Then make a Venn diagram. On it write the ways that carrots and oranges are alike and different.

Venn Diagram

Write ◆ Use the information from your Venn diagram to write a paragraph. Explain how carrots and oranges are alike and different.

Writing in Your Journal

In the Writer's Warm-up you wrote about the five senses. Then you learned how your senses help you enjoy nature. Think about the story *Through Grandpa's Eyes*. Think about what you learned about Grandpa's "own way of seeing." Describe it in your journal.

BOOKS TO ENJOY

Read More About It

Amy: The Story of a Deaf Child

by Lou Ann Walker

A deaf person cannot hear. But Amy takes part in the same daily activities you do.

Helen Keller

by Stewart and Polly Anne Graff

Helen Keller was blind and deaf. She worked hard to use her other senses. Read this biography to learn how her brilliant teacher, Annie Sullivan, helped Helen speak and read.

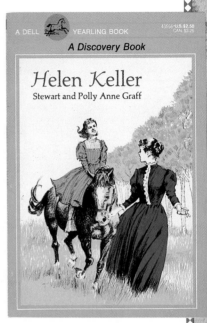

A DELL YEARLING BOOK

A Discovery Book

Helen Keller
Stewart and Polly Anne Graff

Book Report Idea   Senses List

Next time you give a book report, describe parts of it according to the senses.

Make a Senses List ◆ List the five senses along the edge of your paper. For each sense, describe a character or scene in the book that fits. You might tell about a noise that gave an important clue, or a special food one character always ate.

sight	
sound	
smell	A strong smell of smoke told Jenny there was something very wrong.
hearing	
touch	

Unit 7

Adjectives   *pages 332–341*

A. Write each sentence. Underline the adjective.

1. Some frogs live in trees.
2. They have sticky pads on their toes.
3. They make loud calls.
4. Frogs have powerful legs.
5. They can jump three feet.
6. Frogs have long tongues.
7. Insects stick to a wet tongue.
8. Frogs burrow in mud during cold winters.

B. Add *-er* or *-est* to each adjective in (   ). Write the sentences.

9. The great horned owl is the ___ kind of owl. (large)
10. The elf owl is the ___ kind of owl. (big)
11. A barn owl is ___ than a screech owl. (big)
12. An owl has ___ eyesight than most birds. (sharp)
13. Geese are ___ than owls. (smart)
14. An owl is ___ than a goose. (quiet)

C. Write the correct article in (   ).

15. Thomas Edison was (a, an) inventor.
16. His first job was selling newspapers on (a, the) trains.
17. Edison set up (a, an) laboratory.
18. It was in the express car of (a, an) train.

Synonyms   *pages 342–343*

D. Write the synonym in ( ) for each word below.

19. happy (jolly, sad)   **23.** help (aid, hinder)
20. keep (discard, save)   **24.** noise (silence, sound)
21. hurry (delay, rush)   **25.** join (connect, part)
22. make (create, destroy)   **26.** part (whole, bit)

Describing   *pages 354–359*

E. Read the paragraph below. Then write the answer to each question.

It was a stormy night. The howling wind shook the windows. Sleet rattled on the metal roof of the barn. The cattle huddled under the old shed for protection against the raging blizzard. I shivered in my wintry bed. Thick blankets covered my ears against the storm's fury.

27. What does the paragraph describe?
28. Which two words tell how something sounded?
29. Which word describes the blizzard?
30. Which sentence describes where the person is?

Using Your Senses   *pages 356–357*

F. Complete each sentence with the type of adjective shown in ( ). Write each sentence.

31. The bears eat the ____ honey. (taste)
32. You can hear the ____ buzzing of the bees. (sound)
33. The tiny bees are no match for the ____ bear. (size)
34. The bear has ____ fur. (touch)
35. Soon its ____ fur is covered with bees. (color)
36. The nearby campfire has a ____ scent. (smell)

Tongue Twisters

Make up tongue twisters. Think of a noun that is a little bit silly, such as *toes*. Then write adjectives that begin with the same sound that the noun begins with.

tiny	**tender**	**tacky**	**tan**
two	**ticklish**	**tidy**	**tingly**

Experiment with the different tongue twisters the adjectives and noun can make.

tiny, ticklish, tan toes   two tingly, tender toes

Ask a classmate to say your tongue twisters quickly.

Adjective Building Blocks

Look at the four trees named below. Use the blue letters to write a five-letter adjective that describes trees. Use the red letters to write a four-letter adjective that also describes trees.

p i n e   e l m   w a l n u t   o r a n g e

Make a puzzle like the one above to share with your classmates. Use months, animals, or people instead of trees.

Unit 7 Extra Practice

1 Writing with Adjectives
p. 332

A. Copy each sentence. Draw one line under each adjective. Draw two lines under the noun that the adjective describes.

EXAMPLE: **April has warm days.**

ANSWER: **April has <u>warm</u> <u>days</u>.**

1. Kaloma and Ellie walked by little streams.
2. Tiny plants floated in water.
3. I spotted green frogs.
4. They sat on flat rocks.
5. Frogs jumped over large logs.
6. They blinked at shiny beetles.
7. Golden butterflies passed near them.
8. Ellie looked for pretty rocks.
9. Kaloma picked up empty shells.
10. Lazy snails had left them behind.
11. Hungry robins flew by.
12. They spied fat worms.
13. Robins landed beside muddy footprints.
14. Everyone enjoys lovely days in spring.

B. Write each sentence. Add an adjective.

15. We saw a ____ tree.
16. It was a ____ day.
17. We sat in ____ grass.
18. A ____ fly buzzed.
19. I smelled ____ roses.
20. Sam ate a ____ pear.
21. I had ____ grapes.
22. A ____ dog ran by.
23. It had a ____ tail.
24. My ____ pal yawned.
25. A ____ bird sang.
26. The ____ sun set.

2 Adjectives That Tell *How Many*

p. 334

A. Write each adjective that tells *how many*.

1. Two classes had a book fair last Friday.
2. Sixty people looked at new and old books.
3. Some students exchanged books.
4. Hans Christian Andersen wrote many stories.
5. My book has twelve tales by this Danish man.
6. Two brothers from Germany also wrote tales.
7. The Grimm brothers wrote about several animals.
8. Ed likes the story about three billy goats.
9. Another story is about a tailor and seven flies.
10. You read about Cinderella's two stepsisters.
11. This story has thirty pages.
12. Many children know about the Grimm brothers.
13. I read five tales by Hans Christian Andersen.
14. He was born many years ago in Denmark.
15. One story by Andersen is about a little mermaid.
16. Some people have seen her statue in Denmark.
17. Fifteen people laughed when I said Andersen was a great Dane.

B. Use a different adjective that tells *how many* in each sentence. Write each sentence.

18. Bonnie read ____ stories.
19. The first story told about ____ children.
20. The children had ____ adventures.
21. They traveled for ____ days.
22. They met ____ animals who helped them.

3 Adjectives That Tell What Kind

p. 336

A. Write each adjective that tells *what kind*.

1. The bus passed by tall skyscrapers.
2. It crossed over a busy bridge.
3. We heard a loud siren.
4. A red truck hurried by on its way to a fire.
5. I saw a spotted dog on the truck.
6. Once my bus went on a bumpy road to a wonderful park.
7. We had a picnic near a round lake.
8. Our friendly driver told funny stories.
9. Lars rode the tan bus to the library.
10. It was a rainy day.
11. A new neighbor named Pete got on the bus.
12. He wore a shiny slicker.
13. He carried a small backpack.
14. Pete gave Lars a shy smile.
15. He sat in the empty seat beside Lars.
16. The bus stopped near brick steps.
17. Lars shared his green umbrella with Pete.
18. They walked into the square building together.

B. Think of another adjective that tells *what kind* to take the place of each underlined word. Write the new paragraph.

The bus passed many interesting sights. New cars rolled out of a noisy factory. Busy workers were building a skyscraper. They walked on narrow platforms and carried heavy loads. One worker waved a red flag at the traffic. He wore a hard helmet.

4 Adjectives That Compare   *p. 338*

A. Write the missing form of each adjective.

1. slow, slower, _____
2. steep, _____ , steepest
3. cold, colder, _____
4. _____ , newer, newest
5. hard, _____ , hardest
6. high, _____ , highest

B. Write each sentence. Use the correct adjective in ( ).

7. Rhode Island is the (smaller, smallest) state of all.
8. Hawaii is a (smaller, smallest) state than Alaska.
9. Alaska is (larger, largest) than Texas, too.
10. The (higher, highest) waterfall in the United States is in Yosemite National Park.
11. The Mississippi River is (longer, longest) than the Ohio River.
12. Maine has (cooler, coolest) summers than Texas.
13. America's (older, oldest) zoo is in Philadelphia.

C. Add *-er* or *-est* to each adjective in ( ). Write each sentence.

14. California redwoods are the world's (tall) trees.
15. Georgia has (warm) winters than Indiana.
16. Western Oregon is (green) than eastern Oregon.
17. Death Valley is the (low) spot in the nation.
18. America's (old) city is in Florida.
19. The Grand Canyon is (deep) than Bryce Canyon.
20. Louisiana has the world's (long) railroad bridge.
21. Iowa has a (great) amount of snow than Arizona.
22. The (short) street in the world is in Ohio.
23. Alaska has (cold) winters than Alabama.

5 Using *a*, *an*, and *the*

p. 340

A. Write which articles may be used before the nouns.

1. ___ brush	**4.** ___ leader	**7.** ___ hands
2. ___ eraser	**5.** ___ pencils	**8.** ___ object
3. ___ pens	**6.** ___ easel	**9.** ___ subject

B. Choose the correct article in ( ) to complete each sentence. Write each sentence.

10. Dana goes to (a, an) school in the city.

11. She is studying to be (a, an) engineer.

12. Engineers plan (a, the) bridges people need.

13. Dana works in (a, an) office, too.

14. She is (a, the) assistant to another engineer.

15. Robert attends (a, an) art school in the city.

16. He watched (a, an) artist work with clay.

17. Robert hopes to become (a, an) photographer.

18. He studies (a, the) animals in the Bronx Zoo.

C. Use *a* or *an* to complete each sentence. Write each sentence.

19. Grandfather takes ___ class in oil painting.

20. He uses ___ stand for his paintings.

21. It is called ___ easel.

22. He paints on ___ board of canvas.

23. He can use ___ canvas more than once.

24. Grandpa's paint comes in ___ tube.

25. Each tube contains ___ color.

26. He painted ___ astronaut's picture.

27. He uses ___ brush with thin stiff hairs.

28. I gave Grandpa ___ apron.

USING LANGUAGE TO
CLASSIFY

PART ONE

Unit Theme   *The Solar System*

Language Awareness   Sentences

PART TWO

Literature   "Sun, Moon, and Planets"

A Reason for Writing   Classifying

Writing
IN YOUR JOURNAL

WRITER'S WARM-UP ◆ What do you know about the sun, the moon, and the stars? Have you ever seen a shooting star or an eclipse of the moon? Can you name any groups of stars in the night sky? What interests you most about the solar system? What questions do you have? Write in your journal. Write what comes to your mind about the solar system.

GETTING STARTED

Say a noun that begins with the same letter as your first name. Have a classmate tell whether your noun names a person, place, or thing.

1 Nouns in Sentences

Remember that the subject of a sentence names someone or something. The subject of each sentence below is shown in blue.

> The <u>sun</u> is a bright star.
> Many <u>stars</u> are visible on a clear night.
> The <u>children</u> watched the stars in the sky.

The main word in each subject above is underlined. Notice that the underlined word is a noun.

> **Summary** ♦ The main word in the subject of a sentence is often a noun.

Guided Practice

Each subject is underlined. Name the main word.

1. The <u>sun</u> gives us light.
2. <u>Sunny days</u> make me happy.
3. <u>Karla</u> feels warmth from the sun.
4. <u>Many astronomers</u> study the sun.
5. <u>A powerful telescope</u> is their most important tool.

Practice

A. The subject is underlined in each sentence. Write the main word in each subject.

    6. <u>The sun</u> heats the earth's land, water, and air.
    7. <u>Much energy</u> comes from the sun.
    8. <u>Green plants</u> take in some of the sun's light.
    9. <u>This sunlight</u> helps the plants grow.
  10. <u>All living organisms</u> need sunlight.

B. Write each sentence. Underline the main word in each subject.

  11. The sun is smaller than most stars.
  12. Hot gases make the sun bright.
  13. The sun heats some houses.
  14. Many scientists study solar energy.
  15. Some homes have solar-heated water.

C. Choose a subject for each word group below. Then write the complete sentence. Underline the main word in each subject.

  The sun   **A ball**   **The earth**

  16. ___ is where we live.
  17. ___ rises in the east.
  18. ___ is shaped like the earth.

Apply • Think and Write

From Your Writing ♦ Read what you wrote for the Writer's Warm-up. List the main words in the subjects of your sentences.

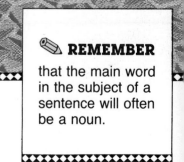

GETTING STARTED

Say a sentence using a friend's name and an action verb.
EXAMPLES: *Derek plays a drum.*
Denise raises the flag.

2 Verbs in Sentences

The predicate of a sentence tells what the subject is or does. The predicate of each sentence below is shown in green.

1. The earth travels around the sun.
2. At least nine planets orbit our sun.

The main word in each predicate above is underlined. Notice that each underlined word is a verb. Verbs are always found in the predicate of a sentence.

Many verbs show action. What are the actions of the earth and the planets in sentences **1** and **2** above?

Summary ◆ The main word in the predicate of a sentence is a verb. Every sentence needs to have a verb in the predicate.

Guided Practice

Name the verb in the predicate of each sentence below.

1. The planets vary in size.
2. Jacy identifies Jupiter as the largest planet.
3. Smaller solar bodies revolve around the sun.
4. Medium-sized stars burn with a yellow color.
5. Comets belong to the solar system, too.

Practice

A. The sentences below tell about the sun and the planets. The predicate in each sentence is underlined. Write the verb in each predicate.

   6. The sun <u>changes in brightness</u>.
   7. Nine planets <u>travel around the sun</u>.
   8. A special force <u>keeps the planets in orbit</u>.
   9. The earth <u>revolves around the sun in 365 days</u>.
 10. Jupiter's year <u>equals about twelve Earth years</u>.

B. Write each sentence. Underline the verb.

 11. Six planets have moons.
 12. Twelve moons travel around Jupiter.
 13. Meteors and comets circle the sun.
 14. Sometimes meteors collide with Earth.
 15. Scientists study the solar system.

C. Change the underlined verb in each sentence below. Write each of the new sentences.

 16. Michelle <u>gazed</u> at the stars.
 17. The stars <u>dance</u> in the sky.
 18. The sun <u>supplies</u> energy.
 19. An eclipse <u>occurs</u> once in a while.
 20. All the planets <u>move</u> in the same direction.

Apply • Think and Write

Creative Writing ♦ Write sentences telling why you would or would not like to visit another planet. Use lively verbs in the predicates of your sentences.

✎ **REMEMBER**

to use verbs
that express
action clearly.

Take turns answering the *where* and *when* questions. Use one word to tell *when*. Use one word to tell *where*.

When is your moon trip? My trip is _____ .
Where do astronauts float? Astronauts float _____ .

3 Writing with Adverbs

The first landing on the moon was a great event. Read about it in the sentences below. Notice the underlined words.

> Once a spacecraft landed on the moon.
> An astronaut placed a flag there.

Each underlined word is an adverb. Adverbs describe verbs. The adverb <u>once</u> tells *when* a spacecraft landed on the moon. The adverb <u>there</u> tells *where* the flag was placed.

Study the adverbs in the chart below.

Adverbs That Tell *When*		Adverbs That Tell *Where*	
early	yesterday	here	someplace
now	today	there	up
soon	tomorrow	everywhere	down
then	always	inside	in
once	often	outside	out

Summary ♦ A word that describes a verb is an **adverb**. Use adverbs that tell *where* or *when* to give more information in your sentences.

Guided Practice

Tell whether each adverb tells *where* or *when*.

1. today   **2.** there   **3.** in   **4.** once   **5.** soon

Practice

A. Write each underlined adverb. Then write *where* or *when*.

> **EXAMPLE:** Spacecraft <u>often</u> carry astronauts.
> **ANSWER:** often, when

6. The spacecraft soars <u>up</u> into the sky.
7. <u>Soon</u> the astronauts are in space.
8. <u>Now</u> they are weightless.
9. The astronauts can float <u>everywhere</u>.

B. Write each sentence. Underline the adverb.

10. Yuri Gagarin once orbited the earth.
11. Soon John Glenn made some orbits.
12. The astronauts looked outside.
13. The space race continues today.

C. Write each sentence. Complete each sentence with an adverb that answers the question in ( ).

> **EXAMPLE:** I will visit the control room ____. (When?)
> **ANSWER:** I will visit the control room soon.

14. The astronauts left ____. (When?)
15. We went ____ to the launching pad. (Where?)
16. The lunar module will land ____. (When?)
17. The spacecraft landed ____. (Where?)

Apply • Think and Write

A Possible Career ◆ Write sentences telling why you would or would not like to be an astronaut. Use some adverbs that tell *where* and some that tell *when*.

> ✎ **REMEMBER**
> that you can use adverbs to add details about time and place.

GETTING
STARTED

Think of words to finish the sentence:
Wandering Willy walked ____ .

EXAMPLES: *Wandering Willy walked slowly.*
Wandering Willy walked calmly.

4 Adverbs That Tell *How*

Adverbs are words that describe verbs. Look at the underlined adverbs below. How does each adverb end?

Mars orbits <u>smoothly</u> around the sun.
Scientists look <u>closely</u> at Mars.

The adverb <u>smoothly</u> describes the verb *orbits*. Smoothly tells *how* Mars orbits around the sun. The adverb <u>closely</u> describes the verb *look*. Closely tells *how* scientists look at Mars. Many adverbs that answer the question "How?" end in *-ly*.

Read the sentence. What adverb tells *how* Mars shines?

■ Mars shines brightly.

> **Summary** ◆ Some adverbs answer the question "How?" Many adverbs that answer the question "How?" end in *-ly*.

Guided Practice

Name the adverb in each sentence.

1. Scientists observe the planets carefully.
2. Astronauts bravely explore space.
3. Cameras photograph the planets clearly.
4. They develop the photographs quickly.
5. Scientists view the pictures eagerly.

Practice

A. Write the adverb in each sentence.

6. People read about Mars curiously.
7. They collect information gladly.
8. Mars is correctly called the Red Planet.
9. It certainly appears rust-red.
10. Windstorms fiercely stir the reddish dust.

B. Add *-ly* to each word in ( ) to form an adverb. Then write each sentence.

11. Green spots increase (sudden) in spring.
12. In winter the polar cap expands (swift).
13. Photographs (plain) show craters and mountains.
14. Dr. Howard speaks (wise) about the planets.
15. He (careful) describes two small moons.

C. Add an adverb that ends in *-ly* to each sentence below. Each adverb will answer the question "How?"

16. Alvaro waits ____ for the telescope.
17. Dr. Howard aims it ____ at Jupiter.
18. Alvaro ____ locates Jupiter's moons.
19. He yells ____ .
20. Dr. Howard is ____ pleased.

Apply • Think and Write

A Creative List ◆ Pretend you are directing a trip to Mars. Prepare a list of rules. Tell how you want people to behave. You may use these adverbs in your rules: *calmly*, *nicely*, *politely*, and *safely*.

> ✎ **REMEMBER**
> that adverbs that tell *how* give details about actions.

◆ GETTING STARTED ◆

One thing sometimes causes something else to happen. Play "Cause and Effect."

EXAMPLES: *I didn't hurry, so I was late.*
I couldn't hear, so I moved closer.

5 Contractions

Remember that a contraction is a shortened form of two words. Each contraction below is made up of a verb and *not*.

■ **I don't like storms.   She doesn't like rain.**

The contraction *don't* is a shorter way to write *do not*. The apostrophe replaces the letter *o* in *not*. What contraction is a shorter way to write *does not*? What letter does the apostrophe replace?

Verb + not = Contraction					
is	+ not = isn't		have	+ not = haven't
are	+ not = aren't		has	+ not = hasn't
was	+ not = wasn't		had	+ not = hadn't
were	+ not = weren't		can	+ not = can't
do	+ not = don't		could	+ not = couldn't
does	+ not = doesn't		would	+ not = wouldn't
did	+ not = didn't		should	+ not = shouldn't

The contraction *won't* is a shorter way to write *will not*.

> **Summary** ◆ Some contractions are formed from a verb and *not*. Contractions can help you write the way people talk.

Guided Practice

Tell what contractions can be formed with these words.

1. was + not   **2.** did + not   **3.** had + not

Practice

A. Find the contraction in each sentence. Write the two words that make up each contraction.

4. The planet Neptune wasn't discovered until 1846.
5. Neptune isn't the smallest planet.
6. Scientists didn't discover Pluto until 1930.
7. They weren't sure there was another planet.
8. Scientists aren't certain of the number of planets.

B. Write the contractions you can make with these words.

9. should + not
10. are + not
11. could + not
12. does + not
13. were + not

14. has + not
15. do + not
16. would + not
17. have + not
18. is + not

C. Write each sentence. Use a contraction in place of the underlined words.

19. Some planets <u>have not</u> been discovered.
20. Astronomers <u>do not</u> know what to expect.
21. They <u>can not</u> see everything.
22. The telescope <u>is not</u> powerful enough.
23. She <u>could not</u> visit the planetarium.

Apply • Think and Write

Dictionary of Knowledge ♦ Read about astronomer Maria Mitchell in the Dictionary of Knowledge. Write about her studies and discoveries. Use some contractions in your sentences.

✎ **REMEMBER**

to use an apostrophe where one or more letters have been left out in a contraction.

How would you describe the feel of sandpaper? How would you describe the feel of glass? Are the words you used opposite in meaning?

VOCABULARY ◆
Antonyms

Some things are opposites.

> Have you ever taken a <u>hot</u> bath and a <u>cold</u> shower?
> Do you think it's wise to take a <u>long</u> walk on a <u>short</u> dock?
> Can you go <u>deep</u>-sea fishing in a <u>shallow</u> stream?

The underlined words above are antonyms. **Antonyms** are words that have opposite meanings. *Hot* is the opposite of *cold*. *Long* is the opposite of *short*. What word is the opposite of *deep*?

Building Your Vocabulary

Look at the picture pairs below. What antonyms do you think of for each pair?

Practice

A. Write the antonyms in the sentences below.

   1. Marcia seemed cheerful, but Mary seemed sad.

   2. Susan loved the movie, but Brenda hated it.

   3. Tomás asked a question, and Sol gave an answer.

   4. One box was heavy, and the other was light.

B. Write the sentences. Use an antonym in place of each underlined word.

   5. Charlie likes to pull weeds.

   6. The sun is much smaller than the moon.

   7. The water flowed uphill.

   8. It's hard to find the sum of 2 plus 2.

C. Complete each rhyme below. Use an antonym for the underlined word.

   9. *Young* is to *old* as hot is to ____ .

   10. *Thick* is to *thin* as lose is to ____ .

   11. *Low* is to *high* as wet is to ____ .

   12. *Cold* is to *heat* as sour is to ____ .

Language Corner ♦ Echo Words

American dogs *bow-wow*, *woof-woof*, and *arf-arf*. Did you know that Spanish dogs *pan-pan*, Italian dogs *bu-bu*, and Chinese dogs *wah-wah*?

What do dogs sound like to you?

How to Combine Sentences

Sentences that have ideas that go together can be combined. You can use a comma and the word *and* to combine them. Combining sentences can add variety to your writing. Read the examples below.

1. Paula looks at the night sky. The stars seem to wink at her.
2. Paula looks at the night sky, and the stars seem to wink at her.

Both examples tell us something about the night sky. Example **2** combines the two sentences about the night sky into one strong sentence.

You can also combine sentences that ask questions by using a comma and the word *and*. Remember to combine them only if they have ideas that go together.

3. Will you watch the stars with me tonight? Can you tell me about them?
4. Will you watch the stars with me tonight, and can you tell me about them?

The Grammar Game ♦ Be a sentence-combining star! Join each pair of sentences into one longer sentence.

♦ Where is the North Star? Can I see it without a telescope?
♦ The Big Dipper is easy to find. A clear night is the best time to see it.

Working Together

By combining sentences, you can join ideas that go together. Work with your group on activities **A** and **B**.

A. Use a comma and the word *and* to combine each pair of sentences. Replace the names with names of group members.

1. Evan swept the floor. The dust disappeared.
2. Barb mowed the lawn. Grass flew everywhere.
3. Will Mary wash the car? Can Greg help?
4. Jo cleaned all day. Now the house sparkles.

B. Use classmates' names to complete the sentences below. Then combine each pair of sentences into one sentence.

5. ___ tells funny jokes. People always laugh.
6. ___ keeps the pencils sharp. We need them often.
7. ___ is a great cook. The treats smell tasty.
8. ___ plays the piano. Everyone sings along.

WRITERS' CORNER ◆ Sentence Variety

Mixing statements, questions, commands, and exclamations makes writing interesting. What kinds of sentences can you find in this ad?

Do you want to travel in space? Perhaps you can become an Astrokid. Don't wait any longer! Send in your application today.

Read what you wrote for the Writer's Warm-up. What kinds of sentences did you use?

LIFT-OFF ON TITAN
painting by Robert McCall.

USING LANGUAGE
TO
CLASSIFY

PART TWO

Literature   "Sun, Moon, and Planets"
A Reason for Writing   Classifying

CREATIVE
Writing

FINE ARTS ◆ There are two astronauts standing in the front of this painting. What are they doing? Why are they there? What do you think they are saying to each other? Write about the conversation they are having.

CRITICAL THINKING ◆
A Strategy for Classifying

A VENN DIAGRAM

Classifying is grouping things that are alike. After this lesson you will read "Sun, Moon, and Planets." You will learn ways the earth, moon, and sun are alike. You will also learn ways they are different. Later you will write about how two things are alike.

Here is part of "Sun, Moon, and Planets." What does it tell you about the moon and the earth?

In some ways the moon and the earth are alike. Both are covered by rocks and soil. . . . But the earth's surface is always being changed. . . . The moon's surface does not change.

What is one way that the moon is like the earth? What is one way that they are different?

Learning the Strategy

You often notice how things are alike or different. Suppose you look at the sky. Why might you think the clouds are like cotton balls? Imagine you meet identical twin girls. They look almost alike. How else might they be alike? How might they be different?

Can you show how two things are alike and different? A Venn diagram is one way to do it. A Venn diagram is two circles that overlap. The example on the next page is about twins named Nan and Fran. The words in the middle show

CRITICAL THINKING: Comparing/Contrasting

how they are alike. The words on the outsides show how they are different. Do you know any twins? What ideas might you add to this Venn diagram?

Nan
different
Likes sports
Dislikes movies
Is friendly

alike
Brown eyes
Dark hair
Warm
smile

Fran
different
Dislikes sports
Loves movies
Is shy

Using the Strategy

A. What are your two favorite foods? Make a Venn diagram. Show how your favorite foods are alike and different.

B. Make a Venn diagram for the earth and the moon. List ways they are alike. List ways they are different. Then read "Sun, Moon, and Planets." See if you find anything to add to your diagram.

Applying the Strategy

- You told how the earth and the moon are alike. How did you figure it out?
- Is it ever important to notice how things are alike? Or different? When?

SUN, MOON, AND PLANETS

The sun is much larger than the moon. But it is much farther from the earth than the moon is. Large bodies like the sun look smaller when they are far away.

The moon does not give off its own light. Instead it reflects light from the sun. The sun is the source of light for the earth and the moon.

In some ways the moon and the earth are alike. Both are covered by rocks and soil. Both have uneven surfaces. Mountains, valleys, and large flat areas are found on both the moon and the earth. But the earth's surface is always being changed by moving water and wind. The moon's surface does not change. Can you tell why?

Reader's Response

Do you think you would like to explore the moon? Tell why.

Excerpt is from *Silver Burdett and Ginn Science 3*, © 1987.

SUN, MOON, AND PLANETS

◆ Responding to Literature

1. Have you ever seen a bright full moon shining in the sky? What does it make you think of?

2. Imagine that you could walk on the moon. Tell what you would see. Tell what you would wear. Show how you would walk in your special clothes.

3. What do you like about the sun? The moon? Fold a piece of paper in half. On one side, draw your favorite thing about the sun. On the other, draw your favorite thing about the moon. Tell about your drawings.

◆ Writing to Learn

Think and Compare ◆ How does the earth compare with the moon? What do you know now that you did not know before this lesson? Copy the diagram below. Add details.

Venn Diagram

Write ◆ Write a paragraph to tell how the earth and the moon are alike. Use details from your diagram.

Each of these pairs of things has a likeness. How are the things alike? *a pen and a pencil, a tablet and a chalkboard, a door and a window*

SPEAKING and LISTENING ◆
Comparisons

Ana explains to the class, "The harvest moon looks like a giant orange in the sky." She uses a comparison to make her explanation clear.

A comparison tells how two things are alike. A harvest moon looks like a giant orange. Both are round and orange-colored. Comparisons can help you when you speak and when you listen. Here are some guidelines for using comparisons.

Making Comparisons	**1.** Use a comparison to describe something.
	    The earth looks like a big blue marble.
	2. Use a comparison to explain something.
	    Walking on the moon is like jumping on a trampoline.
	3. Tell in what way two things are alike.

Being a Critical Listener	**1.** Listen for details that describe. Decide if the details tell how things are alike. **2.** Decide if the comparisons you hear are helpful. Do the comparisons help you draw pictures in your mind? **3.** Ask questions if you do not understand a comparison you hear.

Summary ◆ A **comparison** tells how one thing is like another. Use comparisons when you speak. Listen for comparisons when others speak.

Guided Practice

Tell in what ways the sun and the moon are alike. Think of as many ways as you can.

Practice

A. Tell how each pair of things is alike. How many ways can you give?

1. a puppy and a kitten
2. a newspaper and a magazine
3. an apple and an orange
4. your feet and your hands
5. a bicycle and a car

B. Work with a partner. Take turns making comparisons. Choose something in the room, but don't tell what you choose. Use comparisons to describe the thing or to explain what it is. As the listener, guess what is being described. Here are some sample clues.

6. It looks like a ____ .
7. It is shaped like ____ .
8. It is the same color as ____ .
9. It sounds like ____ .
10. It has ____ like a ____ .

Apply ◆ Think and Write

Remembering Comparisons ◆ What interesting comparisons have you heard? Think of conversations, of radio and television programs, and of commercials. Write at least one comparison you have heard.

> ✏️ **Remember**
> to use comparisons to describe or explain something.

♦ GETTING
STARTED ♦

Ask a riddle about how things are alike.
EXAMPLE: *How is a clock like a person's body?*
ANSWER: *They both have hands.*

WRITING ♦
A Paragraph That Compares

When you classify, you put things that are alike in a certain way in a group. Classifying helps you organize your thoughts and helps you learn. Making comparisons is an important part of classifying.

Here is a paragraph that compares Earth with Venus. Notice how it does this.

Topic sentence

Details

Earth and Venus are alike in several ways. They are both planets traveling around the sun. They are nearly the same size. They both have clouds in their skies, too.

Writing a paragraph that compares two things helps you and your reader see ways in which the things are alike.

Summary ♦ A **paragraph that compares** tells how two things are alike. It begins with a topic sentence. Then it gives details about how the things are alike.

Guided Practice

These three sets of clothing belong to one group. That group is called work clothes. Why do they belong to that group? How are they alike?

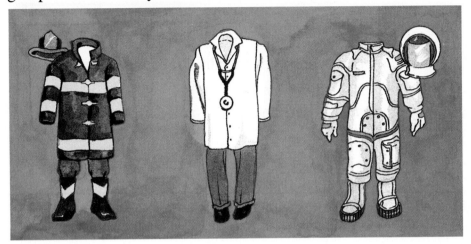

Practice

A. Write one way in which each pair of things is alike.

1. a jet plane and a rocket
2. an astronaut and Christopher Columbus
3. the sky and the ocean
4. a planet and a star
5. the sun and the earth

B. Write a paragraph that compares two things. You may compare two things from **Practice A** if you wish. Remember to begin your paragraph with a topic sentence.

Apply ◆ Think and Write

Dictionary of Knowledge ◆ Read about Mars. Write a paragraph that tells how Mars is like Earth.

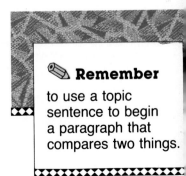

✎ **Remember**
to use a topic sentence to begin a paragraph that compares two things.

Focus on Likenesses

How is the earth like the moon? How is a hurricane like a tornado? How are all insects alike? Scientists can answer such questions. In their work, scientists look for **likenesses.** They study and understand things partly by finding out how things are alike.

You can use likenesses, too. Look for them when you read. Notice how an author compares one thing with another. Make comparisons of your own when you write. Show your reader how things are alike.

Look at these sentences about the earth and the moon. You read them earlier in the unit.

In some ways the moon and the earth are alike. Both are covered by rocks and soil. Both have uneven surfaces. Mountains, valleys, and large flat areas are found on both the moon and the earth.

What things does the author compare? How are they alike?

The Writer's Voice ♦ Look at this photograph of the lunar rover. Astronauts used it to travel on the moon. Compare it with a car. How are the two vehicles alike?

Working Together

Do you often notice the ways that things are alike? When you describe how two things are alike, you are comparing. The things you compare might be the same size. Some things are alike because they are the same color, or the same shape. Sometimes things are alike because they are living, or not living. Work with your group on activities **A** and **B.**

A. With your group, choose two different things in your classroom to compare. Discuss how the two things are alike. List as many likenesses as you can.

B. Work on a paragraph with your group. Compare the two things your group chose in activity **A.** Start with a topic sentence. Add details. Try to keep the same kind of details together. For example, write all the details about what the two things look like first.

In Your Group

- Give your ideas to the group.
- Record everyone's ideas on a list.
- Show appreciation for people's ideas.
- Look at others when they talk.

THESAURUS CORNER ♦ Word Choice

Look up the word *cool* in the Thesaurus. Think of two things that are cool. Then write three sentences to compare the two things. Use a different synonym for *cool* in each of the sentences that you write. Be sure that each synonym fits the meaning of the sentence.

WRITING PROCESS
CLASSIFYING

Writing an Article That Compares

"Sun, Moon, and Planets" compares the earth and the moon. Were you surprised to discover how they are alike? We often learn a lot by comparing things.

Know Your Purpose and Audience

MY PURPOSE

Now you will write an article to compare two things. Your purpose is to tell how they are alike.

MY AUDIENCE

Your audience will be your classmates. Later you might read your article aloud. You might also create a "How Are They Alike?" display.

1 Prewriting

First you must choose two things to compare. They will be your topic. Then you need to gather ideas about your topic.

Choose Your Topic ♦ Think of pairs of things to compare. Start by making a list. Then circle the pair you find most interesting.

Think About It	Talk About It
You might start by naming two things that fly. What are two things that grow? Think of two things you can wear. Which pair will you write about? Which pair has the most likenesses? Circle the pair that you like the best.	Work with your classmates to find things to compare. Brainstorm and then make a list of pairs on the chalkboard. Think of things that seem easy to compare. Then pick the pair that you know the most about.

Topic Ideas

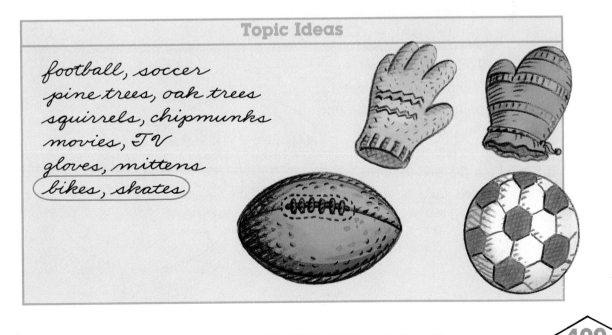

football, soccer
pine trees, oak trees
squirrels, chipmunks
movies, TV
gloves, mittens
bikes, skates

Choose Your Strategy ♦ Here are two ways to get ideas for your article. Use the way you would like to try.

PREWRITING IDEAS

CHOICE ONE

A Comparison Chart

Draw a line down the middle of a piece of paper. Write one item on one side. Write the other item on the other side. List details about each item. Then circle details that are alike for both.

Model

bike	skates
two wheels	four wheels each
pedal it	glide on them
can go fast	can go fast
have to balance	have to balance
it's fun	they are fun

CHOICE TWO

A Venn Diagram

Make a Venn diagram. Draw two overlapping circles. Write one item at the top of each. On the outsides write details that are different. In the middle write details that are alike.

Model

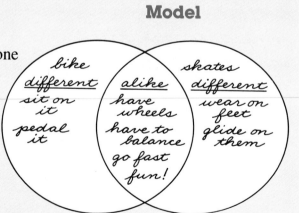

2 Writing

Begin to write your article. Start by saying that the two items are alike. Here are two ways to start.

♦ ___ and ___ are alike in some ways.
♦ Have you noticed how ___ and ___ are alike?

Your comparison chart or Venn diagram can help you write. You will only write about what is alike. Look at details you circled on your comparison chart. Look at details in the middle of your Venn diagram.

Write two paragraphs. Tell about one or two likenesses in each paragraph.

Sample First Draft ♦

A bike and skates are alike.
At first it is hard to balance
on wheels. You have to practess
balancing on your skates or bike.
Both have wheels. If you don't,
you might take a fall.
You can go fast on a bike. You can
go fast on skates, too. I like to
go on my bike or skates. they are
both a lot of fun.

3 Revising

Here is an idea to help improve your article.

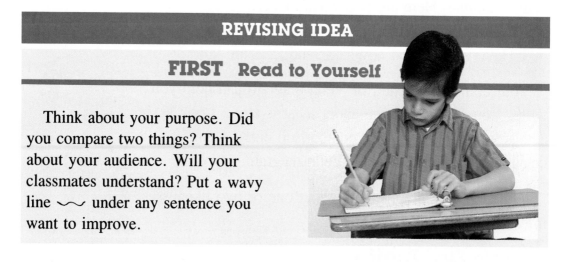

REVISING IDEA

FIRST Read to Yourself

Think about your purpose. Did you compare two things? Think about your audience. Will your classmates understand? Put a wavy line 〰 under any sentence you want to improve.

Focus: To compare is to tell about likenesses. Did you give details about how your items are alike?

THEN Share with a Partner

Sit beside a partner. Read your article aloud as your partner reads silently. Ask your partner for ideas.

The Writer

Guidelines: Thank your partner for helping you.

Sample questions:
- How could I improve my first sentence?
- **Focus question:** Are there more likenesses I can add?

The Writer's Partner

Guidelines: Be polite. Give helpful ideas.

Sample responses:
- In your first sentence you could say ____.
- Another way they are alike is ____.

Revising Model ♦ The article below is being revised.
Notice how the writer is making changes.

The writer added a needed detail.

This fact was in the wrong order.

Tumble is a better word in this sentence.

The writer's partner suggested this addition.

in some ways
A bike and skates are alike.

At first it is hard to balance on wheels. You have to practess balancing on your skates or bike. (Both have wheels.) If you don't, *tumble* you might take a fall.

You can go fast on a bike. You can go fast on skates, too. I like to *everywhere* go on my bike or skates. they are both a lot of fun.

Read the article above with the writer's changes. Then revise your own article.

Grammar Check ♦ Adverbs can add information about *where*, *when*, or *how*.

Word Choice ♦ Is there a more exact word for a word like *fall*? A thesaurus can help you find exact words.

Revising Checklist

☐ **My purpose:** Did I write an article to compare two things?

☐ **Audience:** Will my classmates understand my article?

☐ **Focus:** Did I give details about how my items are alike?

4 Proofreading

Proofreading can help to make your article neat and correct. Then your readers can understand your writing.

Proofreading Model ♦ Here is the article that compares a bike and skates. The proofreading changes are shown in red.

in some ways
A bike and skates are alike.

At first it is hard to balance
practice
on wheels. You have to practess
balancing on your skates or bike.
Both have wheels If you don't,
tumble
you might take a fall.
¶ You can go fast on a bike. You can
go fast on skates, too. I like to
everywhere
go on my bike or skates. they are
both a lot of fun.

PROOFREADING IDEA

Handwriting Check

Don't let your words trail off. Make every letter neatly. The last letter should be as neat as the first.

Now proofread your article and add a title. Then make a neat copy.

5 Publishing

Now you have written an article that compares. Would you like to share it with others? Here are two ideas.

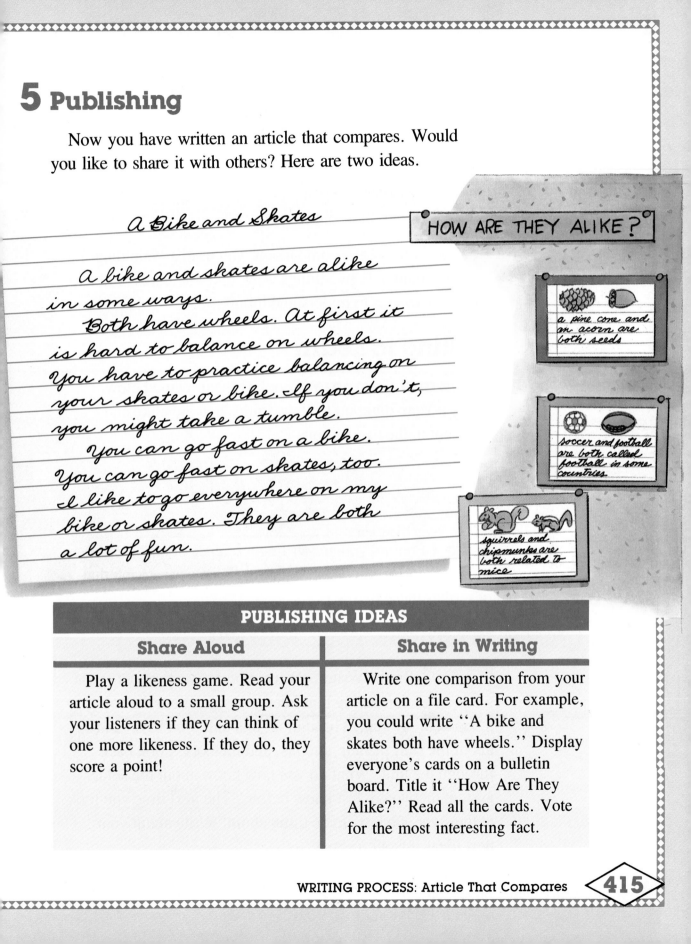

A Bike and Skates

A bike and skates are alike in some ways.

Both have wheels. At first it is hard to balance on wheels. You have to practice balancing on your skates or bike. If you don't, you might take a tumble.

You can go fast on a bike. You can go fast on skates, too. I like to go everywhere on my bike or skates. They are both a lot of fun.

HOW ARE THEY ALIKE?

a pine cone and an acorn are both seeds

soccer and football are both called football in some countries

squirrels and chipmunks are both related to mice

PUBLISHING IDEAS

Share Aloud

Play a likeness game. Read your article aloud to a small group. Ask your listeners if they can think of one more likeness. If they do, they score a point!

Share in Writing

Write one comparison from your article on a file card. For example, you could write "A bike and skates both have wheels." Display everyone's cards on a bulletin board. Title it "How Are They Alike?" Read all the cards. Vote for the most interesting fact.

Writing Across the Curriculum Science

When you wrote a comparison, you used a Venn diagram to understand how two things were alike. Scientists often use comparisons to understand things.

Writing to Learn

Think and Compare ◆ Look at the drawing below. Make a Venn diagram to show things that are alike and different in the two seasons.

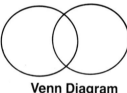

Venn Diagram

Write ◆ Pretend you are writing a science book. Use the information in your Venn diagram. Write a paragraph that describes these two seasons.

Writing in Your Journal

In the Writer's Warm-up you wrote about something that interested you about the solar system. Throughout this unit you have read about the sun, planets, moons, and meteors. Look back through the unit. What do you now know about the solar system that you didn't know before? The next time you look at the stars, what will you think about? Write about your new ideas in your journal.

Read More About It

The Planets in Our Solar System

by Franklyn M. Branley

Our earth is one of nine planets that belong together. Read some interesting facts about planets in this book.

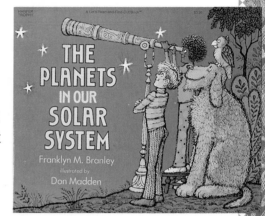

Astronauts *by Norman Barrett*

How do people become astronauts? What do astronauts do up there in space? This book will answer these and other questions.

Book Report Idea Report Rocket

Use a rocket for your next book report.

Create a Rocket Report

Cut a tall rocket shape out of construction paper. Write the title and author on it. Tell interesting details about your book by adding sentences to the rocket. Draw stars to show how much you enjoyed the book. One star means the book is good, and four stars means the book is great.

UNIT REVIEW

Unit 8

Nouns   *pages 382–383*

A. Write the main word in each underlined subject.

1. A cool <u>wind</u> blows.
2. The <u>door</u> bangs shut.
3. The nervous <u>dog</u> jumps.
4. The red <u>towel</u> is mine.
5. My <u>goat</u> sees the towel.
6. His <u>lunchtime</u> is near.

Verbs   *pages 384–385*

B. Write the verb in the predicate of each sentence.

7. My sister calls me.
8. We chase the goat.
9. The goat moves fast.
10. We run into a field.
11. I creep closer to him.
12. The goat swallows strings.

Adverbs   *pages 386–389*

C. Write whether each adverb tells *when* or *where*.

13. tomorrow
14. here
15. early
16. inside
17. soon
18. down
19. someplace
20. out
21. always
22. now
23. there
24. tonight

D. Add *-ly* to each word in ( ) to form an adverb. Then write each sentence.

25. We watched (curious) as the van was unloaded.
26. Cecile waited (impatient) to meet the new neighbors.
27. Later she rushed (excited) into the house.
28. She (joyful) talked about the children.

Contractions   *pages 390–391*

E. Write the contraction for each pair of words.

29. was + not

30. is + not

31. did + not

32. will + not

33. can + not

34. should + not

35. had + not

36. does + not

Antonyms   *pages 392–393*

F. Write the antonym in (   ) for each word below.

37. afraid (brave, dark)

38. bright (shining, dark)

39. let (forbid, grant)

40. fall (rise, drop)

41. dirty (clean, polluted)

42. work (toil, play)

43. change (remain, switch)

44. alone (separate, together)

45. end (finish, start)

46. grow (shrink, expand)

47. cool (chilly, warm)

48. big (tiny, great)

Comparisons   *pages 402–405*

G. Write the correct answer to each question.

49. How are mice and rabbits alike?

   a. Both have long tails.

   b. Both have four feet.

   c. Both are tiny.

   d. Both have long ears.

50. How are boards and bricks alike?

   a. Both have splinters.

   b. Both are for building.

   c. Both come from trees.

   d. Both are made of clay.

CUMULATIVE REVIEW

Sentences *pages 8–17*

A. Write each sentence correctly. Use a capital letter and put the correct mark at the end.

1. did you see the comet
2. we went down to the shore
3. the comet was quite large
4. what a thrill it was to see it

B. Write each sentence. Draw one line under the subject. Draw two lines under the predicate.

5. We saw Halley's comet.
7. Many people saw it.
6. It has a long tail.
8. It will be back.

Nouns *pages 62–71*

C. Write the plural form of each noun.

9. driver   10. bus   11. woman   12. lunch

D. Write the possessive form of each noun.

13. class   15. bowl   17. stories   19. comet
14. turtle   16. benches   18. stars   20. telescope

Capital Letters and Periods *pages 118–123*

E. Write each proper noun correctly.

21. saratoga   23. mrs miniver   25. halloween
22. monday   24. idaho   26. david copperfield

Pronouns *pages 164–173*

F. Change the underlined word or words in each sentence to a pronoun. Write each new sentence.

27. Hazel waved to Brad and me.

28. She and I were jogging.

29. Call Tim and Betsy's mom.

30. Try Joanne's soup.

31. Patricia wrote to Mariah.

32. Look at Robbie's picture.

33. The squirrel sat up.

34. It saw Mike and Mary.

35. The plant flowered.

36. Russ saw a spider.

37. Tim and Jake swim.

38. The gift is for Pete.

Verbs *pages 218–229, 272–273, 278–283*

G. Write the correct present-time form of the verb in ( ). Then write the correct past-time form.

39. Alva ____ to catch the school bus. (hurry)

40. We ____ our homework after supper. (do)

41. The dog ____ her morning walk. (miss)

42. Wendy's friend ____ her sculpture. (admire)

43. Walker ____ the tower on the hill. (see)

44. The eagle ____ out in alarm. (cry)

45. The bald eagle ____ to be a very big bird. (grow)

46. The train ____ at our station last. (stop)

H. Write each sentence. Draw one line under the helping verb. Draw two lines under the main verb.

47. Ken has gone away.

48. He had taken the bus.

49. We have said goodbye.

50. The bus had arrived.

51. Ken has climbed on.

52. We have waved.

53. The driver had smiled.

54. She has signaled.

55. The cars have stopped.

56. The bus had departed.

57. It has gained speed.

58. We have watched it.

I. Write the adjective that describes each underlined noun.

> **59.** A tiger is a wild <u>cat</u>.
> **60.** It has a rough <u>tongue</u>.
> **61.** Every wild cat is a good <u>climber</u>.
> **62.** It pulls back its sharp <u>claws</u> when it walks.

J. Write each pair of words. Underline each adjective.

> **63.** canine teeth   **66.** some leopards   **69.** black panthers
> **64.** striped coat   **67.** fierce animals   **70.** open country
> **65.** orange fur   **68.** few enemies   **71.** many lions

K. Add *-er* or *-est* to each adjective in ( ). Write each sentence.

> **72.** The male lion is (large) than the female.
> **73.** Of all the wild cats, the leopard is the (mean).
> **74.** The puma is (fierce) than the ocelot.
> **75.** The cheetah is the (fast) running animal.
> **76.** It is even (fast) than other wild cats.

L. Choose the correct article in ( ). Write each sentence.

> **77.** Isaac Newton was (a, an) shy man.
> **78.** One day he watched (a, an) apple fall.
> **79.** Newton wrote (a, the) laws of gravity.
> **80.** Later he invented (a, the) special telescope.

Nouns   *pages 382–383*

M. Write the main word in each underlined subject.

81. Your <u>body</u> has many bones.
82. The <u>bones</u> form a frame.
83. The <u>frame</u> holds you up.
84. The <u>jaw bone</u> can move.
85. <u>Other bones</u> can't move.
86. The <u>spine</u> has many bones.

Verbs   *pages 384–385*

N. Write the verb in the predicate of each sentence.

87. Snow covers the ground.
88. The wind blows fiercely.
89. The animals breathe slowly.
90. Bears sleep all winter.
91. They hide in caves.
92. The bears become thin.

Adverbs   *pages 386–389*

O. Write whether each adverb tells *when*, *where*, or *how*.

93. lovingly
94. inside
95. often
96. today
97. up
98. far
99. never
100. wisely

P. Add *-ly* to each word in ( ) to form an adverb. Write each sentence.

101. The bear ate (eager) all summer and fall.
102. Soon it would be sleeping (sound).
103. All winter it would sleep (deep).
104. Scientists have studied sleeping bears (careful).

Contractions   *pages 284–285, 390–391*

Q. Write the two words that make up each contraction.

105. shouldn't
106. weren't
107. I'll
108. doesn't
109. isn't
110. we're

Scrambled Adverbs

Unscramble each set of letters to make an adverb in the box.

1. tisdoue
2. ynlesruvo
3. tnimieaptyl
4. yleimtaimde
5. rcllaey
6. ltpnaasyel
7. yyeeadrts
8. ftiwsyl
9. woromotr
10. xsuoinayl

> pleasantly
> nervously
> tomorrow
> yesterday
> clearly
> anxiously
> swiftly
> outside
> impatiently
> immediately

Adverb Links

The answers to this link puzzle are adverbs that fit this sentence: *I got there _____.* Write the words that fill the links.

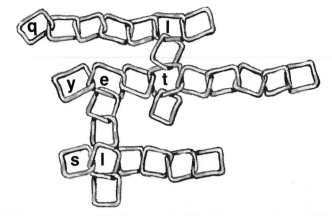

Unit 8 Extra Practice

1 Nouns in Sentences

p. 382

A. The subject is underlined in each sentence. Write the main word in each subject.

1. A large company made two robots in 1939.
2. The electrical robots appeared at the World's Fair.
3. The mechanical man weighed 260 pounds.
4. Elektro counted on his fingers.
5. The electrical dog was named Sparko.
6. A scientist built a mechanical woman in 1940.
7. That inventor lived in California.
8. Isis played a musical instrument.
9. The robot rested on a sofa.
10. Her machinery contained many wheels.

B. Write each sentence. Underline the main word in each subject.

11. The children watched an old movie.
12. A friendly robot knew how to drive.
13. A smart robot appeared on television.
14. Robby helped a lost family.
15. Their spaceship crashed on a strange planet.
16. My sister dreamed about robots.
17. A huge spaceship came from Mars.
18. A short creature carried a suitcase.
19. Strange sounds came from its stomach.
20. The mysterious robot had three eyes.
21. My sister gave it a sandwich.
22. The robot said, "Thank you."

A. Write the verb in each predicate.

1. Ira and Edna unfold the flag.
2. They raise the flag on the flagpole.
3. They lower the flag at sunset.
4. Ira and Edna carefully fold the flag.
5. Edna stores it away every evening.
6. Everyone marches in a parade on June 14.
7. Connie wanted an American flag for Flag Day.
8. She walked to a new store.
9. The store sells flags from different countries.
10. Connie saw many flags with stars.
11. She looked at red, white, and blue flags from England and France.
12. Connie waved Italy's red, green, and white flag.
13. The clerk told her about the United States flag.
14. The American flag has thirteen stripes.
15. Connie carried her new flag proudly.

B. Write each sentence. Underline the verb.

16. Derek makes flags for his friends.
17. He cuts a big rectangle of white paper.
18. Derek pastes seven red stripes on it.
19. He adds a blue square to the upper left corner.
20. He draws fifty white stars.
21. Ramón collects flags from other countries.
22. Aunt Lily gave him a Mexican flag.
23. The flag shows an eagle on it.
24. The eagle stands on a rock.
25. It holds a snake in its mouth.

3 Writing with Adverbs   *p. 386*

A. Write whether each adverb tells *where* or *when*.

1. always	**4.** in	**7.** then	**10.** inside
2. inside	**5.** once	**8.** down	**11.** yesterday
3. early	**6.** there	**9.** today	**12.** out

B. Write each underlined adverb. Then write whether the adverb tells *where* or *when*.

EXAMPLE: **We went down to the bus station.**
ANSWER: **down, where**

13. My family travels everywhere by bus.
14. We always look at the schedule.
15. Once I forgot to check the timetable.
16. I was going someplace by myself.
17. The bus was leaving here at seven o'clock.
18. I arrived late at the terminal.
19. I ran outside to look for the bus.
20. Then I went to the ticket agent.
21. She pointed up at a schedule on the wall.
22. Now I remember to read the timetable!

C. Write each sentence. Underline the adverb.

23. Roberta arrived today.
24. She traveled yesterday on a bus.
25. A taxi brought her here from the station.
26. She put her suitcase inside.
27. We went out to the yard.
28. She will leave tomorrow.
29. I will visit Roberta soon.

4 Adverbs That Tell *How*

p. 388

A. Write the adverb in each sentence.

1. The telephone rang loudly.
2. Floyd answered it quickly.
3. Floyd spoke to Ms. Yamamoto politely.
4. Charles answers the telephone calmly.
5. He takes messages correctly.
6. He writes messages neatly on a pad.
7. Darren uses the telephone nicely.
8. He answers its ring quickly.
9. He listens patiently to the other person.
10. Darren speaks clearly.
11. Then he politely asks the caller to wait.

B. Add -*ly* to each word in ( ) to form an adverb. Then write each sentence.

12. Kiki waited (impatient) by the telephone.
13. Her sister watched her (curious).
14. The phone rang (sudden).
15. (Nervous) Kiki answered it.
16. She listened (quiet) for a moment.
17. She hung up the telephone (silent).
18. Then she (slow) turned around.
19. She clapped her hands (loud).
20. (Proud) she announced that she had won first prize in the Space Age Science Fair.
21. Kiki's sister hugged her (tight).
22. (Quick) they telephoned the news to Mother.
23. She (calm) announced a special celebration.
24. They waited (excited) for her arrival home.

5 Contractions

p. 390

A. Write the contractions you can make with these words.

   1. did + not   **3.** was + not   **5.** are + not

   2. has + not   **4.** does + not   **6.** can + not

B. Find the contraction in each sentence. Write the two words that make up each contraction.

   7. Bicycle riders shouldn't forget safety rules.

   8. Dawn isn't careless on her bicycle.

   9. She doesn't take chances.

   10. Some people don't always stop at corners.

   11. Reggie didn't stay close to the curb.

   12. Margie and Arnold aren't riding safe bicycles.

   13. Pat couldn't remember hand signals for turns.

   14. Ben and Cam hadn't stopped at every stop sign.

   15. They weren't watching for other traffic.

   16. Sheldon wasn't wearing bright clothing at night.

   17. It isn't difficult to remember these rules.

   18. Then you won't have an accident.

C. Write each sentence. Use a contraction in place of the underlined words.

   19. I could not wait for the safety poster contest.

   20. Tom has not followed the contest rules.

   21. He is not making a poster.

   22. I have not finished my large poster.

   23. I hope the paint on my poster does not streak.

   24. My poster would not fit in my desk.

   25. I do not want to lose it before the judging.

   26. The judges will not change the rules.

Acknowledgments continued from page ii.

Permissions: We wish to thank the following authors, publishers, agents, corporations, and individuals for their permission to reprint copyrighted materials. Page 26: "A Curve in the River" from *More Stories Julian Tells* by Ann Cameron. Copyright © 1986 by Ann Cameron. Reprinted by permission of Alfred A. Knopf, Inc. Page 80: "A Way With Wood" reprinted from the October 1987 issue of *Ranger Rick* magazine, with permission from the publisher, The National Wildlife Federation. Copyright 1987 NWF. Page 132: "Little Bird Flitting" by Basho. From *Cricket Songs* Japanese haiku translated by Harry Behn. © 1964 by Harry Behn. All rights reserved. Reprinted by permission of Marian Reiner. "The Wind" from *Once Upon a Time* by David McCord. Copyright 1952 by David McCord. Reprinted by permission of Little, Brown & Company. Page 133: "Caterpillar" from *Blackberry Ink* by Eve Merriam. Copyright © 1985 by Eve Merriam. All rights reserved. Reprinted by permission of Marian Reiner for the author. "Move Over" from *Little Raccoon and Poems from the Woods* by Lilian Moore. Copyright © 1975 by Lilian Moore. Reprinted by permission of Marian Reiner for the author. Page 134: "Lulu, Lulu, I've a Lilo" From *If I Had a Paka* by Charlotte Pomerantz. Used by permission of Greenwillow Books (a division of William Morrow & Co., Inc.). "To a Firefly" by Chippewa Algonquin. Reprinted with permission of Atheneum Publishers, an imprint of Macmillan Publishing Co., from *The Earth is Sore*, adapted by Aline Amon. Copyright © 1981 by Aline Amon Goodrich. Page 138: "The Mirror" by William Jay Smith. From *Laughing Time: Nonsense Poems*, published in 1980 by Delacorte Press, copyright © 1955, 1957, 1980 by William Jay Smith. Reprinted by permission of William Jay Smith. "White Fields" by James Stephens. Reprinted with permission of Macmillan Publishing Co. from *Collected Poems* by James Stephens. Copyright 1915 by Macmillan Publishing Co., renewed 1943 by James Stephens. Reprinted with permission of The Society of Authors. Page 139: "Three" by Elizabeth Coatsworth reprinted by permission of Grosset & Dunlap, Inc., from *The Sparrow Bush* by Elizabeth Coatsworth, copyright © 1966 by Grosset & Dunlap, Inc. Page 140: "Winter Moon" copyright 1926 by Alfred A. Knopf, Inc., and renewed 1954 by Langston Hughes. Reprinted from *Selected Poems* by Langston Hughes, by permission of the publisher. "At Black Mark Farm" From *The Moon and a Star and Other Poems* by Myra Cohn Livingston. © 1965 by Myra Cohn Livingston. Reprinted by permission of Marian Reiner for the author. Page 141: "Taking Turns" by Norma Farber reprinted by permission of Coward, McCann & Geoghegan from *Small Wonders* by Norma Farber, text © 1979 by Norma Farber. Page 142: "Go Wind" by Lilian Moore. Reprinted with permission of Macmillan Publishing Co., from *I Feel the Same Way* by Lilian Moore. Copyright © 1967 by Lilian Moore. "Wild Geese O Wild Geese. . ." by Issa. From *Cherry-Blossoms: Japanese Haiku Series III*. © 1960 by The Peter Pauper Press. Reprinted by permission. Page 182: Excerpt from *Socks* by Beverly Cleary. Text copyright © 1973 by Beverly Cleary. Used by permission of Morrow Junior Books (a division of William Morrow & Co., Inc.). Page 238: Excerpts of text, pp. 74–76 and 79–83 from "The Sleeping Prince," in *Clever Gretchen and Other Forgotten Folktales* retold by Alison Lurie. Text copyright © 1980 by Alison Lurie, reprinted by permission of Harper & Row, Publishers, Inc. Page 294: Excerpt from *Sacagawea* by Wyatt Blassingame. © 1965 by Wyatt Blassingame. Reprinted courtesy of Blassingame, McCauley & Wood. New York, NY. Page 304: From *Of Courage Undaunted* by James Daugherty. Copyright 1951 by James Daugherty. Copyright renewed © 1971 by Charles M. Daugherty. All rights reserved. Reprinted by permission of Viking Penguin, a division of Penguin Books USA, Inc. Page 350: Excerpt from *Through Grandpa's Eyes* by Patricia MacLachlan. Text copyright © 1979 by Patricia MacLachlan. Illustrated by Deborah Ray. Illustrations copyright © 1980 by Ray Studios, Inc. Reprinted by permission of Harper & Row, Publishers, Inc.

Study Skills Lessons

Study Habits

1. **Listen to your teacher.** Make sure that you know what your teacher wants you to do for homework. In a notebook write down what your teacher says.

2. **Have all the homework materials you need.** You may need your textbook. You may also need such things as pencils, pens, erasers, a ruler, and a notebook.

3. **Study in the same place every day.** Try to find a quiet place where other people will not bother you.

4. **Plan your study time.** Decide on the best time of the day for studying. Plan exactly what you will do during that time. Carry out your plan.

Practice

Answer the following questions about study habits.

1. How can you best prepare to do your homework?
2. What kind of place is best for doing homework? What is the best place in your house?
3. How can you improve the way you use your study time?

Test-Taking Tips

1. **Be prepared.** Have several sharp pencils and an eraser. This is your first step.

2. **Read or listen to the directions carefully.** Be sure you know what you are to do.

3. **Answer the easy questions first.** Quickly read all the questions on the page. Then go back to the beginning. Answer the questions you are sure you know. Put a light check next to those you are not sure of or that you do not know.

4. **Next try to answer the questions you are not sure you know.** You may have a choice of answers. If so, narrow your choice. Get rid of answers you know are wrong. Then mark the answer you think is right.

5. **Answer the hardest questions last.** If you can't answer a question at all, go on to the next. Do not stay on one question too long.

6. **Plan your time.** Remember, don't spend too much time on just one question. If you do, you won't have time to answer the others. You will also need to save some time to check your answers.

Practice

Answer the following questions about taking tests.

1. How can you best prepare to take a test?
2. In what order should you answer the questions on a test?
3. What is the last thing to do before completing a test?

Parts of a Book

Some books are meant to be read from cover to cover. Others are not. For example, you read an adventure story from beginning to end. You probably do not read a book of information the same way. You may just read the pages that give the information you need.

How can you find out which pages tell what you want to know? Two parts of a book can help you. They are the **table of contents** and the **index**. The table of contents is at the front of a book. The index is at the back. Study these examples.

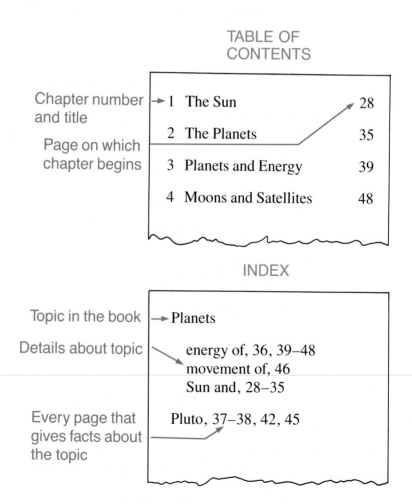

TABLE OF
CONTENTS

Chapter number
and title

Page on which
chapter begins

1 The Sun   28

2 The Planets   35

3 Planets and Energy   39

4 Moons and Satellites   48

INDEX

Topic in the book → Planets

Details about topic

energy of, 36, 39–48
movement of, 46
Sun and, 28–35

Every page that
gives facts about
the topic

Pluto, 37–38, 42, 45

434 STUDY SKILLS: Parts of a Book

Practice

A. Use the examples on page 434 to answer questions **1–5**.

1. What part of a book lists topics in alphabetical order?
2. What part of a book lists chapter titles in order?
3. What part of a book lists all the pages about one topic together?
4. On what page does the chapter "The Sun" begin?
5. What page has information about the movement of the planets?

B. Use the Table of Contents of this book to answer these questions. Write each answer.

6. How many units are in the book?
7. Which part of each unit is the Grammar part?
8. How many Writing Connection lessons are in each unit?
9. On what page does the Unit Review for Unit 4 begin?
10. On what page does the Thesaurus begin?

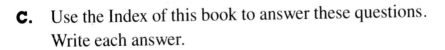

C. Use the Index of this book to answer these questions. Write each answer.

11. What pages tell about writing letters?
12. What pages tell about question marks?
13. Does the book tell anything about adverbs?
14. Is the word *lion* listed in the Index?
15. What pages tell about homophones?

Using an Encyclopedia

You can find information on a topic in an encyclopedia. An **encyclopedia** is a set of books with facts about people, places, and things.

Each book in an encyclopedia is called a **volume**. On the side of each volume, you will see a volume number and one or more letters. As in a dictionary, the entries are in alphabetical order. Each entry has information on a single topic. The letters on the volumes show what entries are in each volume.

Study this illustration. How many volumes does this encyclopedia contain? In which one would you look for information about volcanoes?

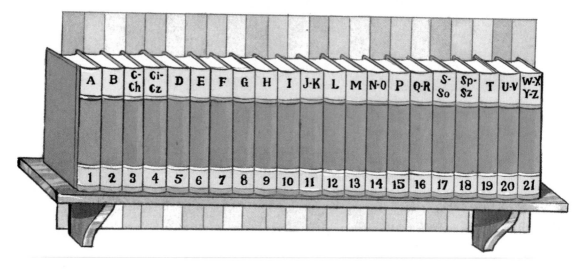

Information about a person is listed by the last name. Ernesto Galarza is a famous Mexican-American writer. Why would you find the entry about him in Volume 8?

Practice

A. Write the volume number for each topic below. Use the encyclopedia on page 436.

1. dolls
2. New Zealand
3. Winston Churchill
4. Indiana
5. llama

6. Jane Addams
7. Florida
8. Casey Jones
9. water
10. Puerto Rico

B. Write each sentence. Fill in the blank with the correct answer. Use the encyclopedia shown.

11. A set of books with facts about people, places, and things is called an ____.
12. Volume 21 contains information about entries beginning with the letters ____.
13. Information about caves is in Volume ____.
14. Entries beginning with the letter *s* are found in Volumes ____ and ____.

C. Which volume of the encyclopedia would you use to answer each question? Write the number of the volume.

15. What is a baby kangaroo called?
16. How tall is the Empire State Building?
17. What is a meteorologist?

Alphabetical Order

You already know that **alphabetical order** is the order of the letters in the alphabet. Alphabetical order is a useful way to list words. It makes them easy to find. Dictionaries list words in alphabetical order. Telephone books list names this way, too.

How to Use Alphabetical Order

1. Look at the first letter of each word. Use the first letter of each word to put the words in order.

   <u>A</u>laska   <u>C</u>olorado   <u>D</u>elaware

2. If the first letters are the same, use the second letter of each word.

   O<u>h</u>io   O<u>k</u>lahoma   O<u>r</u>egon

3. If the first and second letters are the same, use the third letter.

   Mi<u>c</u>higan   Mi<u>n</u>nesota   Mi<u>s</u>souri

Practice

A. Write these lists of words in alphabetical order.

List 1	List 2	List 3
Indiana	Maryland	Arkansas
Georgia	Virginia	Nevada
Texas	Michigan	Arizona
Maine	Vermont	Nebraska

bird

butterfly

B. Write each group of words in alphabetical order.

  1. state, town, city, world
  2. Ohio, Kansas, Utah, Kentucky
  3. river, stream, bay, sea
  4. cottage, cabin, house, hut
  5. Asia, Africa, Australia, America

C. Write each group of words in alphabetical order.

  6. hill, hall, hen, huge, howl
  7. growl, grain, grim, grumble, green
  8. belt, best, begin, beet, beauty
  9. slow, sleet, school, slump, seat
  10. cheese, clash, cellar, comb, chase

cat

dog

D. List the first names of people in your family. Write your list in alphabetical order.

E. List five things that belong together. For example, list five insects, five foods, or five colors. Write your list in alphabetical order. Then ask a classmate to tell why the five things belong together.

donkey

Using a Dictionary

A dictionary has information about words. The words are listed in alphabetical order.

Finding Words Quickly   To find a word quickly, think of a dictionary as having three parts. The word *antelope* is found in the front part. The word *unicorn* is found in the back. Where will you find the word *ostrich*?

Middle: h, i, j, k, l, m, n, o, p

Front: a, b, c, d, e, f, g

Back: q, r, s, t, u, v, w, x, y, z

Practice

A.   Write each word. Then write *front, middle,* or *back* to show where it is found in a dictionary.

1. manner	**4.** effort	**7.** storm	**10.** harp
2. illness	**5.** western	**8.** legend	**11.** bubble
3. clever	**6.** flute	**9.** sluggish	**12.** tickle

Using Guide Words   Two words called guide words appear at the top of each dictionary page. The **guide words** show the first and last words on the page. All other words on the page come between the guide words.

Practice

B. The word *lesson* comes between the guide words shown. Which word below would appear on this page?

label   letter   lend

leopard ——————◇—————— level

C. Read each word. Write the pair of guide words it comes between.

13.	racer	**rabbit–radish**	**relish–repeat**
14.	comet	**class–coat**	**color–cone**
15.	violin	**very–video**	**vine–vision**
16.	grease	**gravy–great**	**greed–gulp**

D. Read each pair of guide words. Write the word that would appear on the same page.

17.	**capital–close**	canyon	clean	crayon
18.	**eggplant–elephant**	eighty	east	enemy
19.	**zigzag–zone**	zebra	zipper	zoom
20.	**jungle–kettle**	just	jump	key

E. **21–23.** Have a classmate write three words from the Dictionary of Knowledge, which begins on page 444. See how quickly you can find the words.

A dictionary gives spellings and meanings of words. Read the sample entry below. It is from the Dictionary of Knowledge, which begins on page 444.

Pronunciation

Part of speech

Entry word — **ar•range** (ə rānj′) *verb.* 1. put in proper — Meanings
order. *Could Mr. Jeffers arrange these books on the bottom shelf?* 2. make plans. *We will arrange to meet at the library.* — Example sentence

Other forms — **arranged, arranging.**

Entry words   These are listed in alphabetical order in dark type. The entry words have dots between syllables. The entry word shows how the word is spelled and how it may be divided at the end of a line of writing.

Pronunciation   This tells how to say the word. It is given in symbols that stand for certain sounds. The Pronunciation Key on page 444 tells the sound for each symbol. For example, the symbol ā stands for the long a sound heard in *arrange.*

Part of speech   This tells how the word may be used in a sentence.

Meanings   Different meanings of a word are numbered.

Example sentence   This shows how the word is used.

Other forms   These are shown when the spelling of the base word changes.

Practice

F. Use the dictionary entries at the right to answer the questions. Write your answers.

24. How many entry words are listed?

25. Which two entry words name foods?

26. Which entry words have more than one meaning?

27. Which word names a musical instrument?

28. Which word means "case filled with feathers"?

29. Which meaning of *pickle* has an example sentence?

30. Which entry has two example sentences?

G. Find *reflect* in the Dictionary of Knowledge. Write the number for the meaning that *reflect* has in each sentence.

31. Let's reflect on that idea.
32. The lake reflects the trees.
33. Light reflects from the water.

pic•co•lo (pik′ə lō) *noun.* a small flute with a high, shrill sound.

pick•le (pik′l) *noun.* 1. salt water, vinegar, or other liquid used to preserve food. 2. cucumber preserved in pickle. 3. trouble or difficulty. *We were in a pickle with that flat tire.*

pic•nic (pik′nik) *noun.* an outdoor meal or party. *They had a picnic in the park.*

pie (pī) *noun.* a round pastry with a fruit, meat, or cream filling.

pil•low (pil′ō) *noun.* a case filled with feathers or other soft material.

pinch (pinch) *verb.* 1. to squeeze between finger and thumb. *She pinched herself to be sure she was awake.* 2. to press or squeeze so that it hurts. *My shoes pinch my feet.*

Dictionary of Knowledge

This Dictionary of Knowledge has two kinds of entries, **word entries** and **encyclopedic entries**. Many of the word entries in this dictionary are taken from the literature pieces found throughout this book. You might use these entries to help you understand the meanings of words. You will use the encyclopedic entries in two "Apply" sections in each unit.

Word Entries ◆ These entries are just like the ones you learned about on pages 442 and 443 of this book. They give the spellings, pronunciations, and meanings of words.

Encyclopedic Entries ◆ These entries are like the articles you find in encyclopedias. Each article gives interesting information about a person or a topic.

Full pronunciation key*   The pronunciation of each word is shown just after the word, in this way:
abbreviate (ə brē′ vē āt).

The letters and signs used are pronounced as in the words below.

The mark ′ is placed after a syllable with a primary or heavy accent as in the example above.

The mark ′ after a syllable shows a secondary or lighter accent, as in **abbreviation** (ə brē′ vē ā′ shən).

SYMBOL	KEY WORDS	SYMBOL	KEY WORDS	SYMBOL	KEY WORDS
a	ask, fat	u	up, cut	n	not, ton
ā	ape, date	ʉr	fur, fern	p	put, tap
ä	car, father			r	red, dear
				s	sell, pass
e	elf, ten	ə	a in ago	t	top, hat
er	berry, care		e in agent	v	vat, have
ē	even, meet		e in father	w	will, always
			i in unity	y	yet, yard
i	is, hit		o in collect	z	zebra, haze
ir	mirror, here		u in focus		
ī	ice, fire				
o	lot, pond	b	bed, dub	ch	chin, arch
ō	open, go	d	did, had	ñg	ring, singer
ô	law, horn	f	fall, off	sh	she, dash
oi	oil, point	g	get, dog	th	thin, truth
͞oo	look, pull	h	he, ahead	th	then, father
o͞o	ooze, tool	j	joy, jump	zh	s in pleasure
yo͞o	unite, cure	k	kill, bake		
yo͞o	cute, few	l	let, ball		
ou	out, crowd	m	met, trim	′	as in (ā′b′l)

*Pronunciation key adapted from *Webster's New World Dictionary, Basic School Edition*, Copyright © 1983 by Simon & Schuster, Inc. Reprinted by permission.

A

An•der•sen, Hans Chris•tian (an′ dər s'n, häns′ kris′ chən) 1805–1875

Hans Christian Andersen is Denmark's most famous author. For more than a hundred years children and adults have enjoyed his fairy tales. The tales are simple enough for children, but many of the stories have hidden meanings for grown-ups.

One of Andersen's most famous stories is "The Ugly Duckling." It tells about a duckling who is hated by the other ducks because he is different looking. No one knows that he is really a baby swan who will grow up to be beautiful.

Some other famous stories by Hans Christian Andersen are "The Emperor's New Clothes" and "The Tinder Box."

an•ger (ang′ gər) *noun.* A feeling of being very annoyed and wanting to fight back at a person or thing that hurts one or is against one; wrath; rage. — *verb.* to make angry. *The tourist's rudeness angered us.*

an•i•ma•tion (an′ ə mā′ shən)

Animation is the making of a movie from drawings. Cartoons are animated movies. A full-length cartoon may use a million drawings. In fact, many drawings have to be made for each tiny movement.

The first step in making an animated movie is creating a giant comic strip with a story and characters. Then the sound and music are recorded. Finally, the drawings are done.

Some of the most famous animated characters are Mickey Mouse, Donald Duck, and Snoopy. Walt Disney is perhaps the most famous animator the world has ever known.

a fat	**er** care	**ī** bite, fire	**oi** oil	**u** up	**th** thin	ə = a *in* ago
ā ape	**ē** even	**o** lot	**oo** look	**ur** fur	***th*** then	e *in* agent
ä car, father	**i** hit	**ō** go	**o͞o** tool	**ch** chin	**zh** leisure	i *in* unity
e ten	**ir** here	**ô** law, horn	**ou** out	**sh** she	**ng** ring	o *in* collect
						u *in* focus

ar•range (ə rānj′) *verb.* **1.** to put in proper order. *Could Mr. Jeffers arrange these books on the bottom shelf?* **2.** to make plans. *We will arrange to meet at the library.* **arranged, arranging**.

B

bed•cham•ber (bed′ chām′ bər) *noun.* a bedroom. *The young princess enjoyed her brightly decorated bedchamber.*

bow¹ (bou) *verb.* **1.** to bend the head or body in respect or greeting. **2.** to give up. *I bow to your wishes.* — *noun.* a bending of the head or body in respect or greeting.

bow² (bou) *noun.* The front part of a ship or boat. *He saw land from the bow of the boat.*

Braille Al•pha•bet (brāl′ al′ fə bet)
The Braille Alphabet is a special system of printing and writing. It is used by blind people. The Braille system uses raised dots on paper for

letters. The writing is printed on a special typewriter called a Braillewriter. Letters in Braille are read by placing fingertips on the raised dots. Each

different grouping of raised dots stands for a different letter.

The Braille Alphabet was created by Louis Braille. Braille was blinded by an accident at age three. As a child, he studied science and music, and he played the organ at the Institute for the Blind. Later on, Braille became a teacher at the school. While there, he invented the Braille Alphabet.

brass (bras) *noun* **1.** a yellow metal that is made of copper and zinc. *This doorknob is made of brass.* **2.** the brass instruments in an orchestra. *plural* **brasses.**

bum•ble•bee (bum′ b'l bē′)
A bumblebee is a large black and yellow bee. This insect flies from flower to flower in the summertime,

buzzing noisily. The name bumblebee comes from the word *bumble,* which means humming. Unlike the honeybee, which stings once and dies, a bumblebee can sting again and again.

The bumblebee is important to farmers. The bumblebee carries pollen from flower to flower, helping many plants grow. These plants are important for feeding farm animals.

Dictionary of Knowledge

bur•ly (bur′ lē) *adjective.* big and strong; husky. *A bumblebee is big and burly.* **burlier, burliest.**

bur•row (bur′ ō) *noun.* a hole or tunnel dug in the ground by an animal. *A mole lives in a burrow.* — *verb.* **1.** to dig a burrow. *Woodchucks burrow into the earth quickly.* **2.** to search or work hard, as if by digging.

C

cat•er•pil•lar (kat′ ər pil′ ər) *noun.* a hairy, wormlike creature that crawls. Later, it forms a cocoon and becomes a moth or butterfly. *A caterpillar is a furry creature.*

cham•pi•on•ship (cham′ pē ən ship′) *noun.* the position or title of being a champion; first place. *My team won the state championship.*

chis•el (chiz′ ′l) *noun.* a tool with a strong blade used for cutting or shaping wood, stone, or metal. *These chisels are old and dull.* — *verb.* to cut or shape with a chisel. *The artist will chisel the stone.*

clo•ver (klō′ vər) *noun.* a low-growing plant with sweet-smelling flowers. Most clovers have leaves in three parts. Once in a while a clover with leaves in four parts can be found. *Some people consider a four-leaf clover a sign of good luck.*

co•coon (kə kōōn′) *noun.* a silky case that a caterpillar spins and lives in while changing into a butterfly or moth. *How long will the caterpillar stay in its cocoon?*

com•pe•ti•tion (kom′ pə tish′ ən) *noun.* the act of taking part in a contest. *The competition will be over soon.*

con•sent (kən sent′) *verb.* to agree with or to approve. *I consent to this deal.* —*noun.* agreement or approval. *I have her consent to go on the trip.*

con•ti•nent (kont′ ′n ənt) *noun,* a very large body of land. *The continents are Asia, Africa, Australia, Europe, North America, South America, and Antarctica.*

D

dash•board (dash′ bôrd) *noun.* the panel in a boat or car that has the controls on it. *The light switch is on the left side of the dashboard.*

dis•a•gree•ment (dis′ ə grē′ mənt) *noun.* **1.** a quarrel or an argument. **2.** a difference of opinion. *We had a disagreement about the movie.*

a fat	**er** care	**ī** bite, fire	**oi** oil	**u** up	**th** thin	ə = a *in* ago
ā ape	**ē** even	**o** lot	**oo** look	**ur** fur	**th** then	e *in* agent
ä car, father	**i** hit	**ō** go	**oo** tool	**ch** chin	**zh** leisure	i *in* unity
e ten	**ir** here	**ô** law, horn	**ou** out	**sh** she	**ng** ring	o *in* collect
						u *in* focus

E

en•ter•prise (en′ tər prīz) *noun*. a business or an undertaking, usually one that takes courage. *Because of their enterprise, the play was a great success.*

F

fire•fly (fīr′ flī)

The firefly is an insect known for its glowing or flashing light. The firefly is also known as a lightning bug. Most fireflies are brown or black, with red, orange, or yellow marks.

The firefly is a member of the beetle family. Like all beetles, fireflies have two pairs of wings. Only the second pair is used for flying.

Fireflies use their lights to find mates. Each type of firefly has its own light signal. A female will signal to a male and wait for him to signal back.

The enemies of fireflies are certain kinds of birds, frogs, lizards, and spiders.

G

gen•er•ous (jen′ ər əs) *adjective*. **1.** willing to give or share; not selfish. *He was generous with his time.* **2.** large; great in amount. *That is a generous portion of turkey.*

Great Ba•sin (grāt′ bās′ ′n)

The Great Basin is a large desert area in the western part of the United States. It mostly lies in the states of Nevada, Idaho, Wyoming, Utah, Oregon, and Arizona. The Great Basin covers about 200,000 square miles.

This desert area is like a basin, or sink, because all of its waters stay in it. They do not flow to other places. Its streams either dry up or flow into one of the basin's lakes and then dry up. Although desert plants do grow there, the area has very few trees. The Great Basin is surrounded by mountains.

greet (grēt) *verb*. **1.** to meet and speak to with polite and friendly words; hail or welcome. *Our host greeted us with a warm "Hello!"* **2.** to meet or receive in a particular way. *The speech was greeted with cheers.* **3.** to come or appear to. *A roaring sound greeted his ears.*

Grimm broth•ers (grim′ bru*th*′ ərz)

Jakob (1785–1863) and Wilhelm (1786–1859) Grimm are best known for their German folktales and fairy tales. The brothers collected the tales from farmers and villagers in Germany. Until the Grimm brothers wrote the stories, the tales only existed by mouth. The brothers tried to write the stories exactly as they heard them. Through the stories, they hoped to keep German folklore alive.

Some of the Grimm brothers' most famous stories are "Hansel and Gretel," "Little Red Riding Hood," "Cinderella," "Sleeping Beauty," and "Rumpelstiltskin."

Their other famous works were a German dictionary and *German Grammar.*

guar•an•tee (gar ən tē′) *noun.* **1.** a promise to return something to a buyer if it doesn't work correctly. *This toaster has a one-year guarantee.* **2.** a promise that something will be done. *You have my guarantee that my work will be done*

on time. — *verb.* **1.** to give a guarantee for. *I guarantee this toaster for one year.* **2.** to promise. *I cannot guarantee that I will be there.* **guaranteed, guaranteeing**.

gup•py (gup′ ē)

A guppy is a kind of tropical fish that is often kept in a home aquarium as a pet. The guppy comes from fresh water in warm places. It is useful because it eats mosquito eggs.

Guppies are tiny, but they make good pets. They are not delicate. The guppy is hardy and energetic and is easily kept. If fed and watered correctly, they will stay healthy in home aquariums. They can be kept in fishbowls or other small containers. Males grow to about one inch in length. Females grow to twice that size. The males can be beautiful. They are often spotted and streaked in rainbow colors. The males love to show off by "dancing" around the females.

						ə = a *in* ago
a fat	**er** care	**ī** bite, fire	**oi** oil	**u** up	**th** thin	e *in* agent
ā ape	**ē** even	**o** lot	**oo** look	**ur** fur	**th** then	i *in* unity
ä car, father	**i** hit	**ō** go	**o͞o** tool	**ch** chin	**zh** leisure	o *in* collect
e ten	**ir** here	**ô** law, horn	**ou** out	**sh** she	**ŋ** ring	u *in* focus

About fifty young guppies are born to a female every four to six weeks. Baby guppies should be separated from the adult guppies. The adults sometimes eat the babies. Guppies live to about three years of age.

I
---

in•spec•tion (in spek′ shən) *noun*. the act of examining or looking at something carefully. *The bunk was ready for inspection.*

in•struc•tion (in struk′ shən) *noun*. **1.** the act of teaching. *Her career involved the instruction of small children.* **2.** a lesson; something taught. *We received swimming instruction from the coach.* **3.** orders or directions. *The model boat came with clear instructions.*

in•sure (in shŏŏr′) *verb*. **1.** to get or give a contract that says money will be paid if someone is hurt or something is destroyed. *We will insure our home against fire.* **2.** to make certain about something. *The guide will insure your safety.*

I•vo•ry Coast (ī′ vər ē kōst′)

The Ivory Coast is a country on the west coast of Africa. It is about the size of New Mexico. The population is mostly black African. The country got its name during the 1400s, when French sailors there traded for ivory. The country has a beautiful tropical forest and a large amount of grassland. It has rolling hills covered by forests.

Most of the people of the Ivory Coast are farmers. Coffee and cacao are the main crops. Palm oil, fruits, and timber are also becoming important.

Once a French colony, French is the main language spoken in this now independent country. The Ivory Coast is growing in wealth, and more people are becoming educated. The country and its people are rapidly changing.

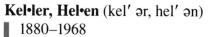
K

Kel•ler, Hel•en (kel′ ər, hel′ ən) 1880–1968

Before age two, an illness took away Helen Keller's sight and hearing. She could not speak. She lived alone in her own world. But she overcame all this to become one of the most famous people in the world.

A teacher named Anne Sullivan taught Helen how to read, write, and speak. It took years of very hard work. It seemed like a miracle.

After college, Helen gave her life to

helping blind people. She wrote many books and received many awards. She traveled all over the world, helping the blind. A famous movie, *The Miracle Worker,* was made about her early life with Anne Sullivan.

M

Mars (märz)

Mars is the seventh largest planet. It is the fourth planet in distance away from the sun. Mars is the only planet whose details can be seen from the earth. Only the planet Venus comes closer to our planet than Mars. The surface conditions of Mars are more like those of the earth than any other planet. Our plants and animals, however, could not live on Mars. It is much colder than the earth. Photos of Mars show signs of deep canyons and dry riverbeds.

Mars and Earth both rotate about once every twenty-four hours. It takes Mars 687 days to go around the sun. It takes Earth only 365 days. The surface of Mars has bright areas, dark areas, and polar caps. Much of the planet's surface has craters and canals. The planet seems dry, but water inside the polar caps might be frozen. Whether or not life exists on Mars is still a mystery to us.

Mars is known for its reddish color. It was named after the red war god Mars.

Mar•tian (mär′ shən) *noun.* an imaginary creature of the planet Mars, as in science fiction. — *adjective.* of Mars, especially the planet Mars.

mat•tress (mat′ ris) *noun.* a casing of strong cloth filled with cotton, foam rubber, coiled springs, etc. and used on a bed.

a fat	er care	ī bite, fire	oi oil	u up	th thin	ə = a *in* ago
ā ape	ē even	o lot	ᴏᴏ look	ᴜr fur	th then	e *in* agent
ä car, father	i hit	ō go	ᴏ̄ᴏ̄ tool	ch chin	zh leisure	i *in* unity
e ten	ir here	ô law, horn	ou out	sh she	ŋ ring	o *in* collect
						u *in* focus

mem•o•ry aid (mem′ ər ē ād′)

A memory aid is a poem, clue, or other "trick" that helps you remember something. Many people use this memory aid. It helps them remember the number of days in each month of the year:

Thirty days hath September,
April, June, and November.
All the rest have thirty-one,
But February which has twenty-eight.

Sometime you might create a memory aid to help you remember something. Here are two simple memory aids that someone made up. They are used for remembering the spellings of February and December.
For February: B<u>rr</u>! Feb<u>r</u>ua<u>r</u>y has two <u>r</u>'s.
For December: See <u>c</u>, not <u>s</u>, in De<u>c</u>ember.

Another term for this kind of memory aid is a mnemonic (nə mon′ ik). How could you remember that the word *mnemonic* begins with a silent *m*?

mer•chan•dise (mʉr′ chən dīz) or (mʉr′ chən dīs) *noun.* goods; things bought and sold. *What kind of merchandise is sold here?* — *verb.* (mʉr′ chən dīz) to buy and sell; to deal in. **merchandised, merchandising**.

Mitch•ell, Ma•ri•a (mich′ əl, mə rē′ ə) 1818–1889

Maria Mitchell was an American astronomer. She is famous for her work with sunspots and the satellites of planets. In 1847, she discovered a new comet. Even though she had little formal education, Maria Mitchell became a professor of astronomy. In 1848, the American Academy of Arts and Sciences invited her to be its first female member. She was elected to the Hall of Fame in 1905.

N

nov•ice (nov′ is) *noun.* **1.** a person who is new at something; a beginner. *Jan is a novice at driving.*

P

pi•rogue (pi rōg′) *noun.* a boat that is like a canoe. *The children paddled the pirogue around the tiny island.*

poul•try (pōl′ trē) *noun.* the birds, such as chickens, ducks, and turkeys, that are raised for food. *Would you prefer fish or poultry for dinner?*

prick (prik) *verb.* to make a small hole in something using a sharp point. *I will prick the edge of the fabric.* — *noun.* a tiny hole made by a sharp point.

R

re•flect (ri flekt′) *verb.* **1.** to throw back or be thrown back, as light, heat, or sound. *Metal may reflect heat.* **2.** to give back a picture, as in a mirror. *The mirror reflects my face.* **3.** to bring blame. *Your poor behavior will reflect on your parents.* **4.** to think seriously about something. *Do you reflect on your past?*

Re•vere, Paul (rə vēr′, pôl) 1735–1818

Paul Revere lived during the time of the American Revolution. He was a patriot who helped fight for our country's independence. He is most famous for a special ride he took one night to Lexington and then Concord, Massachusetts.

In 1775, Revere and other patriots found out that British soldiers were coming. The British were going to arrest them and destroy their supplies. Revere was told to ride to Lexington and Concord to warn other patriots. A signal was planned. A light would be flashed from the steeple of the Old North Church in Boston. Two flashes would mean that the British were coming by water. One flash would mean that they were coming by land. Revere rode fast and warned his friends on time.

During his life, Paul Revere was a soldier, a craftsman, and a businessman.

rov•er (rō′ vər) *noun.* a person who wanders, or roves. *He was a rover from the time he started walking.*

S

sat•is•fac•tion (sat′ is fak′ shən) *noun.* a thing that pleases or meets someone's needs. *Playing the flute gives me satisfaction.*

scorch (skôrch) *verb.* **1.** to burn or be burned slightly. *The pan hanging over the campfire may scorch.* **2.** to dry up

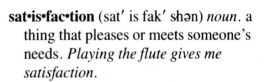

a fat	er care	ī bite, fire	oi oil	u up	th thin	ə = a *in* ago
ā ape	ē even	o lot	oo look	ur fur	th then	e *in* agent
ä car, father	i hit	ō go	oo tool	ch chin	zh leisure	i *in* unity
e ten	ir here	ô law, horn	ou out	sh she	ng ring	o *in* collect
						u *in* focus

by heat. *The sun may scorch the grass.* — *noun.* a slight burn on the surface of something.

Sho·sho·ne In·di·ans (shō shō′ nē in′ dē ənz), *also spelled* Shoshoni

The Shoshone Indians once lived in some of the most barren land in the United States. They couldn't grow crops. They had to move from place to place in small groups, searching for food. They planned their travels carefully. They knew when and where each plant would ripen. They knew where to find small animals to hunt. Each year, they went back to the same areas. The groups were named according to the main foods of an area. There were Seed Eaters, Rabbit Eaters, and so on. When there was a lot of food, the groups willingly shared with other groups.

The Shoshone spent a lot of time singing, dancing, and storytelling. The most famous Shoshone Indian in American history is Sacagawea. Today the Shoshone Indians are farmers and ranchers.

source (sôrs) *noun.* **1.** a spring or fountain that is the starting point of a stream. **2.** a thing or place from which something comes. *An encyclopedia is a source of information.*

trans·ac·tion (tran sak′ shən) *or* (tran zak′ shən) *noun.* a deal, as in a piece of business. *The transaction took a long time.*

Twain, Mark (twān, märk) 1835–1910

Mark Twain was the pen name of Samuel Langhorne Clemens. Twain is one of our country's best known authors. He is also known for his great humor. The ideas for Twain's writing came from things he did and saw. He worked as a riverboat pilot on the Mississippi River. He was a newspaper reporter in San Francisco and a lecturer in Hawaii. Whatever Twain saw, he saw with humor.

Mark Twain's most famous books are *The Adventures of Huckleberry Finn, The Adventures of Tom Sawyer, The Prince and the Pauper*, and *A Connecticut Yankee in King Arthur's*

Court. Twain appreciated funny things, but he also had a sad side. Both feelings can be found in his books.

─────── **U** ───────

un•i•corn (yōō′ nə kôrn)

The unicorn is an imaginary animal. Unicorns appear in many stories and paintings. The unicorn has the head of a horse. It has the legs of a deer and the tail of a lion. It has one long horn in the middle of its forehead. The unicorn is supposed to stand for purity, shyness, and goodness.

No one really knows where the legend of the unicorn started. Some experts believe that it came from early reports of the rhinoceros. Many people once believed that the unicorn had magical powers.

─────── **V** ───────

vi•brate (vī′ brāt) *verb.* **1.** to move very quickly back and forth. *I saw the engine vibrate.* **2.** to echo. *The classroom vibrated with laughter.* **vibrated, vibrating**.

─────── **W** ───────

wild•fowl (wīld′ foul) *noun.* a game bird as a wild duck or goose. *A lot of wildfowl live in the marshland.*

wild•life (wīld′ līf) *noun.* wild animals and birds. *This park protects wildlife.*

a fat	er care	ī bite, fire	oi oil	u up	th thin	ə = a *in* ago
ā ape	ē even	o lot	oo look	ur fur	th then	e *in* agent
ä car, father	i hit	ō go	ōō tool	ch chin	zh leisure	i *in* unity
e ten	ir here	ô law, horn	ou out	sh she	ŋ ring	o *in* collect
						u *in* focus

THESAURUS

A thesaurus contains lists of synonyms and antonyms. You will use this Thesaurus for the thesaurus lesson in Unit 1 and for the Reading–Writing Connection lessons in this book. You can also use the Thesaurus to find synonyms to make your writing more interesting.

Sample Entry

Entry word — **like**–to be pleased with; to have a good feeling for. Carol and her friends <u>like</u> to play computer games.

Example sentence

Synonym — *enjoy*–to get pleasure from; to be happy with. If you <u>enjoy</u> historical places, you should visit Williamsburg.

Antonym — ANTONYM: dislike

How to Use the Thesaurus Index

To find a word, use the Thesaurus Index on pages 457–461. All the entry words, synonyms, and antonyms are listed alphabetically in the Index. Words in dark type are entry words. Words in italic, or slanted, type are synonyms. Words in blue type are antonyms. The page numbers tell you where to find the word you are looking for.

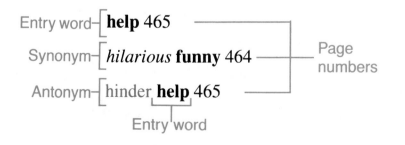

Entry word — **help** 465

Synonym — *hilarious* **funny** 464

Antonym — hinder **help** 465

Page numbers

Entry word

cool 463

correct **right** 471

courteous **nice** 469

crawl **run** 471

create **make** 468

creepy **scary** 471

cry **laugh** 467

current **new** 469

current **old** 469

D

dally **hurry** 466

damp **wet** 473

dark **bright** 463

dash **hurry** 466

decrease **grow** 465

delay **hurry** 466

delayed **quick** 470

delighted **happy** 465

demonstration **show** 472

depart **go** 465

descend **fall** 464

describe **tell** 472

design **make** 468

destroy **make** 468

detached **alone** 462

detain **hurry** 466

detest **like** 468

diagram **picture** 470

dim **bright** 463

dirty 463

disagreeable **nice** 469

discard **keep** 466

disconnect **join** 466

discontent **happy** 465

dishonest **right** 471

dislike **like** 468

disregard **look** 468

divide **join** 466

doze **rest** 471

drag **pull** 470

drop **fall** 464

dry **wet** 473

dull **bright** 463

dull **funny** 464

E

eerie **scary** 471

elderly **old** 469

end 464

enjoy **like** 468

enlarge **grow** 465

enormous **big** 462

entirety **part** 470

examine **look** 468

excellent **bad** 462

exhibit **show** 472

expand **grow** 465

explain **tell** 472

F

faded **bright** 463

fall 464

false **right** 471

fearless **afraid** 462

filthy **dirty** 463

fine **bad** 462

finish **end** 464

flee **leave** 467

follower **leader** 467

forbid **let** 467

fragment **part** 470

fresh **new** 469

frightened **afraid** 462

frown **laugh** 467

frosty **cool** 463

fry **cook** 463

funny 464

G

giant **small** 472

gigantic **big** 462

giggle **laugh** 467

glance **look** 468

glowing **bright** 463

go 465

good **bad** 462

grand **big** 462

grant **let** 467

great **big** 462

great **small** 472

grow 465

H

happy 465

harm **help** 465

harmful **bad** 462

Thesaurus

A

afraid–feeling fear. Some people are afraid of flying in airplanes.

anxious–uneasy from fear of what may happen. Everyone became anxious as flood waters continued to rise.

frightened–filled with sudden fear. The frightened campers heard another noise in the bush.

scared–suddenly becoming afraid. A scared animal will run from danger.

terrified–filled with great fear of danger. The terrified swimmer yelled for help.

timid–easily frightened; afraid to do something. The timid child would not ride the pony.

ANTONYMS: **bold, brave, fearless, unafraid**

alone–being away from or left without others. The rider was alone on the trail.

detached–standing alone. The house has a detached garage.

isolated–kept apart from others, usually for a certain reason. The isolated patient has the mumps.

private–away from the public. The club's meeting place is private.

secluded–removed and shut off from others; undisturbed. The secluded cabin is hidden by trees.

separate–not connected or joined; apart from others. The new books are on a separate shelf.

ANTONYMS: **combined, joint, public**

B

bad–not good; not as good as it should be. It was a bad movie, and everyone was bored.

harmful–causing hurt or damage. Buyers were warned that the new toy might be harmful.

naughty–behaving badly; not obeying. The naughty puppy chewed on the table.

poor–not good in quality; without quality. The tennis player made a poor shot and lost the point.

severe–very harsh. Travelers need to be extra careful in severe weather.

wrong–not right. It is wrong to interrupt someone who is speaking.

ANTONYMS: **excellent, fine, good, right, superior**

big–large in size, amount, or number. A crowd gathered in the big room.

enormous–extremely large or great. Thousands of fans watched the game in the enormous stadium.

gigantic–huge, like a giant. A tour guide talked about the gigantic redwood trees in the national park.

grand–large and very nice-looking. The grand hotel is the oldest building in the city.

great–very big. Years after the shipwreck, divers found a great number of gold pieces.

massive–big and heavy; solid. The airplane looked tiny flying over the massive mountain.

ANTONYMS: **little, slight, small, tiny**

bright–full of light; clear in color. We see bright stars at night.

brilliant–brighter than usual. The artist used brilliant colors in her painting.

glowing–giving off light because of heat; showing strong color. A glowing fire made the room warm and cheerful.

shining–giving off light. The shining lamp of a lighthouse guides ships at night.

sunny–bright with sunshine. The park is filled with people on a warm, sunny day.

vivid–strong and clear in color. It is easy to see the crossing guard in her vivid yellow raincoat.

ANTONYMS: **cloudy, dark, dim, dull, faded**

C

change–**1** to make or become different. We will change our plans if it rains.
2 to move from one place, position, or direction to another. You should change your seat so that we can sit next to each other.

alter–to change slightly. A tailor can alter the jacket to make it shorter.

convert–to change for a different use. The builders will convert the porch into a family room.

shift–to go or move in a different place, position, or direction. Gymnasts must shift their weight properly to keep their balance.

switch–to change place, position, or direction. Due to an engine problem, the passengers must switch airplanes.

vary–to change so that something is not always the same. The cafeteria should vary the food it serves.

ANTONYMS: **remain, stay**

cook–to use heat to prepare food. Will you please cook dinner tonight?

bake–to cook in an oven. Did the pioneers bake their own bread?

barbecue–to cook over an open fire. Wait for the coals to get hot before you barbecue the chicken.

fry–to cook in hot fat over direct heat. While you fry the eggs, I will make the toast.

simmer–to cook slowly with low heat. Put a lid on the vegetables when you simmer them.

toast–to make brown by heating. The campers will toast marshmallows.

cool–having a low temperature. The autumn air feels cool.

brisk–cool and dry; fresh. A brisk morning is a good time for a walk.

chilly–very cool, almost cold. It is too chilly outside to have a picnic.

frosty–cool enough to have frost. Can you see through the frosty window?

shivery–chilly enough to make a person quiver. Hot soup tastes good on a shivery day.

ANTONYMS: **mild, warm**

D

dirty–not clean; not pure. You will need a bucket of soapy water to wash the dirty car.

filthy–completely covered with dirt. After walking in the mud, Brian's shoes were filthy.

polluted–dirty from what is in something. The health department warned people about the polluted drinking water.

smudged–no longer clean from being smeared. The child eating a peanut butter and jelly sandwich has a smudged face.

soiled–needing to be washed. The soiled clothes are in the laundry basket.

stained–discolored in a spot, usually where something has been spilled. The stained tablecloth will have to be washed immediately.

ANTONYMS: clean, pure, spotless, washed

E

end–the last or final part; where something stops. Their house is at the end of the street.

boundary–a line or other marking that shows where something ends. The river forms the northern boundary of the state.

conclusion–the final part of something, such as a book or a play. The audience clapped after the conclusion of the children's concert.

finish–the end of something that has begun or has been started. Everyone stood up to watch the finish of the close race.

limit–a point beyond which something cannot or should not go. We had a two-dollar limit for the gift exchange.

tip–the end of something, usually something that is long and slim. The gardener clipped off the tip of the flower stem.

ANTONYMS: beginning, onset, opening, start

F

fall–to go from a higher place to a lower place. In autumn, leaves fall from the trees.

collapse–to fall in or cave in. If you put those heavy books on that box, it might collapse.

descend–to come down from a higher place. The airplane will slowly descend before landing on the runway.

drop–to fall suddenly. If you bump the table, that bottle of milk might drop and break.

sink–to slowly go lower and lower. A brick or a heavy rock will sink in water.

tumble–to fall accidentally, possibly rolling over and over. The apples will bruise if they tumble out of the sack.

ANTONYMS: ascend, climb, mount, rise, soar

funny–causing laughter. The funny clowns delighted the circus crowd.

amusing–entertaining in a funny way. Shada told an amusing story about her vacation.

comical–funny, almost silly. The most comical hat had bananas on the top.

hilarious–extremely funny. The dancing bears were a hilarious sight.

humorous–laughable and enjoyable. Limericks are humorous poems.

witty–clever and amusing. Her witty remark made the guests feel at home.
ANTONYMS: **boring, dull, serious**

G

go–1 to move or pass along. My bike will not go any faster in this mud. **2** to move away from a place; to leave. The students may go when the bell rings.
advance–to move forward. The people with tickets should advance to the front of the line.
depart–to go away; to leave. What time does your bus depart?
proceed–to continue or go on after a stop. Tomorrow Mr. Wilson will proceed with the science lesson.
progress–to go ahead. The tired runners could not progress swiftly.
retreat–to move back or backward. If the deer becomes frightened, it will retreat into the woods.
ANTONYMS: **arrive, come, remain, stay, stop**

grow–to become bigger in size, amount, or number. The plants will grow taller with water and light.
enlarge–to make or become larger. Will this tent enlarge to fit six people?
expand–to become larger than before. A balloon will expand from hot air.
increase–to make greater. Will my strength increase if I exercise more?
multiply–to grow in number or amount. The small group of people will multiply when the parade begins.
swell–to fill out or puff up. Paul's finger may swell from the bee sting.
ANTONYMS: **decrease, lessen, shrink**

H

happy–feeling glad and having a good time; not sad. The birthday party was a happy occasion.
cheerful–full of gladness; friendly and pleasant. A person with a cheerful smile greeted us at the door.
contented–satisfied with the way things are. The contented baby was soon asleep.
delighted–greatly pleased; very glad. After the spelling bee, the delighted winner accepted his prize.
jolly–full of fun; merry. The jolly singers clapped their hands to the beat of the music.
jubilant–showing much joy and happiness. The jubilant team celebrated their victory.
ANTONYMS: **discontent, miserable, sad, sorrowful, unhappy**

help–to do or give what is needed; to be useful. I will help you carry that heavy box.
advise–to help by giving a suggestion or an opinion. Before the game, the coach will advise the players.
aid–to help by giving relief. The money will aid needy families.
assist–to give help, usually by working with another person. The art teacher will assist the classes with their projects.
benefit–to bring good to; to be good for. Good eating habits will benefit a person's health.
support–to help with comfort and encouragement. Friends support each other.
ANTONYMS: **harm, hinder, hurt, obstruct**

Thesaurus

hurry–to move or act quickly; to move or act more quickly than usual to save time. We will not be late for the show if we hurry.

dash–to move quickly for a short distance. The children always dash into the kitchen at lunchtime.

hustle–to do something fast. When the storm begins, the farmer will hustle the cows into the barn.

rush–to go or do something with speed. If you rush when you do your homework, you may make careless mistakes.

scramble–to move quickly using the hands and feet. A frightened bear cub may scramble up a tree.

ANTONYMS: **dally, delay, detain, linger, loiter**

jump–to go into the air from the ground; to leap. He must jump up to reach the high cupboard.

bound–to jump lightly and quickly along. Frogs often bound from one lily pad to another.

hurdle–to jump over a barrier, usually while running. The young colt would not hurdle the fence.

pounce–to go up suddenly and come down on something. Watch the kitten pounce on the ball.

spring—to move or rise quickly and suddenly. Firefighters spring into action when the alarm rings.

vault–to leap over something using the hands or a pole. They will vault the wall and take a shortcut.

J

join–to put or bring together in order to make or become one. The neighbors will join us for dinner.

assemble–to put the parts or pieces of something together. Did Carla assemble this jigsaw puzzle?

attach–to fasten one thing to another. Can you attach the bike to the top of the car?

clasp–to join in order to hold or keep together. Clasp arms with someone so you do not fall on the ice.

combine–to put or bring together to form a new whole. The cook will combine the salad ingredients.

connect–to join one thing to another. First connect the two wires.

ANTONYMS: **disconnect, divide, part, separate, sever**

K

keep–to have or to hold on to, sometimes for a long time or forever. Ann should keep the shells she finds on the beach.

preserve–to keep from change; to keep safe from harm. The paint will preserve the wood.

reserve–to hold back, usually for a short time only. The librarian will reserve the book for you.

retain–to continue to have. She will retain her part-time job when school starts.

save–to set aside for a special use. Our teacher will save our papers for a bulletin-board display.

store–to put away for later use. You can store your bicycle in the basement.

ANTONYMS: **abandon, discard, lose**

L

laugh–to make sounds that show joy or amusement. Do you laugh at elephant jokes?

chuckle–to laugh quietly. They chuckle over funny cartoons.

giggle–to laugh in a silly or nervous way. Did you giggle when the ride spun you in circles?

roar–to laugh loudly. You will roar when you see the hilarious show.

snicker–to make slight or covered laughing sounds in trying not to laugh aloud. Please do not snicker when someone makes a mistake.

ANTONYMS: **cry, frown, scowl**

leader–a person who guides or tells others what to do; the person in charge. The leader assigned each camper to a cabin.

captain–the head of a group or a team. Marcia is the captain of our team.

chief–the person who has the highest rank. A new police chief will be chosen next month.

commander–a person who gives orders to others. The commander ordered the troops to stand at attention.

conductor–a person who directs music performers. The conductor lifted his baton.

ruler–a person who makes decisions and has control over others. The country honored its new ruler.

ANTONYM: **follower**

leave–to go from; to go away. Our visitors must leave after lunch.

abandon–to go away from, planning never to return. The crew must abandon the sinking ship.

flee–to run away from in a hurry. The animals will flee the burning barn.

part–to leave and separate. My friend and I part on the corner when we walk home from school.

quit–to give up and go away from. She will quit the basketball team and join the band.

vacate–to go away from and leave empty. All swimmers must vacate the pool during a storm.

ANTONYMS: **arrive, come, remain, stay**

let–to allow something to be done or to happen. The teacher will let the students go outside for recess.

admit–to allow to enter or join. They will not admit people into the gym during the rehearsal.

authorize–to give formal permission. Do you think the principal will authorize the field trip?

concede–to give in so something can happen or be done. Did your sister finally concede to helping us with the puppet show?

consent–to agree and give approval or permission. If her father does not consent, she will not be able to go swimming with us.

grant–to give or allow what is asked. Imagine if someone could really grant you three wishes!

ANTONYMS: **ban, bar, forbid, prevent, refuse**

like–to be pleased with; to have a good feeling for. Carol and her friends like to play computer games.

admire–to think of with respect or approval. A good citizen is a person whom people admire.

appreciate–to understand and enjoy. Do you appreciate that artist's work?

enjoy–to get pleasure from; to be happy with. If you enjoy historical places, you should visit Williamsburg.

prefer–to like better than another or others. Some people prefer to live in big cities.

value–to think highly of; to like very much. She will always value the ring given to her by her mother.

ANTONYMS: **detest, dislike, hate, loathe**

look–to turn the eyes to see or watch something. People go to a zoo to look at the animals.

examine–to look at closely and carefully. The doctor will examine Ling's sprained ankle.

glance–to take a quick, almost uninterested look. I'll only glance at the menu, because I'm not hungry.

peek–to look quickly and secretly. Did Tom peek at the present hidden in the closet?

scan–to pass the eyes over quickly, usually to find a certain thing. Everyone should scan the list by the door to find a seat number.

stare–to look directly at for some time. Sometimes I stare out the window and think of faraway places.

ANTONYMS: **disregard, ignore, miss, overlook**

M

make–to form or put together; to bring into being. Will you make some paper flowers for my vase?

construct–to make by putting together; to build. Chris will construct a model car for the contest.

create–to make something new or different. Can we create our own flavor of ice cream?

design—to work out and draw plans for. Mr. Santiago will design the new shopping center in North Carolina.

invent–to think of or make for the first time. Did the Wright Brothers invent the airplane?

manufacture–to make, usually in large amounts, using machines. Many companies manufacture the parts for this computer.

ANTONYMS: **destroy, ruin, wreck**

move–to change from one place or position to another. Move the plant closer to the window.

budge–to move even a little bit. I tried to open the window, but it did not budge.

inch–to move a very short distance at a time. The drivers must inch their way through the deep snow.

push–to move something by using force against it. I will push my bike across the street.

shove–to move by pushing from behind. Can two people shove that heavy crate up the stairs?

transfer–to move or send from one place or person to another. If the closet gets too full, transfer some things to the attic.

N

new–**1** recently made; not old. He showed his new roller skates to his friends. **2** having not existed before. The new highway will go past the airport.

current–having to do with the present time. The newspaper informs readers of current events all over the world.

fresh–not known, seen, or used before. We put a fresh coat of paint on the doghouse.

modern–up-to-date. The modern building is made of glass.

novel–new and unusual. Clarita thought of a novel costume to wear to the party.

original–thought of or done for the first time. We need original ideas for our science projects.

ANTONYMS: **antique, old, old-fashioned, past, used**

nice–kind, thoughtful, or friendly. Some nice people stopped to help us fix the flat tire.

amiable–pleasant and agreeable. She is an amiable person who has many friends.

charming–attractive and delightful. The guest speaker was a charming person with many interests.

congenial–getting along well with others. She was elected team captain because she is congenial.

courteous–thoughtful of others; showing good manners. The courteous child asked to be excused from the table.

warm–showing affection or much interest. He wrote a warm letter telling us how much he missed us.

ANTONYMS: **disagreeable, mean, rude, unfriendly, unpleasant**

noise–a sound that is neither pleasant nor musical; a loud or sharp sound. I cannot read with all that noise in the next room.

blast–a sudden, loud noise. The trumpet player let out a blast with her horn.

clamor–loud, continuing noise, usually voices. The clamor of the party lasted for hours.

racket–clattering noise that is disturbing. The racket outside woke everyone up.

rumble–a deep, heavy, rolling sound. The thunder made a rumble that seemed to shake the windows.

uproar–very loud and mixed-up noise. There was an uproar when the movie star walked into the room.

ANTONYMS: **hush, lull, quiet, silence, stillness**

O

old–**1** having lived or been for a long time; not young. We were afraid to go into the old, deserted house. **2** from long ago; not new. I wore my old shoes because it was raining.

ancient–belonging to times long past; very old. Rome is an ancient city.

antique–very old but still existing or being used. This store sells antique furniture.

elderly–somewhat old in age. The elderly man rides a bicycle to work to keep fit.

historical–having to do with the past. I wrote about a historical event.

outdated–old-fashioned. The people in the photograph were wearing outdated clothing.
ANTONYMS: current, modern, new, recent, young

P

part–not the whole; a piece. A leg is one part of the body.
bit–a small piece. Only a bit of his sandwich was left on the plate.
component–a main or necessary part of something. Joe's radio did not work because one component was missing.
fragment–a piece broken off of something. The scientist examined a fragment of a moon rock.
section–a part that is separated or divided from the whole. My garden is planted in one section of the yard.
share–the part belonging to one person. Each person received an equal share of the reward money.
ANTONYMS: all, entirety, whole

picture–a painting, a drawing, or a photograph. The travel poster has a picture of Hawaii on it.
collage–a picture made by pasting different materials on a surface. We made a collage with pieces of felt, yarn, and tile.

diagram–a drawing that shows the important parts of something and how they work. It would be difficult to assemble the bike without a diagram.
landscape–a picture of a scene on land, which someone might see from one spot. The artist painted a beautiful landscape of wildflowers in a field.
mural–a large picture painted on a wall. You will see the mural as soon as you walk into the room.
portrait–a picture of a person. That is a portrait of my grandfather when he was very young.

pull–to move something toward the person or thing giving the force. Let's pull the wagon up the hill.
drag–to pull along the ground. Your coat will get dirty if you drag it.
haul–to pull with much force. Can you haul the sacks into the shed by yourself?
jerk–to pull quickly and suddenly. The lamp may fall if you jerk the cord.
tow–to use a rope or a chain to pull something. The truck will have to tow the car out of the mud.
tug–to pull hard, usually more than once and stopping between pulls. If the door gets stuck again, tug on it.
ANTONYMS: push, shove

Q

quick–fast or sudden. I made a quick trip to the store to buy milk.
abrupt–changing suddenly with no warning. The animal made an abrupt turn when it spotted danger.

hasty–done quickly and in a hurry, often without thinking first. Leslie wrote a hasty note on her way out the door.

instant–without a delay; immediate. The bright student gave an instant answer to the teacher's difficult question.

prompt–quick and on time. This flower shop has lovely gifts and prompt service.

swift–moving or happening very fast. Pang can get the job done because he is a swift worker.

ANTONYMS: **delayed, lingering, long, slow**

R

rest–to be still or quiet, especially after work; to sleep. Let's rest after we wash the dishes.

doze–to sleep lightly. The audience may doze during a long, boring speech.

lounge–to pass the time relaxing. They will lounge in the backyard on their vacation.

nap–to sleep for a short time. My cats usually nap outside on a sunny day.

pause–to stop and rest briefly. If you are tired, pause at the top of the hill.

relax–to take a rest from work. You should relax and let me finish this job.

ANTONYMS: **labor, stir, toil, work**

right–**1** being good or fair. He did the right thing when he told the truth. **2** not wrong; true. What is the right way to solve this problem?

accurate–exactly right. The reporter's story was accurate.

correct–with no mistakes. Allison raised her hand and gave the correct answer.

just–fair and honest. The judge made a just decision.

proper–right for a certain time or place; fitting. Will it be proper to wear shorts to the party?

valid–true according to the facts. Did they have a valid reason for being late?

ANTONYMS: **dishonest, false, mistaken, unfair, wrong**

run–to move or go along by using quick steps. Lucy must run to catch her bus.

chase–to run after and try to catch. In the game of tag, one person must chase the other players.

jog–to run with a slow, steady pace. Many people jog in the park.

race–to run very fast. The children should not race on the playground.

sprint–to run with as much speed as possible, usually for a short distance. The runners will sprint to the finish.

trot–to run, but not very fast. The two children trot behind their father when they go shopping.

ANTONYMS: **amble, crawl, saunter, stroll, walk**

S

scary–causing fright or fear. I cannot sleep after listening to a scary story.

alarming–causing sudden fear of danger. The animal ran when it heard an alarming noise.

creepy–having a strange feeling from being frightened. The silence in the house made me feel creepy.

eerie–scary because something is odd or strange. Those shadows on the wall are eerie.

horrifying–causing terror. Did anyone scream during that horrifying monster movie?

startling–surprising and frightening. The startling siren awakened us.

show–something presented for people to see or watch. The third-grade class is having a talent show.

demonstration–a showing of how something works or is done. The cooking instructor will give a demonstration next week.

exhibit–a show in which things are displayed for people to look at. Would you like to go to the arts-and-crafts exhibit with me?

pageant–an entertaining show about historical events. Rose played the part of a pilgrim in the pageant.

performance–a show, like a circus or a ballet, given for an audience. What time is the performance tonight?

program–a scheduled show on radio or television. I have been waiting to watch my favorite program.

small–not big in size or number, the opposite of large. She saw a small kitten in the tree.

little–small in size or number. Have you seen my little notebook?

petite–small in body size or height. Some clothes come in petite sizes.

pocket-sized–small; miniature. He carries a pocket-sized radio in his book bag.

tiny–very small in size; not giant. That tiny bird makes a soft sound.

weak–small or soft. Her voice sounded weak.

ANTONYMS: **big, giant, great, huge, large**

T

tell–to say in words to another person. The children begged, "Please tell the story again!"

describe–to tell all about something. Can you describe the jacket that you lost?

explain–to tell so that someone will understand. The science teacher will explain the experiment.

inform–to tell the facts. The report I wrote will inform readers about sharks.

mention–to say or refer to briefly. Did she mention her new pet to you?

recite–to repeat something that has been learned or memorized. My younger brother can recite the alphabet.

ANTONYMS: **ask, inquire, listen, question**

trip–a traveling about from one place to another. We are excited about our trip to the mountains.

jaunt–a short trip for enjoyment. Don asked his friend to join him on a jaunt downtown.

journey–a long trip. The travelers were tired from their journey.

outing–a pleasurable time spent away from home. Everyone agreed that the picnic was a nice outing.

trip (*continued*)

tour–a trip to many different places. A
 guide took the group on a <u>tour</u> of the
 famous sites.
voyage–a long trip by water. The ship
 needs to be repaired before the next
 <u>voyage</u>.

W

wet–covered with water or another liquid;
 not yet dry. Gina used a <u>wet</u> cloth to
 wipe the sticky table.
damp–having some water. These clothes
 are still too <u>damp</u> to wear.
humid–having water vapor in the air. If the
 kitchen is <u>humid</u>, turn on the fan.
moist–slightly wet. Newly planted seeds
 should be kept in <u>moist</u> soil.
soaked–wet throughout. We had <u>soaked</u>
 feet because we forgot to wear <u>boots</u>.
soggy–heavy from being wet. This <u>soggy</u>
 oatmeal tastes awful!
ANTONYMS: **arid, dry, parched**

Reports, Letters, Messages

Book Reports

A **book report** is a way to give information and share opinions about a book. A book report begins with the title of the book and the author's name. The title is underlined. The words in the title begin with capital letters.

> <u>Ramona Quimby, Age 8</u>
> by Beverly Cleary
>
> Many things are different for Ramona in third grade. Now she rides the school bus. She gives herself the nickname Superfoot. Ramona's father goes back to college, so she helps more at home.
> <u>Ramona Quimby, Age 8</u> is a very funny book. My favorite part is Ramona's book report. She gives her report like a TV commercial to the class!

In the first paragraph of her report, Lauren told some facts about the book. In the second, she gave her opinion.

Practice

Write the answers to these questions about Lauren's book report.

1. What is the title of the book Lauren read?
2. What is the author's name?
3. Who is the most important character in the book?
4. What is Lauren's opinion of the book?

Thank-You Notes and Invitations

Thank-you note ♦ A **thank-you note** is a short letter of thanks for a gift or favor.

> 20 Maple Avenue
> Clinton, Utah 84015
> March 3, 1991
>
> Dear Uncle Jim,
> Thanks so much for the soccer ball! I really wanted one. Now my friends and I can play every day.
>
> Love,
> Chris

Invitation ♦ An **invitation** is a note or short letter that invites someone to an event. It should answer these questions: What is happening? Where? When? Who sent the invitation?

> Please come to _my birthday party_
> Place _3 Lenox Avenue_
> Date and time _June 4, 2:00–4:00 P.M._
> From _Your friend, Keri Stein_

Practice

Pretend you are having a birthday party. Write an invitation. Then write a thank-you note for a birthday gift.

Addressing Envelopes

When you address an envelope, you write the return address and the receiver's address.

♦ **Return address**   Write your name and address in the upper left-hand corner. This is the **return address**. It shows where to return the letter if it cannot be delivered.

♦ **Receiver's address**   In the center of the envelope, write the **receiver's address**. This is the address of the person who will receive the letter.

♦ **State abbreviations**   You may use an abbreviation for the name of a state. There is an official two-letter abbreviation for each state name. You can get it from your local post office.

Return
address ——— Jon Parker
34 Harbor Avenue
Charleston, SC 29412

25 USA

Receiver's
address ——— Miss Dana Johnston
127 Saw Mill Road
Wheeling, WV 26003

State
abbreviation

Practice

Use a ruler. Draw an envelope like the sample above. Then write this information where it belongs.

Return address: Jeff Gray   42 Pine Street   Ada, OH 45810
Receiver's address: Mr. I. Taft   5 Oak Way   Rye, NY 10580

Telephone Messages

The telephone is an important way to communicate with other people. When you use the telephone, speak clearly and listen carefully. When you take a telephone message for someone, write the information correctly and completely.

Pat's family has a message pad near the telephone. Pat wrote this message. Check to see if he wrote all the important information.

Practice

Read the information below. Write a message for each exercise.

1. The dentist calls at 3:30 P.M. on Monday. She says Mother has a checkup on Friday morning at 9:15 A.M. Dr. Rose wants Mother to call. The number is 555-1551.

2. Joe Allen calls on Tuesday at 7:00 P.M. He wants Dwight to call him at 555-7171.

A Guide to Spelling

There are a few spelling rules that will help you spell many words correctly. Some of the most useful rules are listed below. Learning them will help you spell words easily. Remember to use these rules when you write.

1. If a word ends in a vowel and *y*, keep the *y* when you add a suffix.

   NOUNS turkey turkeys **VERBS** stay stayed

2. If a word ends in a consonant and *y*, change the *y* to *i* when you add a suffix, unless the suffix begins with *i*.

   NOUNS cherry cherries **VERBS** study studies studied
   baby babies   try trying
   ADJECTIVES muddy muddier muddiest

3. Many words end in one vowel and one consonant. Double that consonant when you add a suffix that begins with a vowel.

   NOUNS swim swimmer **VERBS** stop stopping

4. If a word ends in *e*, drop the *e* when you add a suffix that begins with a vowel.

   VERBS save saving

5. When you choose between *ie* and *ei*, usually choose *ie*.

   pie field

   Use *ei* after *c* or for the long *a* sound.

   receive eight

50 Often Misspelled Words

1.	again	26.	laid
2.	always	27.	many
3.	among	28.	much
4.	answer	29.	often
5.	anything	30.	pretty
6.	been	31.	raise
7.	break	32.	said
8.	busy	33.	shoes
9.	children	34.	since
10.	color	35.	some
11.	coming	36.	sometime
12.	cough	37.	sugar
13.	could	38.	sure
14.	doctor	39.	their
15.	done	40.	there
16.	early	41.	they
17.	easy	42.	threw
18.	every	43.	through
19.	forty	44.	tired
20.	guess	45.	together
21.	hear	46.	too
22.	heard	47.	two
23.	here	48.	very
24.	knew	49.	where
25.	know	50.	writing

Words Often Written

Below are words that many students, like you, have used when writing. When you proofread, you can use this list for help.

1.	a	**14.**	have	**27.**	of	**39.**	they
2.	all	**15.**	he	**28.**	on	**40.**	to
3.	and	**16.**	her	**29.**	one	**41.**	up
4.	are	**17.**	him	**30.**	out	**42.**	was
5.	at	**18.**	his	**31.**	said	**43.**	we
6.	be	**19.**	home	**32.**	saw	**44.**	went
7.	but	**20.**	I	**33.**	she	**45.**	were
8.	day	**21.**	in	**34.**	so	**46.**	when
9.	for	**22.**	is	**35.**	that	**47.**	why
10.	get	**23.**	it	**36.**	the	**48.**	with
11.	go	**24.**	like	**37.**	then	**49.**	would
12.	got	**25.**	me	**38.**	there	**50.**	you
13.	had	**26.**	my				

Another way to help improve your spelling is to keep a notebook of special words. Look for words in the books you read. Find words that you think are interesting or hard to spell. Write these words carefully in your spelling notebook. Then when you need to use one of your words, you can look it up.

Make a notebook page for each letter of the alphabet. Keep the pages in alphabetical order. This will make your special words easy to find. If you use a looseleaf binder, you can add pages as your notebook grows.

Grammar Handbook

Grammar Handbook

Grammar

▶ **adjective**   A word that describes a noun is an adjective.

> <u>Several</u> <u>red</u> birds gathered at <u>the</u> <u>little</u> pond.

adjectives that tell *how many*   Some adjectives answer the question "How many?"

> I heard <u>three</u> new bird songs this morning.

adjectives that tell *what kind*   Some adjectives answer the question "What kind?"

> The <u>brown</u> bird flew over to a <u>tall</u> tree.

adjectives that compare   Adjectives have two different forms that are used to compare.

♦ Use the *-er* form of an adjective to compare two persons, places, or things.

> A frog has <u>fewer</u> legs than a crab.

♦ Use the *-est* form of an adjective to compare three or more persons, places, or things.

> The crab is the <u>fastest</u> animal on this beach.

articles: *a, an, the*   The words *a*, *an*, and *the* are a special kind of adjective. They are called articles.

♦ The articles *a* and *an* are used with singular nouns. Use *a* before words that begin with consonant sounds. Use *an* before words that begin with vowel sounds.

> <u>A</u> honeybee is <u>an</u> insect.

♦ *The* is used before both singular and plural nouns.

It gathers <u>the</u> nectar from <u>the</u> flowers.

▶ **adverb**   A word that describes a verb is an adverb.

adverbs that tell *where* or *when*   Many adverbs answer the question "Where?" or "When?"

A rocket flew to the moon and landed <u>there</u>. (Where?)

An astronaut <u>then</u> placed a flag on the moon. (When?)

adverbs that tell *how*   Some adverbs answer the question "How?" Many adverbs that answer the question "How?" end in *ly*.

Mars shines <u>brightly</u>. (How?)

▶ **noun**   A noun names a person, place, or thing.
We saw <u>Aaron</u> at <u>school</u> with his model <u>train</u>.
        (person) (place)   (thing)

singular noun   A singular noun names one person, place, or thing.

<u>Maria</u> is learning to play the <u>violin</u>.

plural noun   A plural noun names more than one person, place, or thing.

The <u>students</u> painted clay <u>bowls</u>.

♦ Add *-s* to form the plural of most nouns.

plum   plums   apple   apples

♦ Add *-es* to form the plural of nouns that end in *ss*, *x*, *ch*, or *sh*.

glasses   foxes   lunches   bushes

From a writer's point of view ...

Adverbs help me add details to my writing— details about time and place.

From a writer's point of view ...

I use exact nouns to help my readers form clear word pictures.

♦ If a noun ends in a consonant and *y*, change the *y* to *i* and add *-es* to form the plural.

hobby   hobbies   pony   ponies

♦ Some nouns change their spelling to form the plural.

woman   women   man   men   foot   feet

common noun   A common noun names any person, place, or thing.

> The <u>author</u> wrote about an <u>animal</u>.

proper noun   A proper noun names a particular person, place, or thing.

> <u>A.A. Milne</u> wrote about <u>Winnie-the-Pooh</u>.

possessive noun   A possessive noun shows ownership.

♦ To form the possessive of a singular noun, add an apostrophe and *-s* (**'s**).

> The <u>lion's</u> mane is long and fluffy.

♦ To form the possessive of a plural noun that ends in *s*, add an apostrophe (**'**).

> People admire the <u>lions'</u> manes.

▶ pronoun   A pronoun takes the place of a noun or nouns.

> Nouns: **The <u>cat</u> follows the <u>children</u>.**
> Pronouns: **<u>It</u> follows <u>them</u>.**

From a writer's point of view …

Using pronouns helps me add variety to my writing.

singular and plural pronouns A singular pronoun takes the place of a noun that names one person, place, or thing. A plural pronoun takes the place of a noun that names more than one person, place, or thing.

Singular Pronouns	Plural Pronouns
I, you, she, he, it me, her, him	we, you, they us, them

subject pronoun The words *I*, *you*, *she*, *he*, *it*, *we*, and *they* are subject pronouns. Use these pronouns to replace nouns in the subjects of sentences.

   <u>Mr. Tanaka</u> has a shop. <u>He</u> has a shop.

object pronoun The words *me*, *you*, *him*, *her*, *it*, *us*, and *them* are object pronouns. Use object pronouns to replace nouns in the predicates of sentences.

   The cat follows <u>Linda</u>. The cat follows <u>her</u>.

possessive pronoun A possessive pronoun shows ownership.

   <u>Chico's</u> aunt has a pet shop.
   <u>His</u> aunt has a pet shop.

using *I* and *me* Use the pronouns *I* and *me* to talk about yourself. Use *I* in the subject of a sentence. Use a capital letter for the word *I*. Use *me* in the predicate of a sentence.

   Mario and <u>I</u> found Frisky under the bed.
   The kitten hid from Mario and <u>me</u>.

▶ **sentence**   A sentence tells a complete thought.
Not a sentence: **Loved planes.**
Sentence: **Amelia Earhart loved planes.**

statement   A statement is a sentence that tells something. It ends with a period (**.**).
The message was in the bottle.

question   A question is a sentence that asks something. It ends with a question mark (**?**).
Where was the message?

command   A command is a sentence that gives an order. It ends with a period (**.**).
Read the message to me.

exclamation   An exclamation is a sentence that shows strong feeling. It ends with an exclamation mark (**!**).
The message came from across the ocean!

▶ **subjects and predicates**   A sentence has two parts, the subject and the predicate.

subject   The subject of a sentence names someone or something.
The sun gives us light.

♦ The main word in the subject of a sentence is often a noun.
This flower needs sunlight.

♦ The words *I*, *you*, *she*, *he*, *it*, *we*, and *they* are subject pronouns. These pronouns can replace nouns in the subjects of sentences.
It needs sunlight.

predicate   The predicate of a sentence tells what the subject is or does.

At least nine planets <u>orbit our sun</u>.

♦ The main word in the predicate of a sentence is a verb.

The earth <u>travels</u> around the sun.

▶ **verb**   A word that shows action is a verb. An action verb tells what someone or something does.

Cinderella <u>sews</u> her stepsisters' dresses.

the verb *be*   A verb may also show being. Use *am*, *is*, *are*, *was*, and *were* to tell what someone or something is or was.

using forms of *be*   The form of *be* that is used must agree with the subject of the sentence.

Subject	Verb
I	am, was
singular nouns and *she*, *he*, *it*	is, was
plural nouns and *we*, *you*, *they*	are, were

helping verb and **main verb**   A verb can be more than one word. The main verb is the most important verb. A helping verb works with the main verb.

Many people <u>have</u> <u>read</u> fairy tales.
They <u>are</u> <u>known</u> all over the world.

present-time verb   A verb in the present time shows action that happens now.

One *pig* <u>builds</u> his house of straw.

using present-time verbs   A present-time verb must agree with the subject of the sentence.

♦ Verbs in the present time that are used with singular nouns end in *-s* or *-es*. Verbs in the present time used with *he*, *she*, or *it* also end in *-s* or *-es*.

The *wolf* <u>blows</u> down two houses.
***It* (or *he*) <u>blows</u> down two houses.**

♦ Verbs in the present time that are used with plural nouns or with the pronouns *I*, *you*, *we*, or *they* do not add *-s* or *-es*.

The three *pigs* <u>run</u> from the wolf.
***They* <u>run</u> from the wolf.**

spelling present-time verbs   The spelling of some verbs changes when *-es* is added.

♦ When a verb ends in a consonant and *y*, change the *y* to *i* and add *-es*.

cry, cries   **hurry, hurries**

past-time verb   A verb in the past time shows action that already happened. Most verbs in the past time end in *-ed*.

The writer <u>remembered</u> her childhood.

spelling past-time verbs   The spelling of some verbs changes when *-ed* is added.

♦ When a verb ends in a consonant and *y*, change the *y* to *i* before adding *-ed*.

dry, dried   **reply, replied**

♦ When a verb ends in one vowel and one consonant, the final consonant is doubled before *-ed* is added.

hop, hopped   **rap, rapped**

irregular verbs   Irregular verbs do not add -*ed* to show action in the past.

Verb	Past	Past with *have*, *has*, or *had*
begin	began	begun
bring	brought	brought
come	came	come
do	did	done
draw	drew	drawn
eat	ate	eaten
fall	fell	fallen
find	found	found
fly	flew	flown
give	gave	given
go	went	gone
grow	grew	grown
know	knew	known
ride	rode	ridden
run	ran	run
say	said	said
see	saw	seen
take	took	taken
throw	threw	thrown
write	wrote	written

Capitalization

▶ **first word in sentence** The first word in a sentence begins with a capital letter.

    Messages can be written or spoken.

▶ **proper noun** Each important word in a proper noun begins with a capital letter.

names of people and pets The names of people and pets are proper nouns. Each main word in a name begins with a capital letter.

    Walt Whitman   Rin Tin Tin
    Winnie-the-Pooh

titles A title begins with a capital letter. Titles are sometimes used with the names of people. Some titles are **abbreviations**.

    Dr. Chu   Mayor Lindsay
    President Jefferson

place names Each word in the name of a street, town, city, or state begins with a capital letter.

    My cousins live on West Acre Road in Dallas, Texas.

calendar words The name of a day or month begins with a capital letter.

    My birthday is Thursday, December 27.

♦ Each word in the name of a holiday or special day begins with a capital letter.

    October 15 is World Poetry Day.

▶ **initials** An initial is the first letter of a name. It is written with a capital letter and is followed by a period.

    Dr. Helen M. Greer writes about wildlife.

▶ **letters** Capitalize the first word of the greeting and the first word of the closing of a letter.

Dear Emily,   Your friend,

▶ **pronoun _I_** The pronoun _I_ is always written as a capital letter.

Danny and I hiked all day.

▶ **state abbreviations** You may use the United States Postal Service two-letter abbreviations of state names when you write addresses. They have capital letters and no periods.

Alabama	**AL**	Maine	**ME**	Oregon	**OR**
Alaska	**AK**	Maryland	**MD**	Pennsylvania	**PA**
Arizona	**AZ**	Massachusetts	**MA**	Rhode Island	**RI**
Arkansas	**AR**	Michigan	**MI**	South Carolina	**SC**
California	**CA**	Minnesota	**MN**	South Dakota	**SD**
Colorado	**CO**	Mississippi	**MS**	Tennessee	**TN**
Connecticut	**CT**	Missouri	**MO**	Texas	**TX**
Delaware	**DE**	Montana	**MT**	Utah	**UT**
Florida	**FL**	Nebraska	**NE**	Vermont	**VT**
Georgia	**GA**	Nevada	**NV**	Virginia	**VA**
Hawaii	**HI**	New Hampshire	**NH**	Washington	**WA**
Idaho	**ID**	New Jersey	**NJ**	West Virginia	**WV**
Illinois	**IL**	New Mexico	**NM**	Wisconsin	**WI**
Indiana	**IN**	New York	**NY**	Wyoming	**WY**
Iowa	**IA**	North Carolina	**NC**	* * *	
Kansas	**KS**	North Dakota	**ND**	District of	
Kentucky	**KY**	Ohio	**OH**	Columbia	**DC**
Louisiana	**LA**	Oklahoma	**OK**		

▶ **titles of books** Capitalize the first word, the last word, and all of the important words in the titles of books. Underline all the words in the title.

<u>Ramona the Pest</u>   <u>One at a Time</u>

Punctuation

▶ **period**   Use a period (.) at the ends of statements and commands.

> **Messages can be written or spoken.**
> **Read this message.**

◆ An abbreviation is a shortened form of a word. Many abbreviations begin with a capital letter and end with a period.

> **Dr. Jones   Mon. at 2:30 P.M.**

▶ **question mark**   A question mark (?) is a special mark that ends a question. A question is a sentence that asks something.

> **Where was the message?**

▶ **exclamation mark**   An exclamation mark (!) is a special mark that ends an exclamation. An exclamation is a sentence that shows strong feeling.

> **I like this bike!**

▶ **comma**   A comma (,) is a special mark used in sentences. It tells when to stop for a moment between words.

◆ Use a comma to separate words in a series of three or more words.

> **Puppies need food, exercise, water, and love.**

◆ Use a comma after the name of a person spoken to.

> **Jack, may I pet your new puppy?**

From a writer's point of view...

Before I make my final copy, I check the punctuation in my work.

♦ Use a comma after *yes* or *no* at the beginning of a sentence.

Yes, I think he will like you.

♦ Use a comma between the city and state and between the date and the year.

Chicago, Illinois   May 27, 1992

♦ Use a comma after the greeting and the closing in a letter.

Dear Aunt Alice,   Sincerely,

▶ **quotation marks**   A quotation is the exact words someone speaks. Use quotation marks (" ") to show where a speaker's exact words begin and end.

♦ Use a comma to separate the speaker's words from the rest of the sentence. Begin the first word in a quotation with a capital letter. Put the end punctuation inside the quotation marks.

Mom said, "You cannot keep a duck in the house!"

▶ **apostrophe**   Use an apostrophe (') to show where a letter or letters have been left out in a contraction. A contraction is a shortened form of two words.

♦ Some contractions are formed from a pronoun and a verb.

I am   I'm   I have   I've

♦ Some contractions are formed from a verb and *not*.

| **is not** | **isn't** | **have not** | **haven't** |

♦ Use an apostrophe to form a possessive noun.

The puppet's head is carved from wood.

The musicians' instruments are packed.

For more information see **noun: possessive noun**.

Writing and Computers

Along with great ideas, the best friend a writer can have is a computer. It's easy and fun to write using one. You can use it to prewrite, write, revise, and proofread. Then it takes only a few minutes to print a final copy.

Catch the Computer Bug

Many people think that computers are hard to use. Some even think that computers are smart! But a computer is just a machine. The only trick you need to know is how to tell it what to do. You need to know how to put your writing into it. You also need to know how to give it commands. Then the computer can help you revise and proofread your writing.

Every computer is slightly different. But each has a manual, or handbook. The manual tells you how to give the commands. Use the manual for help. This list of computer terms, and the chart of computer commands after it, will help you understand the directions in your manual.

Computer Terms

Character: a single letter, numeral, or space. The word *dog* has three characters; so does the number *134*.

Command: an order, such as PRINT or SAVE, that the user gives to the computer.

Computer program: a list of instructions that tells the computer what to do; software.

Cursor: the blinking line or square on the screen that shows where the next typed character will appear.

Disk: a magnetic object on which information is stored (See *floppy disk* and *hard disk*).

Document: one or more pages of your writing, such as a story, a report, or a poem.

Edit: to change what you type into the computer; to revise.

Floppy disk: a small plastic disk used to save and store documents. Sometimes this is called a diskette.

Floppy Disk

Format: to prepare a blank floppy disk for use (also called *initialize*).

Hard copy: document, or writing, that is printed out from the computer onto paper.

Hard disk: an inside part of the computer where information is stored. This differs from *memory*, which stores information being used at the moment.

Hardware: the machine, including the monitor, computer, and keyboard.

Input: information—text, numbers, and so on—typed into the computer.

Keyboard: part of the computer used to input information. It looks like a typewriter keyboard.

Load: to take information from an information storage device, such as a disk, and put it into a computer's memory.

Menu: a list on the monitor of things the computer does on command, such as SAVE.

Modem: the device that allows computers to communicate over telephone lines.

Monitor: the television-like screen on which input and output can be viewed.

Output: text that the computer displays, on the screen or in hard copy.

Printer: the device that prints output in hard copy.

Printout: a copy of your writing made by the printer.

Program: a disk that contains a group of instructions that tells the computer what to do.

Software: programs that run on a computer to allow it to do word processing, math calculations, and so on.

Virus: a set of instructions, hidden in a computer system, that leaves copies of itself in other programs or disks and can erase stored information.

Computer Commands

Cut ▶ Tells the computer to take out, or "cut," a piece of text.

Delete ▶ Tells the computer to remove selected text.

Find ▶ Tells the computer to find a certain word in the text.

Open ▶ Tells the computer to open a document.

Paste ▶ Tells the computer to insert text in a certain place in the document.

Print ▶ Tells the computer to print out the document in hard copy.

Quit ▶ Tells the computer to close a document.

Return ▶ Tells the computer to move the cursor to the next line.

Save ▶ Tells the computer to save a document by putting it into permanent storage.

Shift ▶ Tells the computer to use a capital letter.

Tab ▶ Tells the computer to indent a line of text, as for a paragraph indent.

The Key to Typing

   The hardest part of writing on a computer can be learning how to type. The first step is learning which fingers hit which keys. Use the finger diagram below. Practice typing "The quick brown fox jumped over the lazy dog." Make sure your fingers are curved over the keys on the keyboard. It may be slow going at first, but with practice you'll soon be typing like a pro.

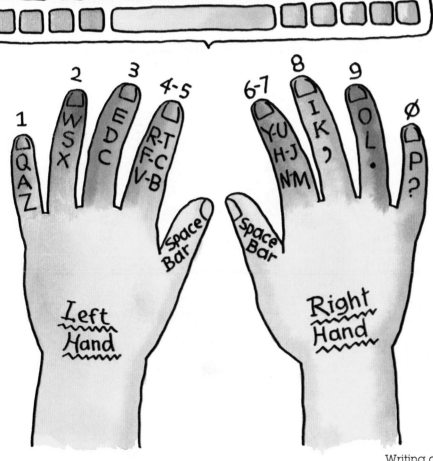

Word Processing

Writing with a computer can make it easier to

- choose topics to write about
- write your first draft
- discover your ideas
- revise your writing
- organize your ideas
- correct your mistakes
- share your writing with others

The word processing program you use will tell you how to use the computer to enter, save, edit, and print your work. Some programs can catch spelling errors. Others can add pictures or borders.

Word processing programs cannot do these things:

- think
- organize your work
- get ideas
- spell words as you write
- choose the best words
- punctuate correctly

You are still in charge of the writing.

Ready, Set, Write!

Now you are ready to prewrite, write, revise, and proofread a piece of writing. Follow these steps.

Create a File and First Draft A file is a group of related documents. In a file folder, you might keep such related papers as prewriting ideas, first draft, revision, and final copy of a story. A computer can also keep a file for you.

- Tell the computer to open a new document.
- Give the document a name. Some computers ask you to name a document with words. Others ask for a series of numbers or letters. For example, you might use *STORY.DR1*, meaning "story, draft 1."
- Type a list of ideas, words that describe your topic, or questions about your topic.
- Type your first draft. Tell the computer to SAVE it.

When you have finished, follow the directions in your manual and create a file. Give it a name, such as *STORY.FILE.* Put your draft in the file. Take a break! Then begin to revise.

Revise and Proofread Your Draft You'll have no more messy papers with arrows and cross-outs when you revise on a computer. You do the thinking; let the computer do the work!

- Make a computer document copy of your first draft.
- Label it—for example, *story revision* or *STORY.REV.* Save the original draft. Use the new copy for revising.
- Move the cursor to a place that needs revising. Give the computer a command. You might tell it to CUT a sentence, move it to another place in your paper, and PASTE the sentence in.
- Check your writing for errors and correct them.

Print your document. Decide how to share your writing.

Index